HOUSES OF THE WORLD

HOUSES OF THE WORLD

© 2000 Könemann Verlagsgesellschaft mbH

Bonner Str. 126, D-50968 Cologne

Author Francisco Asensio Cerver

Publisher Paco Asensio, Arco Editorial, S.A. Barcelona

Editorial coordinator Aurora Cuito

Editor Aurora Cuito

Project coordinator Anabel Martín Encinas

Design Mireia Casanovas Soley

Layout Jaume Martínez Coscojuela

Original title Casas del Mundo

© 2000 for the English edition

Könemann Verlagsgesellschaft mbH

Translation from the Spanish
Wendy Allatson, Alayne Pullen, Martin Reece and
Maggie Rosengarten in association with
First Edition Translations Ltd, Cambridge

Editing Jenny Knight in association with
First Edition Translations Ltd, Cambridge

Typesetting The Write Idea in association with
First Edition Translations Ltd, Cambridge

Project Coordinator Nadja Bremse

Assistant Luke Roskilly

Production Ursula Schümer

Printed in Italy

ISBN 3-8290-4849-1

10 9 8 7 6 5 4 3 2 1

CONTENTS

The introduction to this unprecedented overview of domestic architecture does more than simply establish a clear and precise classification of the trends that have emerged in recent years. Attempting to bring together – in a single volume – some of the best-known designs of a period that is so close to our own contemporary critical standpoint constitutes, in every respect, an exercise in abstraction that is as daring as it is thought provoking. The choice of designs has been limited to a specific decade: the 1990s.

An understanding of domestic architectural design is closely associated with the history of ideas. Through a process of romantic and idealistic simplification, houses have become a physical and spiritual refuge from the strains and stresses of modern life.

In this respect, architecture represents the complex framework of the interaction between the architect and client, a simple concept that illustrates one of the most obvious risk factors in the field of domestic architecture: the creation of the artist versus the preferences and requirements of the end user. On the one hand, the house represents an ideal design opportunity in which the architect can develop experience and creative urges. On the other, excessive imagination can prove disastrous for the client's basic, everyday needs. The simplest way to attain a satisfactory result would therefore be to find a happy medium that achieved a balance between both sets of ideas and transformed the task of designing and creating the house into a mutually interactive process.

Furthermore, a number of other factors

should be taken into account when considering issues related to the living space: the relative importance of context and scale; the fine boundary between the public and private spaces; the spatial construction and formal layout vis-à-vis the realities of domestic life; the concepts of convenience, privacy, and quality of life; the increasing use of technology; social housing, and so on.

The American houses of Frank Lloyd Wright were the first to reflect the new and original style of this period, with their freely extended floor space in which exteriors and interiors are linked by terraces and large projecting roofs. In Europe, the reaction to the excessive ornamentation favored by Adolf Loos had far-reaching consequences that played a decisive role in defining the modern, international style of the architecture of the so-called "century of overcrowding," in which the concepts of utility and correctness take precedence over stylistics. For Le Corbusier, standards of creation were not individual, but met universal architectural criteria in a unique, efficient style for "the machine age." To a certain extent, his style was in direct contrast to that of Walter Gropius, which was characterized by restraint, social awareness, and educational principles. Le Corbusier, on the other hand, favored a virtuosity of design that paid homage to Cubism by confining itself to a style of domestic architecture renowned for its characteristic pure whiteness and clean geometric lines.

The single-family house tends to be

presented as the ultimate stronghold in which the designer can conceive and create with complete freedom of expression. It is, however, a form of affirmation that is somewhat uncertain. The various trends and stances that prevailed toward the end of the 20th century and are continuing into the 21st are, generally speaking, based on a compromise between form and function, between esthetics and pragmatism, in an attempt to achieve a harmonious balance between everyday needs and a broader, more elevated view that is often reduced to a mere exercise in stylistics.

The most recent designs, firmly rooted in the revolutionary theories of the first half of the 20th century, are little more than reinterpretations and variations of the successful creations of Le Corbusier, Wright, Loos, Gropius, Asplund, and Van der Rohe. However, the multidimensionality and heterogeneity of the end of the second millennium proves that architectural design is still very much alive and flourishing.

The modern houses presented in this beautiful volume are based on the same basic objectives: to define environments that are suited to a particular function and lifestyle and adopt an approach that takes into account the needs of the client (in the case of the single-family house) or society (in the case of a community housing project).

Another important aspect considered in **Houses of the World** is the increasing use of the considerable technological advances developed in recent decades. This has led to the creation of a characteristic style that involves the introduction of the very latest technology, devices, and materials into the domestic environment. The use of "high-tech" solutions to solve domestic problems – reflecting the interests and aspirations of an increasingly humane and environmentally aware society – certainly constitutes one of the most interesting creative processes of modern architecture. However, the majority of innovative solutions are adapted to standard architectural forms so that, within the limits of strictly architectural values, they provide a limited range of esthetic and formal solutions.

The substance of the designs contained in the following pages enables us to observe many of the related characteristics that constitute an overview, albeit limited, of the present state of domestic architecture.

First of all, it is relevant to mention the importance of the context in which the residential building is located, whether it is regarded as incongruous or a deliberate attempt to create a contrast with its surroundings. Even so, the single-family house that has been developed as a result of urban overcrowding constitutes an ideal opportunity – within the context of a plan for a first or second home – for the development of complex systems integrated into the rural, maritime, or urban landscape.

The perception of architectural reality is presented to the observer subject to conditions of relief and vegetation. Although it tends to favor a single space, it also makes use of multiple forms and structures that can give rise to better functional distribution (communal, individual, or service areas) and the creation of more expressive imagery.

While the general layout of all these houses to a certain extent presupposes a return to the Georgian ideal of the masculine house as a refuge and place of rest and relaxation, the demands of Dutch and American women for domestic "engineering" should not be forgotten. The combination of these two aspects calls into question the conventional distinction between first and second homes, examples of which can also be found within the international overview which is included in this book.

In all these houses, the essential criteria are an extensive and generous use of space, the use of transparency and light, the conservation – as far as possible – of natural levels and views, and a free and natural interconnection between the different areas of the living space. In the communal areas, there is frequent recourse to the technical strategy of split levels, which creates a feeling of space and comfort. These areas are usually located in close physical and visual proximity to the complementary leisure facilities.

The importance attached to the external areas (mainly the yard and pool) is the logical consequence of designing for leisure, but it can also give rise to certain controversies with regard to the boundaries between public and private spaces.

However, most of the designers featured in this volume have used ingenious strategies and techniques to ensure that the architecture of the house coincides with that of the complementary facilities.

There are two more obvious trends in the classification of the houses chosen for this book: classical and technological, the eternal contradiction between the traditional and ultramodernism that represent the dialectical extremes of all acts of creation. Between these two extremes lies a series of ideas that clearly illustrate the present state of architectural design, based on a number of concepts (traditionalism, postmodernism, and minimalism; the interpretation and revision of rationalist theories; exceptional buildings) whose presentation is often interrelated to emphasize the sheer effervescence of this overview of world architecture.

Other designs are situated in more ambiguous and less easily defined areas. However, they all reflect a knowledge gained from experience and the adaptation of indigenous traditions to the domestic needs of modern life.

All the examples in this overview of domestic architecture are characterized by creative vitality. However, they also reflect the difficulties raised by their chronological proximity and the absence of a critical method that would make it possible to establish a clear and cohesive classification of the various stances, attitudes, and trends of the late 20th century. The 1,000 pages of the book constitute an inevitably incomplete reflection of some of the ideas that, in my opinion, most significantly express the multidimensional nature of domestic architecture within the international context of the last decade.

Francisco Asensio Cerver

HOUSES IN THE CITY

The origin of urban settlements appears to be closely linked to the development of agriculture. A study of the ruins of Stone-Age houses in the Near East has shown that many dwellings consisted of an open structure with no walls. The first permanent sites also date from this period. Perhaps the most obvious reason for creating sedentary settlements was the gradual realization that the life led by agricultural tribes was much easier than that of their nomadic counterparts. Other reasons that led to the establishment of this type of settlement were the need for special places (rather like shrines) in which to carry out rituals dedicated to the dead; for the creation of ceremonial centers for practicing religion and magic, and performing social activities; and, thirdly, for the improved security of the community.

By contrast, the essential activities of the earlier way of life were limited to hunting and maintaining the cohesion of the tribal group, so that the energy of its members was devoted primarily to survival. Although these nomadic tribes enjoyed occasional surpluses, preserving and transporting these surpluses required further expenditure of effort. It could therefore be argued that the accumulation of human energy released by the agricultural revolution was channeled into the development of urban settlements, which in turn gave rise to the sanctification of property rights and even the creation of aggressive war. Until the 18th century, the largest district in the world's major towns and cities was in fact the administrative center of the governing power. Because there were no rapid means of communication, the mechanisms of government had to be brought together within the capital, while a large part of the army was camped nearby. Furthermore, much of the state's business was conducted in the vicinity of these urban centers.

It was not until the industrial revolution and the development of the factory system that the pressures of urban settlement began to take effect. Thousands of workers were needed for the huge, recently developed industrial buildings, while the establishment of a great many independent suppliers in these towns also contributed to their expansion. They often developed from what was originally an administrative center, or grew up around industrial settlements, which were often dirty and unsightly. Soon, faster means of transport – due to the advent of modern motor vehicles – and the rising costs for urban companies, made this last type of town redundant as an industrial center. Today, new factories are rarely built within a town or city, and it is in fact quite common for companies to ask the relevant municipal authority for permission to build them outside the town or city boundary, so that they do not have to meet the high cost of urban land. This is why, from a purely economic point of view, the idea of replacing inner-city slums with modern factories is not at present feasible. It is possible to consider the mechanisms of urban growth on the basis of a central town theory, and its relationship to the size and distance between regional commercial centers. At the lowest level of the hierarchy are the towns supplying basic necessities to those regions isolated from the large urban settlements, and which are distributed throughout the surrounding area. The range of activity of these towns depends on the predominant means of transport. In this way, the towns increase in size as their surrounding regions expand and overlap with other regions from which they are technically distinct.

M House

Location: *Tokyo, Japan*
Year of construction: *1997*
Architects: *Kazuyo Sejima, Ryue Nishizawa*
Photography: *Shinkenchiku-Sha*

The site is bounded by a street to the south and by houses on the other three sides. Because these houses open onto the street, many have walls and screens around them to create a private space. The paradox of opening up a space which then had to be enclosed, meant that the relationship between the house and its surroundings and the creation of privacy were key elements of the design.

The excavation of the site and creation of a patio that lit and aerated the basement level, while at the same time linking it with the upper level, the street, and the sky, are two of the devices used to divide up the living space. The floor at street level is divided transversally by corridors, staircases, and a patio. It incorporates areas that need to be self-contained, for example the garage, the double bedroom, and the guest room. The living space on the lower floor, based on a more unitary design, is organized around the patio and characterized by freedom of movement between the different areas. The kitchen, dining room, and den are some of the areas that coexist on this level. The layout of the house has the advantage of being tailored to suit the clients, a working couple.

The architects' work on the potential of the layout, the development of everyday activities, the screening of the house from the surrounding area, and the desire for light, air, and privacy led to the creation of this homogeneous space known as the M House, which combines all these functions by means of a complex process that produced a formal design of truly breathtaking simplicity.

The attention to architectural detail and the choice of lightweight materials create a restrained and sophisticated living space characterized by luminosity and elegance. As well as being functional, the layout had to incorporate large, flexible spaces that would be able to accommodate various activities: workrooms, dens, and a room for entertaining. *Left*: The light, airy patio provides a direct link with the exterior.

The house is situated in an upper-class residential district in the center of Tokyo. The area is becoming increasingly densely populated as the building land is divided into small plots of around 2,150 sq ft (200 m²), like the one on which the M House was built.

Two studies, several bathrooms, and two parking spaces enable the occupants of the house to maintain their own privacy and independence. Furthermore, discussions between the architects and clients led to the conclusion that a room for entertaining would be ideal, since both partners entertain a great deal in connection with their work. A future family was also catered for in the form of a children's room.

Double House

Location: *Utrecht, the Netherlands*
Year of construction: *1997*
Architects: *Bjarne Mastenbroek, MVRDV*
Photography: *Christian Richters*

The Double House is situated on a street that surrounds a magnificent 19th-century park on the outskirts of Utrecht. Two families share the single building that represents a three-dimensional assemblage of the clashes and compromises between the lifestyles and requirements of its different owners. The mediatory role of the architects gave rise to the original and uncompromising design.

As in other projects, MVRDV decided to limit the number of variables involved in the design in order to simplify a potentially complicated situation. After producing numerous plans for the layout, it was decided to reduce the depth of the house in order to free up the plot and allocate more space to the yard. The strategy gave the design greater physical presence and spatial potential, as well as much better views of the neighbouring park.

The house became a tall, slender unit. Then, sections replaced stories as the battlefield on which the two houses were spatially defined and fitted together. The trajectory of the party wall is like a negotiable boundary that is designed as a surface of uniform thickness. As it rises it becomes a vertical wall to which the noncomplementary layout of both parts of the house are appended.

Initially, this interdependency threatened to paralyze all formal and conceptual progress. Paradoxically, however, architects and clients have produced a final result that is much more successful than it would have been had they all worked individually.

Right-hand page:
The strategy of interior
distribution aimed to create fluid
spaces. Pillars and the vertical
coincidence of the walls were
eliminated. The concrete structure
distributes the loads diagonally.

The two families living in the
house wanted to enjoy the
views of the nearby park.
Access from the street to the
yard and terrace had to be
straightforward.

The architects suggested a
house with a minimum depth,
with the result that the layout
is distributed over five stories,
leaving maximum space for
the yard.

Zorn Residence

Location: *Chicago, United States*
Year of construction: *1995*
Architects: *Krueck & Sexton*
Photography: *Korab Hedrich Blessing*

The Zorn Residence is situated in a residential district in north Chicago. Its position on the site is such that it breaks the rhythm of the adjacent facades and maximizes the views to the south. The owners, a couple with two sons, were dissatisfied with the small rooms and lack of light in their previous house.

The house was designed as a simple brick and glass structure, the interior of which is centered around a split-level area which forms the common living space.

The south-facing facade is the most transparent since it was important to introduce the maximum amount of light. On the west side of the house is a long, narrow, vertical window that projects slightly from the surface of the facade and offers views of the street. It is extended along the roof to provide overhead light, which is diffused into the central area of the upper story.

As in all Krueck and Sexton projects, each section and its location is designed in a way that reaffirms the overall concept. According to the architects, the initial, intuitive, and approximate designs should, at a given moment and after numerous modifications, achieve a unity that reintegrates the elements that were previously distinct. At this point, the design process ceases to be subjective and, as each part takes its place within the whole, achieves objectivity.

The south-facing facade is the most transparent.

From the front, the Zorn Residence is reminiscent of one of Piet Mondrian's geometric creations.

Following pages:
The house is organized around a split-level, central living space.

The concept of the rectangle provides the departure point for the architecture of Krueck and Sexton. Originally conceived as a pure rectangle, the house was modified, becoming slightly irregular and offset, and various superposed elements were added. The breaks and offsetting sometimes occur vertically and sometimes horizontally.

Koechlin House

The architects themselves admit that, unlike most of their work, in this instance they did not have a clear idea of what the house would look like until a long time after work had begun, several months in fact. This may seem strange, since Herzog and de Meuron have deservedly acquired an international reputation precisely for their exterior treatment of buildings.

Unusually, the Koechlin House was built from the inside out. The architects began to work on the idea of a central patio around which all the living spaces of the house would revolve. The patio can be either open or closed. It is closed by means of a sliding glass roof panel that enables the occupants to enjoy the patio area when temperatures are on the cool side.

Later in the year, the patio can be converted into a winter garden. It does not have definite boundaries but can merge into and become part of the living room on the first floor, with a facade window, or it can incorporate one edge of the floor slabs on the second floor to create a terrace. In fact, its boundaries are completely variable since, depending on the areas that are open, it can occupy the entire first floor or confine itself exclusively to the central core of the house.

Location: *Mies, Switzerland*
Year of construction: *1996*
Builder: *W. Ferreira*
Architects: *Herzog & de Meuron*
Photography: *Margherita Spiluttini*

View from the street. The lower floor is partly below ground level.

View of the house from the back yard. The window runners are fixed onto the outside of the house so that the glass surfaces project slightly from the gray cement walls.

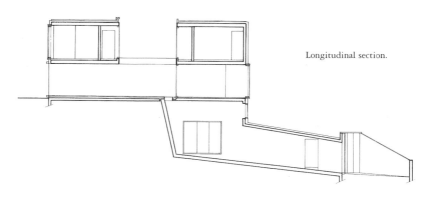

Longitudinal section.

The boundaries of the patio can vary depending on whether the glass doors are open or closed.

The triangular, funnel shape and sloping floor of the entrance create a visual effect that makes this small entrance corridor look much larger that it actually is. This device was widely used during the Baroque period.

The retaining walls of the basement have been left unrendered.

Moerkerke House

Location: *London, Great Britain*
Year of construction: *1996*
Architect: *John Pawson*
Photography: *Richard Glover*

This traditional Victorian mews cottage has been converted into a house for three people. To make maximum use of the limited amount of space available, the kitchen, bathroom, and staircase were relocated. The first floor, comprising the kitchen, living room, and dining room, was left as open as possible by creating a large continuous space that can be divided up whenever necessary.

Two elements were also added to modify the interior space and accommodate the service areas of the house: a chimney breast containing the staircase, and a wall that defines and screens the kitchen, with a stainless steel air filter. The staircase, contained within the chimney breast, is lit by a skylight that sheds light onto the stairs. The flooring on both floors is cherry wood, while the white-painted walls create an atmosphere of reflective tranquillity. The white fabric window shades filter the light and create a visual barrier between the inside of the house and the exterior.

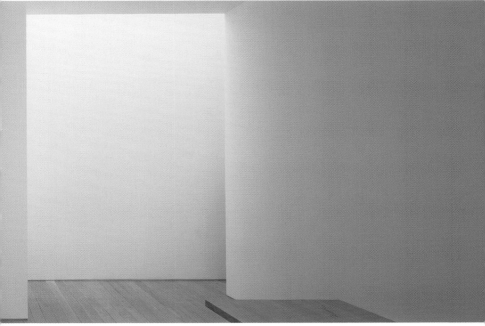

The sparse pieces of furniture that punctuate the living spaces are designer originals: the dining chairs are by Wegner and the armchairs by Christian Liagre.

Grooves at the top and bottom of the vertical partitions prevent them touching the floor and ceiling, making them appear light and delicate.

Right-hand page:
The service areas, which are usually dominated by a number of appliances, are treated like the rest of the house. In the kitchen and in the bathroom, minimalism and formality are very much in evidence.

Stein Residence

Location: *Kensington, London, Great Britain*
Year of construction: *1996*
Architect: *Seth Stein*
Photography: *Richard Davies*

An old stable and a site that was largely undeveloped were incorporated into Seth Stein's design for his own house. Stein did not want to create a contrast with the existing building or the typology and traditional appearance of the surrounding structures. He prefers to establish a dialogue and maintain continuity with the past, integrating it into his designs. The first stage involved the painstaking restoration of all the existing buildings that would be incorporated into the new structure.

The living area of the house follows the natural contours of the site. The first-floor accommodation comprises a long interior patio and a transitional area from the street, where the car can be left. Next to one of the walls of this outdoor vestibule, several dark, wooden planks form a walkway leading to the house and the entrance proper.

The interior patio is the central element of the design. It enables natural light to be introduced into all the main living spaces of the house, constitutes a visual focus, and provides privacy from the surrounding houses. Seth Stein designed it, not as a yard, but as an exterior room, a protected area where children can play in the open air, an eating area, or, quite simply, a contemplative space. The living room – an irregular space of some 97 sq ft (9 m²) – is half covered by a structure of glass windows and a light structure of tensioned steel, set within the U-shape formed by the brick facades of the second floor. In one of the corners, the flight of steps leading to the level of the bedrooms follows the line of an existing curved wall.

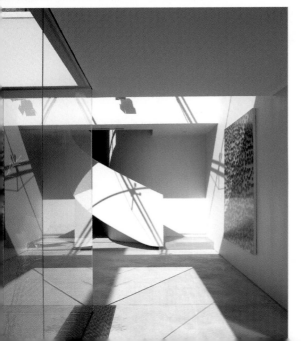

The greater part of the flooring in the house is pale gray concrete, hand finished to give it an orange-peel texture. Most of the walls have been painted in a dull, mat white verging on ivory. The floor of the kitchen is in American oak, while the patio and steps are paved with green Spanish limestone, which is interspersed with areas of grass.

Right-hand page:
On the floor of the dining room, sisal matting (natural fiber) defines the space around the table. The wall behind the table combines wooden paneling and the original tiles bearing the names of the horses that once occupied the building.

The gray Tuscan stone of the bathroom floors and some of the fittings creates an atmosphere of serenity and calm.

The bedroom floors are covered with wool and sisal rugs and carpets in natural tones.

House-studio in Islington

Location: *London, Great Britain*
Year of construction: *1994*
Architects: *Adam Caruso, Peter St. John*
Associates: *Alan Baxter and Associates*
(structural engineers)
Photography: *Hélène Bisnet*

Most of the effort and budget for this design were devoted to improving the existing building (brick surfaces and wooden floors) and introducing natural light into the interior.

As the window openings were very small, Caruso and St. John decided to replace the old facade with a glass wall. During the day, the new facade looks completely closed, as if it were covered with metal sheeting. At night, it is transformed into a lamp that lights up the street.

One of the other surprising things about the facade is its structure. It is divided into horizontal sections of unequal width, defined by the metal strips that support the glass panes. The height of the sections increases, from the storeroom at street level that houses the company meters, to the upper floor.

At the rear of the house, Caruso and St. John have done something completely different, although still with the aim of introducing natural

light very much in mind. They have removed some of the roof tiles and built a lantern the size of a room in the roof to create a well of light. This area contains the kitchen, the bathroom, and the staircase.

There is no attempt to hide the rough finishes of the former warehouse. On the contrary, they set the tone for the type of materials used in the new elements of the house. The end result of the project is a modestly formal and completely inward-looking space. The design consists of a catalogue of "renouncements": minimum division of space, minimum relationship with the street, minimum furniture, minimum finishes on the walls. In this respect, the architects have certainly taken a huge risk: it takes an unusual type of person to live in such a space and whoever lives here must fully subscribe to the same precepts.

The overall outline of the house is not perfectly rectangular: the old brick wall of the facade is irregular and the upper section offset. Thus, in spite of the decidedly geometric and monochromatic nature of the design, minor irregularities sabotaged any attempt to simplify it. The possibilities of the unusually complex, concealed entrance – disguised as an industrial or warehouse door – are increased by the effect of light.

Bjornson House

Location: *Los Angeles, California, United States*
Year of construction: *1989*
Architect: *Arata Isozaki*
Photography: *Richard Bryant/Arcaid*

Arata Isozaki met Teresa Bjornson while he was working on the design for the Museum of Contemporary Art in Los Angeles. Her greatest desire was to build a studio house where she could live and work.

In creating the house, the Japanese architect carefully considered the natural surroundings and type of buildings in this part of Los Angeles. The facades are stuccoed while the interior wall facings are in white-painted *Gypsum* wood. To create the Bjornson House, Isozaki decided to use all these local materials in exactly the same way. As well as taking into account the buildings that would surround the new studio house, the designer also faithfully met the requirements of the American art lover: a structure that had large spaces and harmonious proportions, and — above all — let in a great deal of light.

However, the realization of the design presented certain administrative problems. Isozaki's work was subject to restrictions imposed by architectural regulations, for example, the limitation on the height of the building and its situation at the end of a street leading to the sea. The result was a two-story structure with a rectangular floor plan, divided into three cubic areas each of 24 ft (7.25 m) square. Skylights, in the form of isosceles triangles, are set at an angle at each of the four corners of the copper roof.

Detail of the north-facing facade with the main entrance door. The patio is paved with concrete.

The studio–living room serves as a gallery where the owner of the house, Teresa Bjornson, can exhibit the pieces in her art collection.

The works on display include:
Accelerazione Motocicletta (motorbike) by
Mario Merz, *For Aqua* (bathtub) by
Robert Rauschenberg, and *90% Devil
10% Angel SEX* by Edward Rusha.

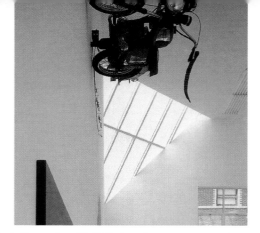

Inside the house, Arata Isozaki has continued to remain faithful to the principle of using local building materials. Thus, the floors in the studio, kitchen, and bedroom are in American maple, while the walls and ceiling throughout the entire house are in painted *Gypsum* wood. In the bathroom, however, the floor has been covered with terrazzo and the walls are partly covered in ceramic tiles and partly in the type of wood that has been used for the ceiling.

The kitchen seen from the dining room.

View of the bedroom with its table-like bed.

View of the bathroom.

Casa Turégano

Location: *Pozuelo de Alarcón, Madrid, España*
Year of construction: *1988*
Architect: *Alberto Campo Baeza*
Photography: *Lluís Casals*

In terms of an architect's creative work, it is possibly the design for their own house that most clearly illustrates their characteristic style. The Casa Turégano, by Alberto Campo Baeza, is a perfect reflection of the personality and aspirations of its owner. The house enabled him to give concrete form to his ideals and concepts of beauty, creating a coherent design and giving substance to thought constructed as form and idea. For the architect, designing his own house meant finally being able to inhabit an ideal, a dream that had become reality.

When designing this white house situated in the district of Pozuelo de Alarcón, in Madrid, Alberto Campo Baeza had to contend with a steeply sloping rectangular plot of some 5,380 sq ft (500 m²). The building has a reticulated, reinforced-concrete structure, and forms a perfect cube with a total floor area of 1,075 sq ft (100 m²) and a volume of 35,300 cubic ft (1,000 m³). It stands at the north end of the site, while the yard and swimming pool are at the opposite end, in front of the south-facing facade. The yard gives access to the spacious living room through two large identical doors, set side by side, that let the necessary amount of light and maximum sunlight into the interior of the building.

The cubic house is surmounted by a smaller prism-shape structure sheltered on one side by a curved wall – the building's only exterior curve – that breaks up the predominant linearity of the design.

The interior, with its snow-white walls and Lucena limestone floors, is characterized by large split-level areas and carefully chosen furniture. Only the furniture breaks the chromatic harmony since even the living room drapes blend with the dominant color.

The Flower House

Location: *London, Great Britain*
Year of construction: *1997*
Builder: *Ralph Pryke Partnership*
Architect: *Peter Romaniuk*
Associates: *Tim McFarlane (structural engineer),*
Jeff Parkes (installations)
Photography: *Dennis Gilbert/VIEW*

Peter Romaniuk, one of the partners in the architectural firm Michael Hopkins and Partners, and his wife Paula Pryke, a well-known London florist, wanted to live in a single-family house in the center of London. At the same time, it had to function as a florist's store and studio.

They found a site in Cynthia Street, between adjoining houses, that measured just under 40 ft (12 m) wide by almost 50 ft (15 m) deep. Obviously, the principal theme of the architectural design focused on defining the relationship between the house and the urban setting: the street, the neighbors, and the noise. Although the couple liked large, open spaces, they had to erect several boundaries that would ensure the privacy of their domestic space.

The building is primarily designed in sections. The first floor is completely occupied by a space that functions as a studio, store, and school of floristry: a total area of 2,260 sq ft (210 m²).

Above the studio are the two floors of the living space. This part of the house is set back from the street, creating a large front terrace – 36 feet (11 m) deep, with an area of 1,400 sq ft (130 m²) – on the roof of the studio. The terrace not only represents the only exterior space, but also acts as a buffer that insulates the house from the street and the neighbors. In certain respects, Peter Romaniuk has built a chalet in the heart of London, but he has done it by redefining the site and creating an unusual relationship between it and the house (in terms of area and height), so as not to be affected by the disadvantages of living in a large city center.

The kitchen is centered around a free-standing, blue bar-counter along the back wall of the house. All the elements of the kitchen – work surfaces, appliances, refrigerator, and oven – are in stainless steel.

View of the central
corridor on the upper
floor, where the
individual bathrooms
have been placed beneath
three skylights that let in
natural light through
the roof.

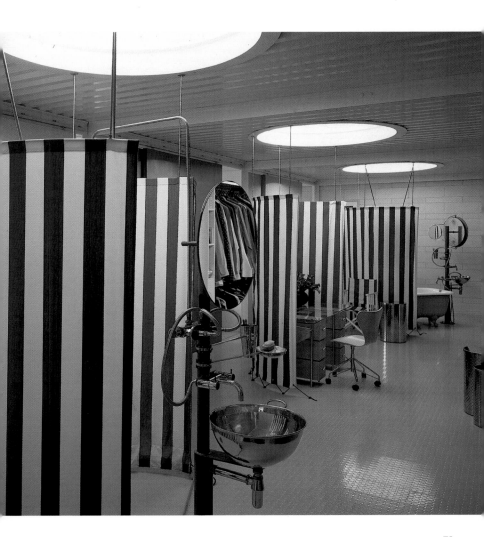

O House

Location: *Tokyo, Japan*
Year of construction: *1994*
Builder: *Fuji-ken*
Architect: *Yoshihiko Iida*
Associates: *SIGLO Structural Engineering,*
        Dan Mechanical Engineering
Photography: *Koumei Tanaka*

Views of the entrance from the street. The main floor is raised above street level to maximize visual and acoustic insulation. The garage acts as a screen that protects the patio and the interior of the house.

This house is situated in a district in Tokyo that has a wide range of single-family houses of all shapes and sizes, garages, and all kinds of commercial buildings. It stands in an arbitrary and haphazard urban landscape of strongly contrasting images: there are no laws governing the type or size of the buildings. Everything is possible and nothing is clearly defined.

Faced with this hostile environment, Yoshihiko Iida decided to build an inward-looking house, with its own particular and private landscape. The Japanese architect has introduced exterior spaces into the house, a device that has a number of advantages. Firstly, the rooms have the benefit of natural light and good ventilation. Secondly, views are created in a controlled environment and designed by the architect himself. Finally, the terraces and patios form ideal open-air living spaces – weather permitting.

Iida has placed three patios at strategic points within the site: in front of the entrance, at the junction of the two wings of the building, and at the far end of the house. The garage is an independent structure that runs parallel to the street and protects the yard from the curiosity of passers-by.

The diversity created by the different settings and levels within the house echoes the diversity that exists beyond its boundaries, in the district, and in this city of kaleidoscopic images.

Left-hand page:
Views of the *tatami* (mat) room
and the master bedroom.

Yoshihiko Iida has used a variety
of materials – wood, marble,
granite – for the floors, while
most of the walls are finished in
polished concrete.

House and Studio

Location: *London, Great Britain*
Year of construction: *1995*
Architects: *Orefelt Associates*
Photography: *Alberto Ferrero*

The building is divided into two well-defined areas – the studio and the house – each with independent access from the yard. From the outside, they both look totally different: the studio has a curved, zinc-plated facade and circular windows, while the house is a white-painted, rectilinear structure made from light concrete blocks.

The house opens onto the south-facing yard. Two bedrooms, a bathroom, and a guest washroom share the first-floor space with the parking area, a storeroom, and two smaller storage areas (one containing the boiler). By contrast, on the second-floor, the dining room and the living room – which overlook the lively Portobello Market – occupy a single,

elongated space, with the kitchen at one end and the den at the other.

Taken overall, the design offers a wide variety of different spaces and atmospheres. Its success is partly due to the many devices used to highlight the different parts of the structure: the creation of an interior patio, an interconnecting spiral staircase, a small second-floor terrace.

Orefelt Associates have successfully combined two distinct and very different functional areas – workspace and living space – within one design. Their interpretation of this simple device has produced a perfectly balanced interaction between the two areas.

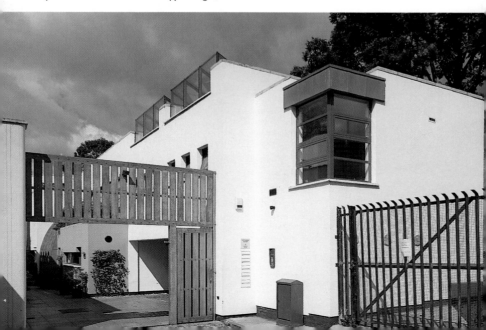

The split-level studio is linked
to the house by a spiral staircase.
It gives access to the gallery-
library that opens onto the
dining room.

Right-hand page:
The design is characterized by the
incorporation of two functional areas
into a single building. The designer,
Gunnar Orefelt, specializes in the
restoration and renovation of old
industrial buildings. By using full and
empty spaces, he has successfully
juxtaposed and connected the two
environments, as well as creating a
transition between the interior and
exterior of the building.

The types of material used in the building were kept to a minimum. The limestone for the kitchen and studio floors, and the birch plywood used as a facing for the studio were possibly the most extensively used. Gunnar Orefelt designed the living room tables, although most of the rest of the furniture was created by other designers, including Aero, Bruno Mattson, MDF, and Conran Design.

Rosenthal House

Color is a fundamental element of this geometrically complex house. It defines spaces and delineates the boundaries between one space and another – slightly offset or pivoted – space. The movement of the design is highlighted by different textures and shades, and by the way that light is reflected by the various surfaces.

It was decided that a two-story, L-shape house would best meet the requirements of the project. Along the western edge of the site, one arm of the L protects the yard from the street and provides areas of shade. The other arm, containing the communal areas of the house, was offset and pivoted in relation to the first. This created an interplay of pivoted spaces that reflect the spaces of the interior, the yard, and the street.

The entrance is located to one side of the parking area, the only part of the previous building to be retained.

Location: *Santa Monica, California, United States*
Year of construction: *1996*
Builder: *G.M. Construction*
Architect: *J. Frank Fitzgibbons*
Associates: *Gimmy Tranquillo (design), Niver Engineering (structural engineers)*
Photography: *Toshi Yoshimi*

At the back of the site, the open-plan kitchen, dining room, some of the service areas, and a living room open onto the most secluded part of the yard. On the second floor are the bedrooms, together with a semiprivate room that overlooks the split level.

A series of terraces give access to the exterior of the house at the various levels, and also provide an overview of this colorful and multidimensional structure.

On both the inside and outside, color is one of the key elements of the design.

The outside of the house is painted in bright colors – yellow, pink, violet, and white – that echo the colors of the flowers in the yard. Inside, chairs, lamps, carpets, balustrades, interior wall coverings, and backgrounds in white, yellow, lilac, orange, and gray create the three-dimensional and flat colors of the interior.

The angle formed by the two "arms" of the building makes the central vestibule a rich and complex space.

Check House

Location: *2 Cluny Park, Singapore*
Year of construction: *1995*
Architects: *KNTA (Kay Ngee Tan, Teck Kiam Tan)*
Associates: *Ove Arup & Partners–Singapore*
(structural engineers), Ee Chiang & Co. (Pte)
Ltd. (main contractors)
Photography: *Dennis Gilbert*

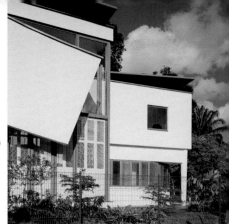

The designs of KNTA, who work in London
and Singapore, are characterized by a dual
identity, a close association of eastern and
western architectural styles. As the architects
themselves state, theirs is not a heterogeneous
combination of different esthetic elements, but a
synthesis that has been gradually developed from
personal experience that coincides with their
own influences and interests.

The extremely elongated site of the Check
House is reflected in the design of both the
house and yard. The spaces are linked together
in a succession of dynamic areas that form a
continuous dialogue. On the first floor, forms
are fluid and curvilinear, while on the second
floor the straight, angular lines create separate
and independent units.

The design of the living space was inspired by
the lifestyle of the occupants. It was conceived
as a natural progression of "journeys and
destinations" in which the rooms are linked and
connected by the movement of the occupants.

In spite of having had to contend with an
extremely long and narrow site, KNTA have
successfully created a dynamic design in which
the almost obligatory linearity has been
reworked and transformed. Every aspect of their
architecture – spaces, materials, colors, and
forms – is pervaded by enthusiasm.

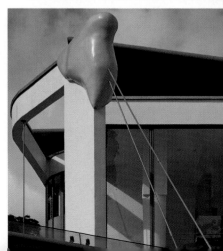

The spaces in this house are meant to be
enjoyed and, as a result, they communicate the
spirit of freedom in which they were conceived.

As well as reducing the effect
of the sun's rays, the double
roof is also one of the
architectural elements with the
greatest visual impact.

The access ramp to the dining room. The false ceiling creates a very distinctive shape.

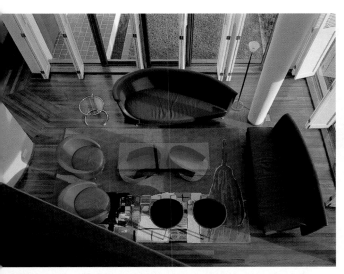

The design of the sitting room incorporates a number of different areas. At the far end are the entrance area and the staircase leading to the second floor.

The furniture was carefully chosen. Each element has a particular form and color that enhances the heterogeneous but harmonious whole.

Detail of the bathtub.

View of the bathroom on
the second floor.

View of the entrance
with its circular,
illuminated wall.

Right-hand page:
General view of the living
room. The slatted window
shades can be used to shut
out the outside world.

House with Studio in Rotterdam

Location: *Rotterdam, the Netherlands*
Year of construction: *1991*
Architects: *Mecanoo architekten b.v.*
Associates: *Theo Kupers, Bjarne Mastenbroek, Cock Peterse, Inma Fernández Puig, Birgit Jürgenhake, Marjolijn Adriaansche; Van Omme & De Groot b.v., Rotterdam (contractors)*
Photography: *Scagliola, Brakkee, Francine Houben*

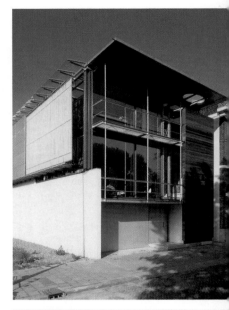

The Dutch architects Erik van Egeraat and Francine Houben, members of the Mecanoo architekten (Delft) practice, designed their own house near Kralinge Plas, a small lake on the outskirts of Rotterdam.

The building is situated at the end of a row of 19th-century houses, surrounded by single-family houses and apartment blocks designed by some of the Netherlands' leading modern architects. Its orientation enables it to enjoy views of the Kralinge Plas, in one direction, and of a canal that runs parallel to the row of houses, in the other. This double view has had a determining influence on the organization of the living space and the composition of the facades. The building is detached from its older neighbors, with the intervening space providing alternative access on the first floor and presenting a blind wall on the upper floors. The entire house is one continuous space, both physically and visually: staircases, walkways, split levels, and alternative doorways connect the spaces vertically and horizontally and offer various possibilities for movement between the different areas.

The textures and colors of the simple materials used in the house – metal, glass, concrete, wood, and bamboo – are arranged and combined to create a single, harmonious environment. The owners' taste for architectural detail appears in every corner of the house (door handles, panels, floors, lighting) and the yard, whose design was undoubtedly influenced by a study trip to Japan.

The concrete flooring and glass walls
create a perfect transition between the
den and the back yard.

Rocks in the yard that was inspired
by traditional Japanese gardens. The
area around the pool is particularly
tranquil and secluded.

Split levels unite the space of the two
upper stories. On the outside, the
continuous bamboo panel reinforces
the continuity.

Detail of the yard lighting.

Right-hand page:
On the second floor, the
communal areas – living
room, dining room, and
kitchen – form a single space
that is projected beyond the
confines of the house along
both lines of vision.

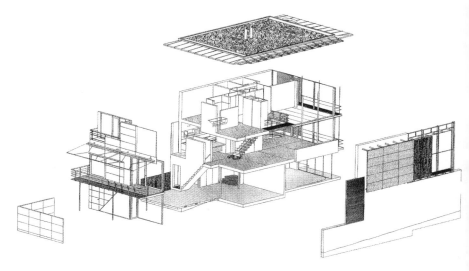

Axonometric projection of the
house showing its various
components.

The spectacular view of the
Kralinge Plas from the library.

The main staircase leads from the
ground floor to the living room.

Right-hand page.
Detail of the metal staircase
leading to the top floor. It
is supported on the wooden
facing of the wall.

The lake seen from the
living room, with the split
level in the foreground.

Little House

Location: *Fukuoka, Japan*
Year of construction: *1996*
Architect: *Naoyuki Shirakawa*
Photography: *Koji Kobayashi, Nobuaki Nakagawa*

Right-hand pag
The south facade see
from the southeas

The area of the actual building is 1,045 sq ft (97 m^2), and the total area of the living space 1,195 sq ft (111 m^2). Because of its location, the first floor is enclosed on all four sides, while the second floor has windows facing east and west.

There are two fundamental elements in the design of the Little House: the cross section that determines the elevations, and the handrails that run throughout the building.

When considering the various spaces required within the house, it was essential to ensure ease of movement from one room to the next and, in particular, to allow for the possibility that one of the couples living there might become physically incapacitated at some point in the future. For this reason, a series of painted, tubular-steel handrails runs from one area to another.

The entrance door, in the east wall of the house, opens onto a fairly large patio that occupies the south end of the living space and gives the house a sense of seclusion. Access to the interior of the house is through the glass doors that open onto the patio.

The architect and his clients agreed that the bedrooms should offer various sources of interest and stimulation in the event of long periods of convalescence or illness. To this end, special equipment and accessories have been installed and consideration has been given to the possibility of moving one of the beds to the south end of the house where there is more movement.

Two areas, along the long wall of the house, are designed as kitchen work surfaces and as closets for storage.

Detail of the east facade

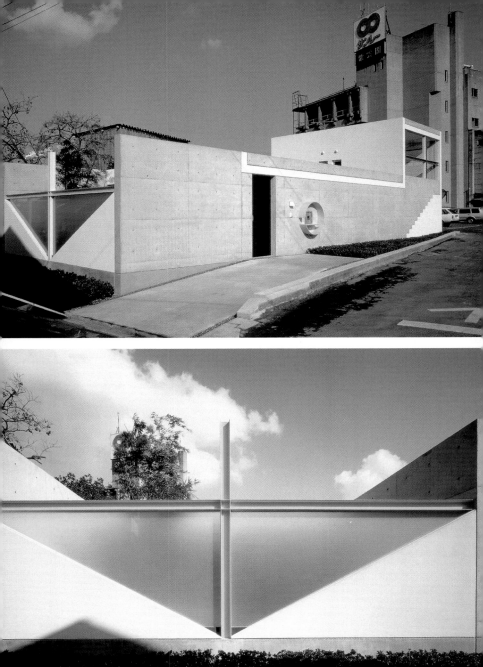

Detail of the staircase.

The living room, dining room, and kitchen.

The bedroom at the north end of the house.

View to the east from the second floor.

Right-hand page:
The dining room, at the south end of the house.

Cube House

Location: *Tokyo, Japan*
Year of construction: *1992*
Architect: *Naoyuki Shirakawa*
Photography: *Koji Kobayashi*

The house is built in the center of Tokyo, on a narrow site with an area of 755 sq ft (70 m²). It is built in the form of a cube: 19½ x 19½ x 19½ feet (6 x 6 x 6 m).

Geometry forms the basis of the design, with the position of each element based on geometric principles or analytical processes. For example, the circumference of the circle in the entrance facade has been carefully calculated so that the face joints that delineate the plane of the facade form tangents to the circle. This circular hole is the entrance, on the second floor, to the patio that gives access to the living room. The architectural elements – windows, doors, and staircases – are treated as abstract forms that are used to create compositions whose principles challenge the conventional use of the basic elements of the design. For example, the table in the living room is a large, flat surface that projects over the staircase: you have to pass beneath the table to reach the second floor.

Apart from the plain concrete of the walls, the predominant material used in the interior is pale-colored wood. Its polished surface provides a contrast with the roughness of the concrete.

The living room, on the second floor, is extremely light and airy. By contrast, the room on the first floor does not have as much light and is rather dark and gloomy. However, Naoyuki Shirakawa considers it important to have both light and darkness in a house, primarily for the element of surprise produced by the contrast between the two. In the words of the architect: "The darkness enables us to see the light."

Left-hand page:
The table of the main
living room, with the
cooking area.

The sink, between the
table and the wall.

The staircase.

The *tatami* (mat) room has
the largest east-facing
window. The translucent
paneling filters and
softens the light.

Circle House

Location: *Fukuoka, Japan*
Year of construction: *1996*
Architect: *Naoyuki Shirakawa*
Photography: *Koji Kobayashi*

The house – with a total area of 3,080 sq ft (286 m²) and an interior area of 1,215 sq ft (113 m²) – is occupied by an elderly widow. The hospital founded by her husband is today run by their two sons, both doctors. The design for this cylindrical building, situated next to the old hospital, allocates the first two floors to the hospital extension and the third to the house proper. This unusual location involves unusual solutions in terms of accommodating overlapping functions within the same building: for example, the separation of access to the hospital extension and access to the house. Both areas relate differently to the structure of the building and to the exterior. Whereas the hospital floors have a continuous line of windows, the third floor is closed to the outside world. Half the surface area of this floor is occupied by a yard onto which all the rooms in the house open.

The house has no windows on the outside and the impression of solidity and compactness is accentuated by its dark color, echoing that of the framework of the old hospital facades.

The interior of the house occupies a rectangular area whose geometry has been superposed onto the external form of the building. The intersection of these simple forms – the rectangle and the circle – gave rise to the organization of the living space.

The most surprising thing about the design is the contrast between the interior and the blind facade. It is an inward-looking house where the activity takes place within an enclosed – and invisible – space. It is designed to provide silence within the city.

The dining room seen from the living room.

View of the yard from the entrance.

Right-hand page (below): View from the dining room toward the *tatami* (mat) room, which can be closed off or remain completely open.

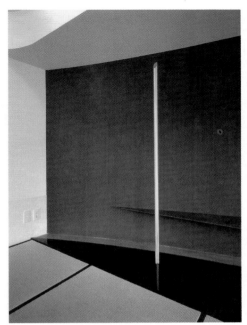

Charlotte House

Location: *Stuttgart, Germany*
Year of construction: *1993*
Architects: *Behnisch & Partner*

The house had to be constructed in such a way that the materials, architectural elements, and techniques used made the least possible impact on the local inhabitants and the environment. In other words, it had to respect the principles of "green" architecture as far as possible, for example by using such eco-friendly materials as colors and lacquers derived from natural resins. Neither the wooden floor nor the built-in closets were sealed or protected with industrial chemicals, but were treated and polished with oil. This ecological approach to the design was nothing new for Behnisch. He had already explored, albeit in a different way, the possibility of combining natural and artificial materials in the Munich stadium. For that project, structural engineers worked in association with landscape designers.

On the first floor, the kitchen, dining room, and living room form a large, continuous space that can be connected, if necessary, with the work area behind a sliding screen. The bedrooms are located on the next two floors, within the space of the semicircular roof. Below ground level, the natural basement has several installations and a swimming pool. It is lit by natural light since the contours of the site enabled windows to be incorporated at the south end of this level.

This design for the house is imaginative and pays a great deal of attention to detail. Like the rest of Behnisch's architecture, it needs to be seen from the inside to be fully appreciated.

This partial view of the facade illustrates the care taken in the choice of materials and the attention to detail.

View of the steps leading to the side entrance.

Right-hand page.
View of the dining-living room from the staircase. At the far end is the terrace with its decking and a bench that also acts as a balustrade.

In the foreground, detail of the fireplace and a small area of the living room. The kitchen is at the far end.

Although the interior is dominated by the use of wood for both the floors and furniture, this does not exclude more traditional pieces of furniture.

Right-hand page: The attic is reached from two of the bedrooms via a steep, ladder-like staircase.

House in Sakuragoaka

Location: *Sakuragoaka, Japan*
Year of construction: *1992*
Architect: *Kunihiko Hayakawa*
Photography: *Toshiwaru Kitajima*

Writing on the subject of the city and perception, Hayakawa describes the city as an instrument of learning. He sees it as a landscape that educates us, transforms our awareness, and leads us to modify the way in which we see things.

Instead of regarding cities as directly opposed to nature, they can be perceived as a natural environment, while the works of architecture that develop within them are like natural organisms that are therefore subject to the same need to grow and evolve.

The house is occupied by two generations: the parents live in house "A" and their son and his family in house "B." The main living room and bedroom adjoining house "A" are separated by translucent panels that can be opened as required. By contrast, the living room and bedroom of house "B" are separated by a bridge.

The external walls are in smooth, plain concrete, with 30% of the surface area covered by windows. This is a higher than average percentage for a private house. The idea was to create a spatial continuity between the interior and exterior space.

Two views of house "A" from the yard.

Looking south from the interior, across the patio.

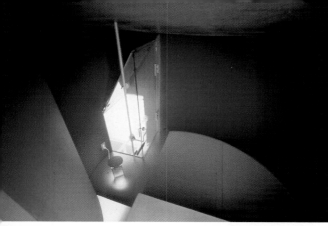

The *tatami* (mat) room is contained within the blue cylinder located in the main living area of house "B." The kitchen is located on the third floor of the cylinder and the *tatami* room on the fourth floor.

Main living area of house "A."

Main living area of house "B."

Casa Margarida

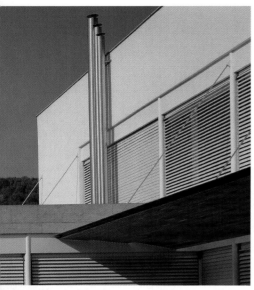

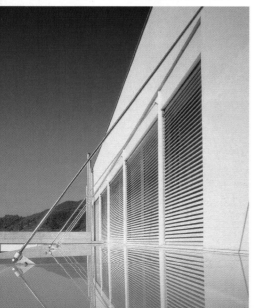

Location: *Olot, Spain*
Year of construction: *1996*
Architects: *Aranda, Pigem, Vilalta arquitectes*
Photography: *Eugeni Pons*

The Casa Margarida is a single-family house constructed as a main residence in the Spanish town of Olot.

The design is defined by the unusual location and the type of buildings suggested by the surroundings. The site is characterized by two main factors: firstly, its orientation, that is best in the direction of the street and, secondly, the very steep slope of the street.

The architecture is simple and austere, and uses a limited range of forms, elements, and materials. The composition is dominated by a taste for simplicity, and the richness of the design lies in the way in which the space is interrelated. The structural forms are clearly defined and all of the architectural details are skillfully executed.

The preoccupation with light, the constant superposition of different layers that filter light and create a subtle relationship between the interior and exterior space, is repeated throughout the house.

The large areas of glass completely open up the house to the yard and the surrounding views, while the smaller windows form precisely cut openings framed by the lawn, a tree, or some other feature. The architects have applied the same care with which they created the design for the house to ensure that the exterior is a visual extension of the interior space.

The house at night, seen
from the swimming pool.
The yard and pool are
located on the same level as
the house and the highest
point of the street.

Right-hand pag
View of the living room fro.
the kitchen. The shadov
created by the slatted windo
shades are projected into t
interior spaces. The interpl
of light and shadow depen
on their various positions ar
whether the shades th
protect the large areas of gla
from the sun's rays a
open or close

View of the heart of the house, a split-level area that opens onto the dining room.

The living room.

Detail of the bathroom.

View from the den.

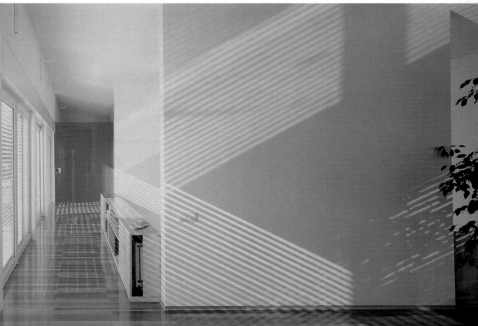

Lawson-Westen House

Right-hand page
The colored, stucco façade
overlooking the yard. In the
foreground are the wooden
beams that support the dome
of the rectangular section of
the building and whose
unfinished ends project
beyond the roof space

Location: *Los Angeles, United States*
Year of construction: *1994*
Architect: *Eric Owen Moss*
Photography: *Tom Bonner*

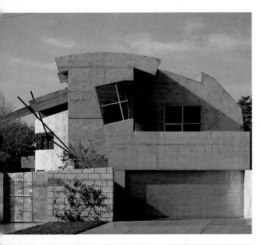

Contrary to possible first impressions, the Lawson-Westen House is not just an architectural *tour de force* or a piece of visual theater generated by arbitrary flights of fancy. The clients' ideas on function, space, and, in some cases, even form were taken up and interpreted by the architect, and became the very premises for the basis of the design. Thus the experimentation with space and form is in fact the architectural representation of a number of earlier ideas.

The unusual layout of the house means that the kitchen has become the real nerve center, both from a functional and a spatial point of view. It is surmounted – and emphasized – by a conical roof that constitutes the main structural feature of the building, not only in terms of its size, but as the catalyst for other external elements of the house.

The form of the interior spaces and the facades represents the application of some very positive ideas on domestic space. It achieves some powerful effects that nevertheless reflect a preoccupation with detail and the overall design in a conceptual dissection of the various levels of the house.

The use and combination of different materials such as wood, glass, and metal reflects a particular attention to detail in the design of elements such as the entrance to the property, the fireplace in the living room, the wooden sections of the vaulted roof, and a wide and varied range of large windows. All these elements contribute individually and collectively to the definition of this highly individual house.

The living room below the vaulted section of the building is crossed by a walkway on the second floor that connects the two parts of the house and provides a visual and spatial link with the kitchen and dining room.

The master bedroom, where an elongated window in the conical roof creates an effective glass panel that is incorporated into the adjoining bathroom.

Right-hand page
The space above the kitchen is crisscrossed by staircases, bridges, balconies, and structural elements that convert the upward space into a visual hullabaloo.

Taylor House

Location: *125 High Road,*
Sirius Cove, Australia
Year of construction: *1996*
Builder: *Mckencie and Ass.*
Architect: *Ed Lippmann*
Associates: *Ted Burner & P.Hammath*
Photography: *Peter Hyatt*

If there is one type of house associated exclusively with the 20th century, it is the house with large areas of glass and open floor space. Some of the best-known houses of that century belong to this category, for example Mies van der Rohe's Fansworth House, or the house of the architect Philip Johnson. Taylor House also belongs to this modern tradition.

Ed Lippmann received the commission for the house shortly after he and his wife returned from the United States and Europe. During their trip, they had visited some of the best-known works of modern masters (Wright, Mies, Johnson, Chareau) and some of the most famous architects of the present day (Nouvel, Foster, Rogers). They had been particularly interested in those built in glass, for example the Cartier building in Paris and the TV offices of Channel 4 in Great Britain. As Lippmann himself admitted, many of the impressions and images of the trip were still going around in his head when he drew up the plans for Taylor House.

The house stands on a shallow, broad site and lies along a north–south axis. However, it slopes fairly steeply in an east–west direction since it is located on a west-facing hillside. In fact, the slope means that the house has beautiful views to the west and the first floor enjoys a magnificent panoramic view of the town of Sirius Cove above the roof of the house next door. As a result, Taylor House has two main facades: the north facade that looks onto the street and the west facade that can be seen from the valley. Both are glass and steel structures, while the south and east facades are masonry walls.

The fact that the garage is in line with the street increases the privacy of the front garden.

The south facade at night. In Australia, south-facing facades receive the least amount of sunlight.

Sliding doors, and the use of wooden flooring in the living room and on the terrace, mean that the boundaries of the house are flexible.

As you might expect, most of the
furniture is designed by modern
masters: chairs and sofa by Le
Corbusier, Barcelona armchair and
chair by Brno de Mies van der Rohe.
In this way, Lippmann pays homage
to the architects that he
most admires.

Like all the other elements in the
house, the steel and glass staircase
creates the effect of transparency
and lightness.

The transparent glass walls are
divided into horizontal sections.
According to Lippmann, this creates a
much greater feeling of serenity and
greater harmony with the landscape
than if they were divided vertically.

The slatted blinds of the central skylight make it possible to regulate the sun's rays.

Casa Hakuei

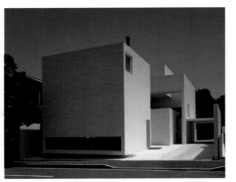

As well as closing off the southern edge of the site, the wall plays a major role within the overall design, defining both the patio and the organization of space within the house.

Following page:
Detail of the entrance to the studio.

Location: *Tokyo, Japan*
Year of construction: *1997*
Builder: *M. Mikuhaki*
Architect: *Akira Sakamoto*
Photography: *Nacasa*

Hakuei House stands on a relatively small, narrow site in the suburbs of Tokyo. Sakamoto's design for a building with simple lines and white walls has created a visual silence within the city that offers passers-by a moment's respite.

The architect did not build the house in the center of the site but, apart from a small yard opposite the entrance and a patio at the back, has extended the building almost to the boundaries. In so doing, he created an interior patio whose definition even took precedence over the composition of the spaces within the house. It was designed as an exterior but very private space that forms the focal point for the everyday life of the occupants.

To this end, one of the first things that Akira Sakamoto decided to do was build a lateral wall that crossed the site from the entrance to the rear boundary. The wall is situated at the eastern end of the site, so that the afternoon sun shines onto its surface and is reflected into every part of the house.

Opposite the wall, the architect decided to build three white boxes. The two largest — identical — boxes are situated at either end of the wall and enclose the patio. The smaller, third box adds complexity and richness to a space that would otherwise be uninteresting.

In this respect, Akira Sakamoto can be said to be adopting a minimalist strategy. In other words, not only do the finishes and overall appearance of the house tend to be extremely sober and restrained, but the principles of its composition are based on considerations that are closely associated with Minimal Art: the relationship between elements, the scale, materials, and the use of light.

The use of natural light, the visual relationship between the rooms, the height of the ceilings, and the split levels ensure that no two spaces in the house look the same, even though all the rooms have virtually the same finish.

The *tatami* (mat) room opens onto a narrow yard at the back of the house.

The communal areas – living room, dining room, and kitchen – are linked by a complex network of interconnecting levels.

Wooden slats are used for the flooring and the sliding doors throughout the house.

Milledge Residence

Location: *Sidney, Australia*
Year of construction: *1995*
Architect: *Jim Milledge*
Associates: *Simon Swaney, Sally Draper*
Photography: *Peter Hyatt*

When passing through the residential areas on the outskirts of large cities, you realize that, in the majority of cases, a great deal of imagination, effort, and money has been wasted on Victorian entrances, classical columns, jacuzzis, and rounded bathtubs, rather than good-quality architecture that incorporates sunny, welcoming, and pleasant spaces.

In the case of the Milledge Residence, the architect was also the client. Although Jim Milledge had his own ideas about the house and materials, he asked two of his friends and colleagues – Simon Swaney and Sally Draper – to work with him on the design and give him the benefit of their ideas and experience.

Every house has to be adapted to suit the particular topography, surroundings, and orientation of the site. For this reason, it is extremely difficult, if not inadvisable, to embark upon a project with preconceived ideas and the firm intention of imposing images seen or imagined in advance.

The house has a single floor, divided into three pavilions that form a U-shape around three sides of the patio area. On the fourth side is a lattice fence that screens the house from the neighboring property.

Each of the three pavilions has a pitched roof with a separate, internal framework. The longest and most spacious pavilion forms the central nucleus of the house. It lies parallel to the swimming pool and incorporates the communal areas: living rooms, dining room, and kitchen.

The house is not in line with the front boundary of the site. The entrance has been set back several yards in order to accommodate a porch where cars can be parked.

The centrally located pool occupies
a key position within the design. As
well as providing an ideal leisure
area in summer, it is a constant
point of reference for all areas of the
house throughout the year.

The Milledge Residence
shares many of the features
of the houses designed in
the purest modern
tradition by Brno Mies van
der Rohe, Richard Neutra,
and Rudolph Schindler.
However, one obvious
difference is the fact that it
has a pitched roof rather
than the typically flat roof
of these houses.

Many of the materials
used for the house are
recyclable and/or
environmentally friendly.
This aspect was also taken
into account when
designing the – entirely
natural – mechanisms for
controlling temperature.

iews of the kitchen. Its
ermanent fixtures consist of
wo parallel fitted units and
wo sliding doors that can
ose off the area if required.

House in Civita Castellana

Location: *Civita Castellana, Rome, Italy*
Year of construction: *1990*
Architect: *Maximiliano Fuksas*
Associate: *Anna Maria Saconi*
Photography: *Massimo Brugé*

The building – conceived by the architect Maximiliano Fuksas as a combination of distinct architectural units – represents an experiment in design that was open to new and innovative interpretations.

The house is situated in the town of Civita Castellana, near Rome. It has an irregular layout and is divided into two distinct areas: the main building and a spiral wing. In the wing, the various rooms (living room, dining room) form series of spaces that have no form of physical barrier separating or delimiting them, while its three levels are linked by a spiral staircase. The entire basement forms a huge circular games room and recreation area. The first floor houses the kitchen, living room, and dining room, while the second floor comprises the master bedroom and a huge den with direct access to a terrace.

The principal building also has three levels: the garage and service areas on the lower level, two bedrooms with a bathroom on the first floor, and two more bedrooms with a bathroom linked by terraces on the third floor.

Maximiliano Fuksas conceived this architectural project as the combination – at the level of geometric structure and spatial organization – of two different elements. He therefore decided to design two adjacent buildings, one in the form of a spiral centered around a cylindrical glass pillar and with a roof in the form of an inverted dome, a sort of upside-down pantheon. Next to and rising above it, stands the traditional house, a rectangular building with a more standard roof

The basic geometric form of this part of the building is the spiral. On the outside, it constitutes one of the principal elements of the design. On the inside, it is reflected in a number of details, for example the spiral staircase that links the various levels of the "turret."

The bottom of the staircase at the base of the huge, central pillar (*above*).

The top of the staircase opens onto the upper terrace that offers magnificent views of the surrounding area.

The huge windows that cover most of the external facades let in vast amounts of natural light that flood through the various spaces of the building. They also reflect the surrounding landscape, creating a spontaneous transition between the interior and external spaces.

All the walls and ceilings in the
house are painted in white, the
dominant color of the design.
The floors are covered in wood
and tiles that, on the first floor,
create an alternating pattern of
gray and white.

Casa Pedreño

Location: *Vallvidrera, Barcelona, Spain*
Year of construction: *1989*
Architects: *Artigues & Sanabria*
Photography: *Francesc Tur*

The central theme of the architects' design was to respect the natural features that dominated the site. However, it was ultimately the scale of the structure that organized and distributed the space, and gave function and form to the house. In certain respects, the design seems to be deeply rooted in the site, following its natural contours. In others, it seems to subscribe to a more spontaneous interpretation and tries to break away from these topographical constraints in an attempt to express its own individuality.

The house is situated in Vallvidrera, on the slopes of the Collserola mountains to the north of Barcelona. The steeply sloping site, the magnificent views of the city, and a nearby wood of indigenous pines are the characteristic elements of the surroundings that played an active role in determining the final form of the building.

The space of the house is organized on three distinct levels. The garage, the entrance, and a den that opens onto a south-facing terrace are situated on the upper (third) floor, at street level. On the intermediate (second) floor, the bedrooms and their respective dressing rooms and bathrooms occupy the south facade, while the north facade houses the games room and service areas. Finally, on the lower (first-floor) level are the living room, dining room, kitchen, and two patios that let natural light into the interior space.

Right-hand pa
View of the split lev
from the living room. T
owner of the house w
directly involved in t
interior design and t
choice of furnitu

The exterior porch lets
natural light into the
interior space.

The house is bounded by a
stone wall. The steps in the
yard are softened by plants.

The corner windows offer
extensive views of the
surrounding landscape.

Right-hand page
A broad roof protects the
house from the external
light and creates areas of
shade both inside and
outside the house

View of the staircase that
links the different levels.
The floor is parquet and
the walls are plain brick.

The kitchen looks directly
onto the yard.

Some of the walls have
been painted in warm,
creamy tones to provide a
contrast with the austerity
of the brick.

Donadio Residence

Location: *Pisa, Italia*
Year of construction: *1990*
Architect: *Gabriella Ioli Carmassi*
Photography: *Mario Ciampi*

The enclosed brick structure and long, narrow windows of this unusual building would appear to make it an unlikely design for a single-family house. However, Gabriella Ioli Carmassi used these strange external characteristics in response to two major disadvantages. She solved the first – an extremely small site – by building upward, and the second – the close proximity of the surrounding houses – by reinforcing the structure with solid brick walls and incorporating a number of narrow openings that form large windows when seen from the inside. The building stands in a residential district, near the historic center of the Italian city of Pisa.

Although the ground plan of the actual house is perfectly rectangular, the location of the staircase at one end creates an L-shape. The main facade, which incorporates the entrance, is vertically dissected by five of the openings that give the exterior its distinctive appearance. Their distribution is irregular, with four of these elongated windows on one side of the entrance, and only one on the other.

The building has three stories, with another that lies partially below ground level and houses the garage, utility area, and studio. The function of each floor has been clearly defined by the occupants, who have made the first floor a day area, with the entrance hall, kitchen, living room, and dining room. The second floor houses the bedrooms while, on the third, the den is bounded by terraces that provide this visually enclosed structure with an open area.

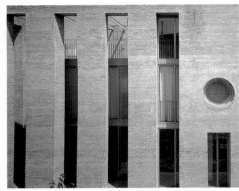

The main entrance has the same elongated shape as the windows. It is surmounted by a circular opening reminiscent of a rose window, the only nonlinear element to break the continuity of the straight lines that dominate the exterior of the building.

The plain brick of the four elevations that form the framework of the building is reflected by the brick of the interior walls.

The different levels of the house are linked by the staircase, enclosed on one side by one of the masonry facades and, on the other, by a transparent glass wall forming a gallery through which the natural light floods into the building. The cylindrical, polished-metal tube that forms the framework of the staircase echoes the characteristic lightness of the interior of the house.

left-hand page:
rays of sunlight enter through the
windows; solid, polished columns
support the framework of the
building; the floor is paved with
terrazzo that echoes the interior
walls and external elevations.

Some of the interior
walls are covered with
wood paneling.

The interior is dominated
by straight lines. The
narrow load-bearing walls
are in plain brick, while
the rest of the structure
consists of huge
transparent walls that
form a glass framework.

House Arango-Berry

Location: *Los Angeles, California, United States*
Year of construction: *1991*
Architect: *Franklin D. Israel*
Photography: *Richard Bryant/Arcaid*

The design for the House Arango-Berry in Beverly Hills is based on an original 1950s structure that has been redesigned and completely renovated.

The ground plan of the original structure consisted of two rectangles joined on one of their long sides. The extension work was carried out in the parallelogram opposite to the one incorporating the entrance, and consisted primarily of building a bathroom and dressing rooms. The galvanized metal sheeting used for both these structures was also used to cover the roof of the entire building.

The extension and renovation work created a huge structure consisting of two massive, rectangular parallelepipeds united by the large roof. The heating, air conditioning, and air vents were installed in the roof space.

Although Franklin D. Israel's design retained the existing swimming pool, the surrounding brick wall was extended to the new, blue-stuccoed concrete wall that forms the boundary of the yard. This blue-stucco facing is the most important constituent element of the exterior space. As well as using it to link the new garage with the main entrance, the architect also used it to border the gallery leading to the living area, incorporating it in the interior space.

The slightly different interior levels of this single-story house are linked by flights of steps.

Partial view of the original
roof and pool of the house, a
typical example of southern
Californian architecture.

Right-hand page:
This panoramic view of the living
room shows the exceptional lighting
provided by the spotlights on the
wooden beams.

Detail of the metal shelving on the
wall of the corridor.

An original piece of furniture with an
abstract painting in the foreground.

The kitchen seen from the living
room. The wooden sculpture is a
symbol of welcome.

The original structure of the 1950s interior has been retained. Large glass windows and translucent concrete panels offer views of the modern city.

The interior decoration has been renovated. For example, the unit containing the television and hi-fi, the fireplace, and even the bed in the master bedroom are made of polished steel paneling.

Craven Residence

Location: *Los Angeles, California, United States*
Year of construction: *1989*
Architect: *Frank Fitzgibbons*
Photography: *Julie Phipps*

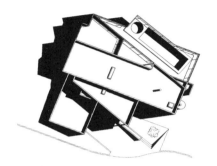

The house was built on three levels that echoed the natural contours of the site. The entrance level comprises the living room, dining room, and a kitchen that incorporates a family breakfast room. The kitchen also gives access to a service room, the utility area, and a staircase leading down to a family living room that opens directly onto the pool. The main entrance dominates the design of this floor, giving access to the communal areas (dining and living rooms) or leading straight ahead to the south-facing wall that overlooks the roof-terrace pool suspended high above the city of Los Angeles. The floor below comprises the swimming pool, two living rooms, a dining terrace, a bar, and the boiler room. The areas requiring more peace and tranquillity, for example the bedrooms (each with its own veranda) and the library, are on the top floor.

The interior walls do not touch the ceiling, leaving the vertical surfaces incomplete and creating the effect of large, open spaces and an atmosphere of cool transparency.

The entire building is governed by the principles of *Yin* and *Yang*, from the architectural structure to the interior design. Frank Fitzgibbons has developed the relationship between the interior and exterior space, as well as the concepts of present, past, and future, to achieve this brilliant architectural design.

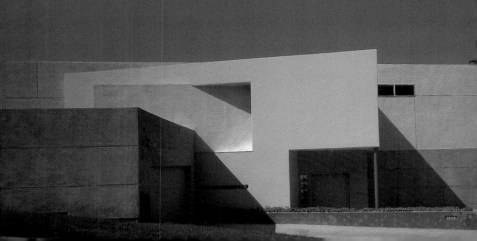

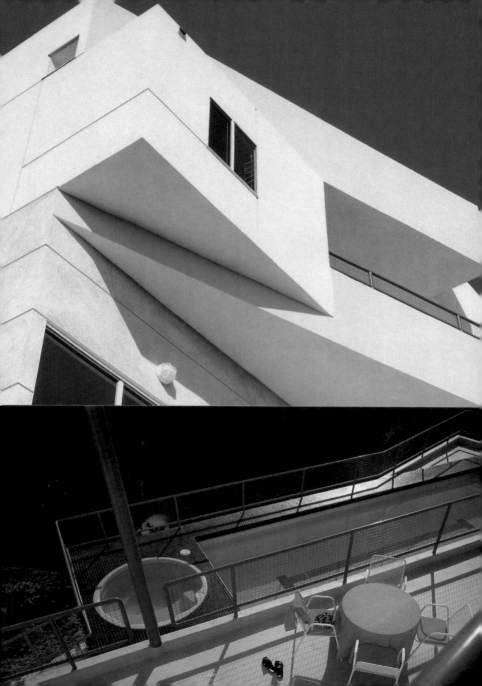

Left-hand page:
Beyond the dining-room
table with its undulating
metal supports, the window
offers a view of the city of
Los Angeles.

Views of the living room,
with the fireplace in the
background.

The living room occupies an
extensive, split-level area.
The natural light enters the
room through the large
windows placed vertically
one above the other. This
large living area not only
acts as a pivotal space around
which the upper and lower
floors are structured, but also
as a link between the
interior and exterior spaces.

House in Rochester Place

Location: *London, Great Britain*
Year of construction: *1988*
Architect: *David Wild*
Photography: *Richard Bryant/Arcaid*

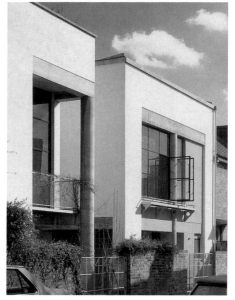

The house of the architect David Wild stands in Rochester Place, in a residential district of the city of London. The architect designed and built the house himself in the late 1980s. Five years later, a private commission to design and build a single-family house along the same lines inspired him to create a pair of houses and build the second next to his own. However, the new building was different from the first in a number of ways.

Seen from the south, the two houses appear as two blocks of white color, the restrained architecture of their facades dominated by large windows overlooking the street. On the opposite side, at the back, the two houses open conventionally onto the exterior space via balconies, doors, and windows. Although both buildings have a rectangular floor plan, there is a difference in the dimensions: the architect's house is much larger, longer, and narrower. It has a small back yard overflowing with plants and shrubs, and a small pool.

Although the houses are only about 15–20 ft (5–6 m) apart, they are linked by a small, grayish building. This single-story annex connects the two houses and maintains their visual unity.

Detail of the structure
supporting the balcony
of the house at
42 Rochester Place

The facade of no. 42. The
house is squarer and more
regularly shaped than its
neighbor at no. 44

ews of the house at no. 44.

e dining table seen from the
ttom of the staircase. Above the
ble, the original structure of the
iling is also visible.

rtial view of a bedroom, whose walls
e painted in a pleasant shade of pink.

rridor and view of the wooden
aircase leading to the second floor.

This view of the spacious living room highlights the original design of the stove that blends harmoniously with the wooden floor.

Wabbel House

Location: *Wittlaer, Germany*
Year of construction: *1990*
Architect: *Wolfgang Döring*
Photography: *Elmar Joeressen*

This unusual house looks more like a modern industrial building than a residential living space. It is situated in the small German town of Wittlaer, but also enjoys the many advantages offered by the nearby city of Düsseldorf.

The family living in the house entertains a great deal and needs a spacious interior. Wolfgang Döring bore this requirement very much in mind when he designed the interior of the house, eliminating all unnecessary walls and only partitioning off those areas requiring their own privacy. The idea of virtually creating one vast, multifunctional room inspired the architect to give the building an industrial, high-tech look.

Wolfgang Döring designed the house in Wittlaer as a rectangular pavilion with a terrace at one end. The garage lies parallel to one of the long sides of the terrace. Above this first-floor level, he added a prism-shape structure that houses the master bedroom and two smaller, adjoining rooms. Next to this tower-like structure, a centrally located metal cylinder contains the spiral staircase linking the two levels.

On the outside, the building is surrounded by red-painted metal framework that gives it its characteristic industrial appearance.

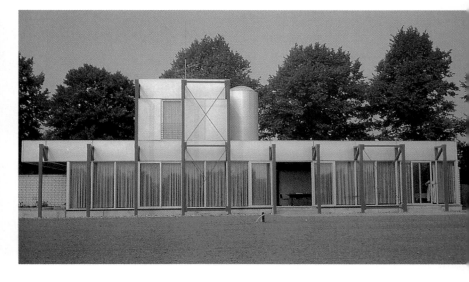

Left: The northeast elevation is completely closed off from the road by masonry panels. The only opening on this side of the house is the main entrance to the building: a narrow salmon-colored door whose yellow canopy creates an interesting note of contrast.

Above: On the southwest elevation, huge windows supported by an aluminum framework create a visual transition between the interior and exterior spaces.

The kitchen was conceived as a physical and visual barrier. Next t it, a metal cylinder acts a a closet.

Döring designed the house as a huge horizont; block of metal in which the different areas interconnect freely. Physical and visual barriers have been kept t a minimum, leaving the interior as open as possible. This all-embracing desire for spac is reflected in the fluid transition between the entrance hall, the main living room, and the dining area.

Right-hand pag
The decor is dominate
by contemporary-sty;
furniture in black ar
dark gray. However,
touch of warmth
provided by the salmo
drapes that help to offse
the coldness of th
ultraspacious hous;

Kidosaki House

Location: *Tokyo, Japan*
Year of construction: *1988*
Architect: *Tadao Ando*
Photography: *Richard Bryant/Arcaid*

This original building, whose form and function are both very specific, stands in the peaceful residential district of Setagaya Ward, in Tokyo. In modern Japanese society, some of the deep-rooted, ancestral traditions that have molded eastern characteristics and behaviour patterns are still very much alive. For example, it is not uncommon to find several generations of the same family living together under one roof in the interest of family unity. In this instance, Tadao Ando had to design a house that would be occupied by three generations of the same family, while taking into account the requirements of a modern lifestyle that demands privacy as well as social living.

Kidosaki House was commissioned for Japanese occupants and the architect's design reflects the traditional Japanese architectural style: a horizontal concept of space and irregular dimensions. However, he also incorporated elements of western architecture, creating a unified and transcendental whole by combining the static geometry and dynamic upward movement of western buildings with oriental architectural principles.

The main body of the building, which stands on an irregular-shape site, is a perfect cube – 40 ft (12 m) square – around which the rest of the structure is articulated.

The transparent glass
walls not only give a clear
view into the interior of
the house, but also
provide pleasant natural
lighting. Kidosaki House
is a formless structure
that is naturally
incorporated into an
almost floating space.

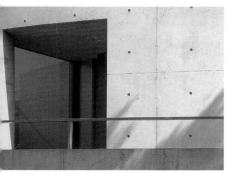

The south facade and the central cube form the boundaries of a patio where restful grays and greens make it an ideal place to relax.

Detail of a wall showing the tiny holes distributed symmetrically over the facades and interior walls.

lean, simple lines define the austere, unembellished interior, in accordance with the principles of traditional Japanese design. The spaces are uninterrupted and open, extensive and uncluttered. The few, carefully selected items of furniture and ornaments enhance the effect of pure space which the present is essential. The furniture, too, is simple, elegant, and distinctly modern in style.

Casa Ca Nostra

Location: *Pont d'Inca, Mallorca, Spain*
Year of construction: *1991*
Architect: *Antonio Vila Ramis*
Photography: *Gabriel Ramón*

Antonio Vila's design for the project was based on an existing structure that incorporated an architect's studio. He conceived the idea of a house and leisure area adjacent to the original building. Casa Ca Nostra is situated on the island of Mallorca, where light and climate are determining factors. The site is located in a busy district that has, however, retained the peaceful residential atmosphere of days gone by. It also has the advantage of a nearby pine wood owned by a local convent. Town-planning regulations were specific and required the facades of the houses in the street to be kept the same.

Because of these restrictions, the architect decided to close the house to the street with a windowless facade that created a completely private space.

The layout of the site is square and incorporates several buildings – the architect's studio, a guest area, and the house itself – arranged around a landscaped patio and pool.

The L-shape of the house forms a patio, covered by a skylight, that acts as a transitional area between the various units and spaces.

The living space is distributed on two floors, with the bedrooms and a special children's area on the second floor. The first floor includes the living room, dining room, kitchen, and service areas.

The house is adapted to the island's local customs and traditions and respects the general atmosphere of its surroundings.

The various units are situated around the edge of the site, forming a large central area of patios and gardens. Recesses in the walls overlooking this area let natural light into the interior of the house.

The principal types of
materials used in the
building were the local
Marés sandstone,
terracotta tiles, and wood.

The concrete beams of the
ceilings are painted white.
The kitchen, bedrooms, and
washroom are lined with
marble. The bathroom
furniture is by Roca
Gondola and the accessories
by Arne Jacobsen.

Right-hand page:
View of the main
living room.

House in Kumamoto

Location: *Kumamoto, Japan*
Year of construction: *1990*
Architects: *Antonio Citterio, Terry Dwan*
Photography: *Joshio Shiratori*

When building this experimental house, Antonio Citterio and Terry Dwan were forced to confront an architectural dichotomy: the mistaken belief that eastern and western houses are totally different from each other.

The building stands on the outskirts of the city of Kumamoto in Japan, in an area devoid of any particular urban characteristics. The architects wanted to adapt the house to its surroundings, while incorporating magnificent views of the neighboring hills.

The ground plan of the house is long and rectangular, and the two floors are very different. The first floor includes the living room, dining room, kitchen, and service areas, and forms the central nucleus of family life. The bedrooms are on the second floor. In the space between the two blocks, a staircase giving access from the street is lit from above by a skylight. The main entrance is located in the middle of the west facade.

The first stage of the project involved evaluating the suburban environment into which the house would be incorporated. The area is characterized by typical suburban houses and it was almost impossible not to follow such urban preconceptions as the type of paving, green spaces, and social areas. The architects also noticed that the houses in the area resembled American suburban houses – representing both the colonial and the provincial architectural styles. However, the interiors were typically Japanese, with low ceilings and small rooms.

By contrast, this house has high ceilings and structural focuses that are typically European. The principal type of material used in the building was wood. The bedrooms were designed on a smaller scale which helped to create a feeling of privacy.

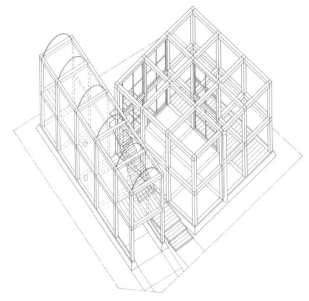

Axonometric projection c
the house.

View of the house's
wooden staircase.

The corridor leading to t
living room is lit by a
circular window (*left*).

The main entrance is
located on the west facade
at the center of the
building. The principal
types of materials used fo
the exterior were wood fo
the framework and
polyurethane-coated pane
for the walls.

The living room has obvious Oriental connotations. However, a European-style sofa provides a contrast with the Japanese table and screen at the far end. The wooden floors – made from local pine – are covered with *tatami* (mats), while the doors and window frames are in white-painted aluminum.

Casa Aznar

Location: *Esplugues de Llobregat, Barcelona, Spain*
Year of construction: *1992*
Architect: *Carlos García Delgado*
Photography: *Francesc Tur*

The Casa Aznar, designed by the architect Carlos García Delgado, is less remarkable for its straight lines than for its undulating curves, its homogeneous appearance, and its different structural levels. It is situated on an irregular-shape, hillside site in the district of Esplugues de Llobregat, on the outskirts of Barcelona. Privacy in this wealthy residential district is maintained by the distance between the houses.

The steep slope and high altitude of the irregular site afford magnificent panoramic views of the surrounding area. The building accounts for 4,300 sq ft (400 m²) of the total surface area – 12,900 sq ft (1200 m²) – while the rest is occupied by a carefully landscaped yard.

In his design for the Casa Aznar, the architect deliberately avoided the tendency to create complex structures, individual features, and distinctive architectural forms that characterize the surrounding houses. He rejected the concept of complexity as a starting point and simplified the ideas that inspired his design: he limited the type of materials used on the outside of the house and based the structure around two levels. He then carefully designed an exterior landscaped area.

The house basically consists of two separate and stylistically distinct units. The lower unit is built in concrete and is geometrically defined by straight lines and angles. The organic forms and curved lines of the upper unit are materialized by a natural stone finish.

The yard, planted with cypresses and palms, plays a key role in the overall perception of the design. Excavation work was kept to a minimum and the design has respected the natural contours of the original site.

Concrete, sandstone, and glass
were used for the facades and
exterior walls of the building.

Right-hand page
View of the pool that is a
integral part of the
living room

Palms have been planted i
the lawn surrounding the
pool, while cypresses define
the boundary of the site

The pool extends along the
rear facade of the house

The curvilinear form of some of the furniture – the table and sofa for example – echoes the curved lines of some of the structural elements of the house.

A huge circular light dominates the top of the staircase linking the two floors of the house.

‎w from the top of the
‎ircase, showing the
‎oden treads.

‎w of the bathroom.
‎e exterior concrete wall
‎ be seen beyond the
‎rble bathtub.

‎e curvilinear lines
‎the interior reflect
‎ external contours
‎the house.

House in Yokohama

Location: *Yokohama, Japan*
Year of construction: *1990*
Architect: *Kazuo Shinohara*
Photography: *Richard Bryant/Arcaid*

This house – which stands high on a steep hillside, in a peaceful part of Yokohama – was designed as an extension to an existing wooden building. The original site was covered by huge trees, and was sensitively created with minimum impact on the environment. To continue to preserve as many trees as possible, the house was built on part of the original plot.

The extension adjoins the existing structure, rectangular, uniform building. The first floor incorporates the entrance (located between the two buildings), the main living room, the *tatami* (mat) room, and a bathroom. The second floor houses the kitchen, the dining room, and also a small storeroom.

The main part of the new extension is in the form of a quarter circle, which meant that only one window had to be removed from the original structure during its construction. One of the central ideas of Kazuo Shinohara's design was to create a spatial link between the two different areas, an impartial and objective articulation between disparate and separate architectural visions.

The architect also explored ways of linking the interior and exterior spaces, and successfully provided a series of logically unrelated solutions that enable all parts of the house to enjoy an extremely pleasant outlook.

Kazuo Shinohara also gave free rein to his imagination when he designed the interior of the house: triangles and squares complement and contrast with circles and semicircles to create a strong visual impact. One of the most striking elements is this bicolored chair and table in black and white.

rge windows create an
most complete transition
tween the interior and
terior spaces.

e design of the kitchen
not only extremely
nctional, but also lets
a great deal of
tural light.

House in Florence

Location: *Florence, Italy*
Year of construction: *1991*
Architect: *Elio Di Franco*
Photography: *Mario Ciampi*

The natural and architectural features of the location – the city of Florence – led the architect to examine the close relationship between the house and the site. This was why Elio Di Franco decided to transform what was an introverted residence into an outward-looking living space.

The house is situated on the Via di San Leonardo, near the Forte di Belvedere. It enjoys views across the city to the northeast, and is dominated by the hill and church of San Miniato al Monte to the southwest.

The irregular-shape house stands on a rectangular platform. Its interior space is distributed over two stories, and it also has a self-contained studio-apartment. The entrance is located on the northeast facade and gives access to the central section of the house. The first floor – comprising the living room, dining room, kitchen, and a bedroom – is the focus of family life. A magnificent spiral staircase leads to the second floor, occupied by the master bedroom, den, and a truly amazing bathroom. Access to the terrace is via an exterior flight of steps on the southeast facade.

Elio Di Franco decided to create a dynamic interaction between the interior and exterior spaces by extending the boundaries of this extremely elegant building to include the pool, the vineyard, and the terraces.

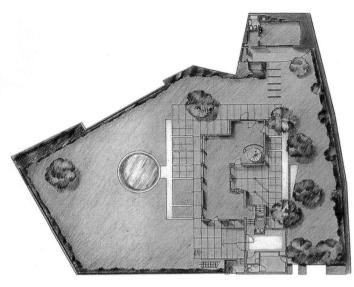

The ground pl[a]
of the hous[e]

The interconnected faca[de]
and pool by night. Th[e]
spacious terrace to the rig[ht]
is an ideal place to enj[oy]
pleasant lunches an[d]
alfresco suppe[rs]

Right-hand pag[e]
View of the southwe[st]
facade. The exterior pavin[g]
is in Serena stone, wi[th]
details in Carrara marbl[e]

The steps leadin[g]
to the terrac[e]

Detail of a triangular st[ep]
in the yar[d]

Right-hand pag
The transition betwee
the exterior and interi
spaces is made by th
repetition of elements of
similar shape and size
both areas. For examp
the rug in the living roo
echoes the shape of th
pool in the yar

View of the bathroor
Beyond the mosa
bathtub, a large windc
offers views across the ci
of Florenc

The same materials are
used outside and inside
the house: Serena stone on
the first floor, and Carrara
marble on the second.

Detail of the staircase
linking the two levels of
the house. Its spiral form
breaks the linear design
that dominates the rest of
the house.

House in Reykjavik

Location: *Reykjavik, Iceland*
Year of construction: *1989*
Architect: *Maggi Jónsson*
Photography: *Axel Sölvasson*

The various wood
elements on the outsi
of the house offs
the coldness of t
metal sheetin

The guiding principle of Maggi Jónsson's desig
for this house was the need to create a space
where the occupants had a sense of community
while at the same time retaining a feeling of
freedom and independence.

The building stands in a corner of a busy part
of Reykjavik, in southwest Iceland. It is
surrounded by detached houses, terraces, and
the occasional two- or three-story apartment
block. Views are fairly limited, since the fairly
steep slope interrupts lines of vision. However, i
is possible to see part of the city, the mountains
and the ocean in the distance.

The two-story house has an irregular ground
plan. The family areas – the dining room, kitchen
and living room – are on the first floor, while th
bedrooms and main bathroom are upstairs on
the second floor.

The building had to be conceived as a
complete unit. Although the family members
carry out their various activities in different
parts of the house, the overall design enables
them to feel in close proximity to each other.
The form and distribution of the interior space
are based on this social and functional concept.

Materials and techniques used inside the hous
are fairly basic: wood for the floors and ceilings,
and light-colored plaster for the walls.

Right-hand pag
The pleasant warmth
the interior desig
provides a strikin
contrast to the cold meta
of the exterior. Glas
panels in the roof let i
the maximum amount c
sunlight: a rar
commodity in thes
northern latitude

Interior view of the
kitchen. The butterfly
design on the glass door
can be seen from the street.

View of the large windows
surrounding the dining
and living rooms. Beyond
the glass doors is the
original stone paving
leading to the yard.

The distribution of space
and the irregular
positioning of the walls
within the house are fairly
unconventional.

House in Highgate

Location: *London, Great Britain*
Year of construction: *1989*
Architects: *John Jenkins, John Moore*
Photography: *Dennis Gilbert*

This house designed by John Jenkins and John Moore is a fine example of the exploration of new modern architectural elements in the tradition of Richard Meier. It stands on a steeply sloping street of Victorian houses in the Highgate district of London. Although it echoes their proportions, it does not echo the style of the surrounding houses.

The structural design was not chosen at random, but reflects the distribution of the communal and private areas within the house. It has a rectangular ground plan and a typical functional distribution of interior space: the kitchen and dining room on the first floor, the living room on the second, and the bedrooms on the top floor. The master bedroom has a stainless steel balcony that offers magnificent views of London. All the rooms are linked by staircases, both inside and outside the house.

The exterior space is divided into three distinct yards: one in front of the house that can be seen from the street, one along one side of the house, and, finally, the south-facing back yard that provides total privacy behind the house.

Originally, the abstract design was going to be emphasized by white walls, but in the end it was built in the same brick as was used for the surrounding houses. A great deal of attention was paid to the architectural detail to create a feeling of lightness and space.

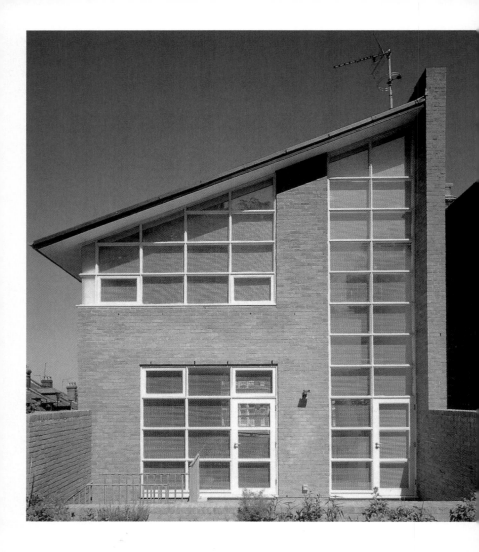

On two of the three visible sides of the house, huge windows let in natural light. The walls are built of London brick to create a design that, as far as possible, is homogeneous with the surrounding area.

View from the top of the stairs. The use of the same type of wood for both the floors and the stair treads provides continuity.

The windows and Venetian blinds give horizontal and vertical continuity to the interior space. The walls are painted white with some of the detail in wood. The doors, handrails, and window frames are all in stainless steel.

House in Santa Monica

Location: *Los Angeles, California, United States*
Year of construction: *1988*
Architect: *Frank Dimster*
Photography: *Reiner Blunck*

The two-story house occupies an irregular site, high on a steep hill. It enjoys magnificent views of the Pacific Ocean, the city of Los Angeles, and the Santa Monica mountains. Before building could begin, the site had to be modified, and three terraces were built.

The excavation work carried out on the site was the starting point for the architectural design. The earth removed, the area modified by excavation, and the drainage system were an integral part of the concepts that formed the project's basis. The architect's response to the context determined the final form of the building.

The irregular first floor of the house is the focus of family life. It comprises the kitchen, a den, the living room, and the split-level dining room. The garage and service areas are also situated on the first floor. The second floor houses the bedrooms, which all have access to the terraces.

Large windows create the transition between the inside of the house and the landscaped areas, offering magnificent views of the surrounding area and effacing the barriers between the interior and the exterior spaces.

The facades combine natural stone with beige painted surfaces. The woodwork, the metal staircase, and the handrails are all painted white.

The spiral staircase linking
the pool with the main
terrace provides a striking
contrast to the linear design
of the house. In the distance,
a beautiful view of Los
Angeles by night.

't-hand page:
rtial view of the various
els of the house.

e extremely functional
:chen opens directly
to one of the terraces.

e problem of too much
:ural light entering the
use through the large
ndows is solved by the
stallation of slatted
nds that filter sunlight.

Some areas have parquet
flooring, while others –
ncluding the stairs – are
peted in gray. The walls
and interior facings are
painted in white.

Detail of the spacious
bathroom, with its
panoramic view of the
anta Monica mountains.

House in Los Angeles

Location: *Los Angeles, California, United States*
Year of construction: *1988*
Architects: *Morphosis Architects*
Photography: *Reiner Blunk*

This three-story house has a slightly irregular ground plan. The interior space is organized in totally unusual way, with the daytime area on the top floor and the bedrooms and service areas on the first two floors. This means that, instead of being overshadowed by the row of houses on the other side of the coast road, the living room enjoys a view of the Pacific Ocean. The plans also clearly show the intersection of two separate areas: a central section that houses the bathrooms, the kitchen, and the elevator, while the rest of the rooms are located in the other diagonal – section.

Particular emphasis has been placed on the circular-shape entrance located on one side of the central block of the building. It gives access to a family living room that opens onto a patio, on the left, and a guest area with a bathroom and sauna opposite, on the right. The next floor houses the den, with access to a patio, and a bedroom with its own closet and en suite facilities that also has access to exterior space. On the top floor are the main living room, the dining room, and the kitchen. A narrow corridor leads onto a vast, open terrace. Finally, the basement houses the garage, storehouse, and the service area.

The windows are placed so as to offer views of the surrounding landscape, as well as being a source of privacy and light. The view is toward the west, the Pacific Ocean, and the private yards of the first and third floors. A single operative window in the kitchen, and a series of three large windows on the north side of the house, provide indirect light to the central space

i-hand page:

e kitchen, located on e third floor of the itral block, is the most mplex space in the use. It is a point of ivergence for structural ments, high-tech pliances, and mplicated systems of :ess to the various cernal areas of the house.

In the interior of the house, the simplicity of the materials offsets the spatial complexity: the loors are tiled, the walls istempered, and the top oor has beautiful wood-paneled ceilings.

House in Vicenza

Location: *Thiene, Vicenza, Italy*
Year of construction: *1990*
Architect: *Franco Stella*
Associate: *Flavio Albanese*
Photography: *Studio Azzurro*

The significance of this design lies primarily in a calculated transformation of topographic disadvantages into an unusual but highly effective layout of functional areas. The fact of raising the building on a dichotomy of presence and absence, empty and full, addition and subtraction constitutes a singularly elegant esthetic achievement that is complemented by the careful articulation of the building lines to define the stratification of the various floors.

The starting point of the structure is the formal and conceptual attempt to set an isolated, serene, almost timeless site that ignores the constraints of its surroundings. The designer achieves his aim by making the annexes an integral part of the layout of the building and giving the substructure unusual importance. The idea of a single family home stems, right from the start, from the need to create optimum space for the individual. For this reason, Stella produces architecture on a human scale that does not reject the values of his craft.

The method he chose to solve the problem of the unexpressive nature of the plot was to take advantage of the flat ground to create a construction on several levels. In this way, he succeeded in taking maximum advantage of the size of the whole space, as well as achieving a perfect distribution of areas, locating the body of the dwelling at the highest point (level with the access road) and the rest of the building on the lower level.

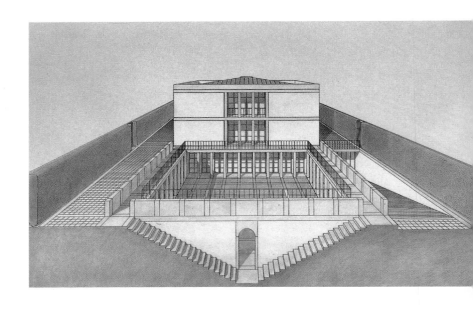

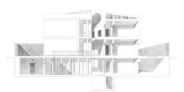

The building rises as a combination of two
antithetical figures, an addition and a
subtraction, of a similar quadrangular
shape. In conventional terms, these two
sections translate into a three-floor house,
two visible and one underground, plus a
sunken patio.

derground, the
gitudinal line is based
the columned room
sing the swimming
l, with five glass doors
provide light for the
er patio.

Schnabel House

Location: *Brentwood, Los Angeles, United States*
Year of construction: *1988*
Architect: *Frank O. Gehry*

The unusual shape of the building, its atypical typology, and the unusual choice of materials were only possible thanks to the understanding of the clients, who were more concerned with the esthetic, cultural, and pragmatic aspects of how they were to live than with submission to conventional dwellings and common styles of domestic architecture.

The selected site is a plot of approximately 5,700 sq ft (530 m²) without any noticeable topographical features. At one end, the rectangular plot terminates in an irregular, trapezoidal area where the slope evens out to form a secluded terrace at a lower level. The absence of any significant external conditioning factors provided the architect with greater freedom to design the project with the advantages of the plot in mind.

Frank O. Gehry was guided by the elaborate building plan (a private area, service area, and recreation area as well as a garage and outbuildings) to a solution based on independe structures that treats each element as a separat unit. This extends to the design and esthetics o the structure. The change in shape and surface each of the buildings maintains its own specific architectural style. Its elements complement ar contrast in an expressive, spatial dialogue.

Right-hand pa
View of the interior of the fi
floor of the house. The gl
wall housing the main entran
allows an abundance of natu
light to enter and offer
direct view of the ya

General view of the Schnabel House
from the back of the plot. The
ingenious treatment of water and
planting is in harmony with the
conceptual atmosphere of the whole.

HOUSES IN THE SUBURBS

In view of the space restrictions that many of the major international town centers now impose, architects have been forced to seek alternative solutions to enable cities to continue along their normal growth path.

Obviously the concept of urban nucleus is changing and previous trends are giving way to different lines of action necessarily directed toward areas further away from the center as these offer greater opportunities and considerable savings on the cost of the plot on which the dwelling is to be built. The problems of increased density of occupation and elimination of unprofitable activities inevitably have an effect on the quality of the areas available for building – areas already choked by congestion, strangled with traffic, and suffering from lack of facilities, community resources, and recreation areas. In effect, population increase determines how far the city expands. The overflow spills into the suburbs, by means of town planning processes that are the result of numerous unrelated actions. In some places, the authorities intervene in regulating these operations and impose standards or lay down guidelines for the development and programming that they judge the population will require. In other situations, dwellings are built on illegally occupied land, and the new suburbs are precariously consolidated by the construction of various types of substandard housing, with all the problems inherent in the lack of minimum services. The process of metamorphosis, ongoing in the nerve centers of major cities, is

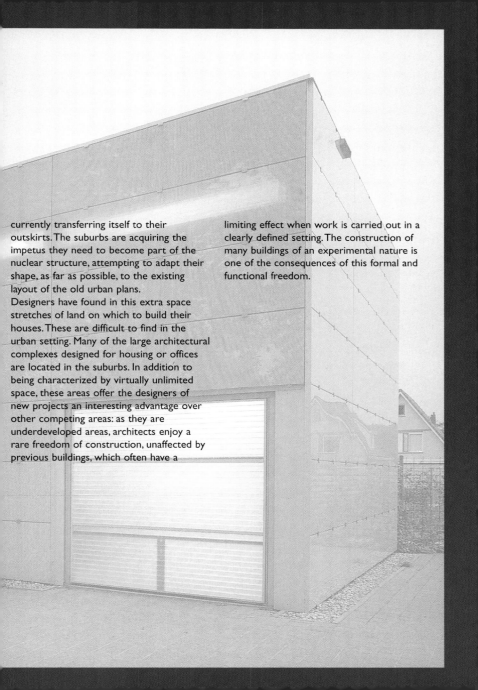

currently transferring itself to their
outskirts. The suburbs are acquiring the
impetus they need to become part of the
nuclear structure, attempting to adapt their
shape, as far as possible, to the existing
layout of the old urban plans.
Designers have found in this extra space
stretches of land on which to build their
houses. These are difficult to find in the
urban setting. Many of the large architectural
complexes designed for housing or offices
are located in the suburbs. In addition to
being characterized by virtually unlimited
space, these areas offer the designers of
new projects an interesting advantage over
other competing areas: as they are
underdeveloped areas, architects enjoy a
rare freedom of construction, unaffected by
previous buildings, which often have a

limiting effect when work is carried out in a
clearly defined setting. The construction of
many buildings of an experimental nature is
one of the consequences of this formal and
functional freedom.

Wall-less House

Location: *Karuizawa, Nagano, Japan*
Year of construction: *1997*
Architect: *Shigeru Ban*
Photography: *Hiroyuki Hirai*

This house is one of a series of experimental projects that the architect calls "Case Study Houses." Built on a slope, so as to minimize excavation work, the rear half of the house gives the appearance of being built into the landscape. The floor curves up at one end to meet the roof slab that is otherwise supported by only three very slender round pillars. The basic idea on which this house has been designed is that of achieving spatial continuity both inside and out. Two planes defined by the floor and the roof mark out and frame the horizon. Boundaries have been eliminated, the interior space has no divisions, visibility is total – even in places as private as the bathroom, which is open to view. Only the kitchen fittings, a bench, and a few items of furniture suggest slight outlines of areas inside a single smooth, homogeneous space.

The dwelling can be altered using sliding panels, making it suitable for different uses while at the same time giving each room a new character. Curved lines are extremely simple, the structure almost disappears, and the total transparency of the outer boundaries make the house seem to blend into its surroundings.

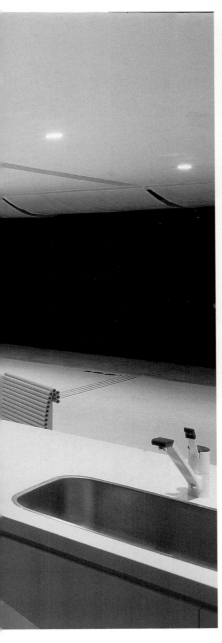

Earth movement was carried out from bottom to top. The intention was not to interfere with the landscape in any way.

Although the underlying
concepts of the project go
against functionality, they
involve theoretical forces
that serve as an example
for other designers.

Russ House

Location: *Constance, Switzerland*
Year of construction: *1994*
Architect: *Ernst Giselbrecht*
Photography: *Peter Eder*

Detail of yard with t
swimming pool in t
foreground and La
Constance in t
backgrour

Right-hand pa
The glass areas have be
treated to filter sunlig
during the summ

Giselbrecht designed the house to have panoramic views. The view of the lake from every room becomes a constant point of reference, a backdrop against which the whole house revolves.

The architect built a retaining wall that enabl him to have a flat area on which to site both th swimming pool and the house. On this platform the house is built like a small two-floor glasshouse: the first floor houses the communa areas and the second floor the bedrooms. Obviously, there is a clear difference between the front facade (with views over the lake) and the back wall.

As can be seen from studying Russ House, Giselbrecht combines strictness of constructio and fondness for detail with considerable form restraint. His buildings are nearly always built c the basis of simple geometric shapes and abstract facades. In this one, apart from the volume of glass, the only additional element is narrow balcony that runs along the whole of th main facade, with an extension at one end, as i it were a lookout post.

View of the double
height living room
All metalwork
white lacquered

The glass walls of the study
provide a visual link with
the living room.

The panoramic view of the
lake is a constant reference
point from every room in
the house.

House Schickert

Location: *Meerbusch, Germany*
Year of construction: *1998*
Architects: *Döring, Dahmen, Joeressen*
Photography: *Manos Meisen*

Ingenuity is the basic ingredient of House Schickert. Wolfgang Döring responds intelligently and subtly to both what was already there and the requirements of the project. He surprises with specific mechanisms that not only develop the virtues of the design, but also reduce the disadvantages of the plot.

At first sight, the house looks like a typical single-family residence: a conventional design within a simple contemporary building surrounded by a generous yard. The design details turn the house into a collection of "architectural winks" conceived for the delight of the occupants.

The main objective was to close those inside off, with their backs turned on the outside, in a private space full of esthetic and constructive distractions designed for the comfort of the occupants. To achieve this, some of the windows are of restricted height so that an observer sitting in the dining room can see only images of the yard.

The way in which the house is built is strictly organized: light, insulating blocks combine with the expansive windows and the metal framework supporting the terrace level. The yard design completes a house that claims to be a reflection of the lifestyle of its occupants and the true freedom of light and space.

The museum-like interior
houses several works of art
and the surface finishes are
clean and elegant. The windows
and reflections play a very
important role in the perception
of the house.

Previous pages:
The pond is bounded by a
polished black granite wall that
appears to have no purpose other
than the purely esthetic. Döring
provides yet another surprise
here, because it is nothing but a
way of being able to see a
reflection of the fish in the pond
from the living room.

Access to the buildin
from the street on th
north side is by
rectangular patio. Th
first open space acts like
screen between the publ
urban space and th
privacy of the dwellin

Casa Huete

Location: *Madrid, Spain*
Year of construction: *1998*
Architects: *Vicens/Ramos*
Photography: *Eugeni Pons*

Having a magnificent plot, a boundless budget, and diligent clients is no guarantee of success. Of course, all these factors make the production process easier but they become pitfalls because the architect may lapse into opulence, extravagance, and the materialization of his most absurd whims. Vicens and Ramos knew how to avoid these temptations, made use of the advantages of their commission, and designed a house of striking shapes and exquisite finishes.

The living area consists of expansive spaces, divided by timber walls that do not reach the ceiling, and contains strategically placed opening to establish specific visual relations. The finishes differentiate the roles of the various partitions: on the one hand, the solid, plastered walls are structural and, on the other, the timber partitio▮ walls – like folding screens – give the area a warm feel. The layout of the cross section is very important in the upper areas of the house and allows overhead light inside.

To a large extent, the cross section of the plan determines the various areas. Firstly, it determines contact with the ground. Secondly, it creates a feeling of fullness and emptiness that gives a sensorial richness to the variety of environments.

House in Dazaifu

Location: *Dazaifu, Japan*
Year of construction: *1995*
Architect: *Hiroyuki Arima*
Photography: *Koji Okamoto*

Japanese architecture creates the dichotomy of a very special cultural setting: futuristic, esthetic and functional. It is profoundly influenced by an ancestral tradition that gives the plans an exquisite sensitivity not found in western architecture. The most radically vanguard buildings are perceived as future advances but do not lose the awareness of belonging to an ancient culture.

Immersed in this special setting, Hiroyuki Arima proposed a dwelling that takes maximum advantage of the setting and light, although to the detriment of the functionality of the house.

The objective of the project has nothing to do with economy or profit, but with the perception of areas designed to be enjoyed by the senses.

Although the house is located near the Temple of Dazaifu, the surroundings are tranquil and do not form part of the bustling activity of the tourist area. Bamboo shrubs and other indigenous trees cover the gently sloping ground. The house is set out as two sections, on sloping ground, the highest and lowest points of which differ by 33 ft (10 m).

Apart from exquisite attention to detail (refined woodwork, light entering at strategic points, sculptured staircases etc. ...), the project enjoys almost sensuous finishes that complete a dwelling designed for perceptive diversity and enjoyment of nature in all its splendor.

With no drapes or window shades, the house offers little privacy. Some things have to be given up in order to make the most of the views and the surroundings.

The steep slope determines the location of the floors on different levels, linked by staircases and walkways. The value of the space lies in the way it includes nature rather than focusing on the functionality and efficiency of the house. With these priorities Arima distances himself from Japanese residential trends of the end of the 19th century that seek to achieve the maximum yield from built areas.

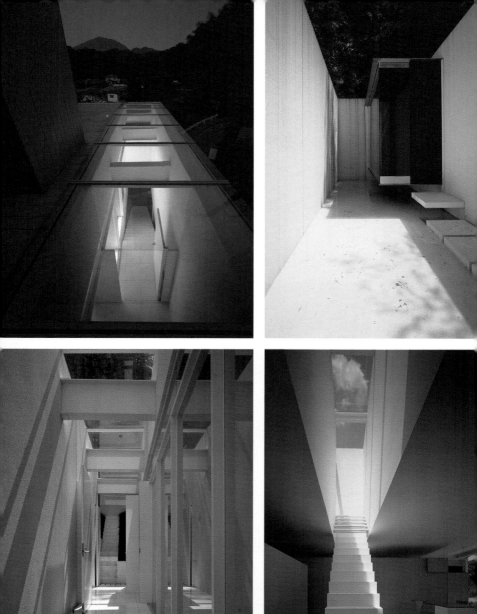

The staircases are carefully designed. Ascent always gives a direct view of the sky, like a metaphor. The last few steps are translucent, allowing overhead light to enter.

Hiroyuki Arima and his Urban Fourth studio achieve areas that are intimately linked to the outside. His choice is striking: to incorporate light, views, and wind into the rooms of the house. Nature percolates physically and perceptively through every opening.

Casa Schöner

Location: *El Pedregal de San Ángel, Mexico*
Year of construction: *1995*
Architects: *Alfonso López Baz, Javier Calleja Ariñ*
Associates: *Raúl Pulido, Octavio Cardozo*
Photography: *Fernando Cordero*

This house is part of a set of three, with the same circular drive and a shared wall of volcanic rock. The plot slopes steeply in a west to east direction – in other words, from the back of the house to the driveway.

This is a completely introverted project that ignores its surroundings. Despite being located on a sloping plot, practically the whole of the building is on the same plane at ground level. This is all due to an initial decision that conditions the whole of the project: building the house around a courtyard.

In contrast to this sealing off from the outside, the interior is expansive and open, with visual lines more than 66 ft (20 m) long. The house is arranged in three strips at right angles to the dividing walls. The first is the social area: the communal area of the house. The first floor accommodates the living room, kitchen, and the rest of the services. On the second floor is a more secluded lounge.

The architects endeavored to give every room its own particular image. In this way, the architecture responds to the different activities that occur at the same time in one house.

One of the most characteristic features of this house is the two huge steel gates, one at each end of the courtyard. The base of the pillars is an equilateral triangle with one point facing towards the courtyard.

Right-hand p
The floors are mai
timber and patter
travertine mar

The fireplace acts
divide between the liv
room and the passage t
runs from the entranc
the corridor crossing
courty

House in Querétaro

Location: *Querétaro, Mexico*
Year of construction: *1997*
Architects: *Bosco Gutiérrez Cortina, Fernando*
  Cárdenas González, Emilio Guerrero y
  Ramos, Alejandro Medina Macías
Associates: *Roberto Stark (structure)*
Photography: *Alberto Moreno Guzmán*

Opposite the fam
room, near the bedroc
area, are a small pond a
a cobalt blue wa

Despite the fact that his architecture is frequently said to be an attempt to recreate local tradition, in our opinion the work of Gutiérrez Cortina is part of one of the great artistic traditions of the 20th century: abstract. His concern for geometric composition with perfectly defined planes and clear spaces makes his work similar to that of Gerrit Rietveld, Piet Mondrian, Barnett Newman, Sol Lewitt, and Frank Stella. Like them, he makes a search for harmony based on a combination of color and shape as well as the conviction that the abstract in itself is capable of evoking emotions.

This is an extensive plot: 100 ft (30 m) wide by 165 ft (50 m) deep, in other words, a completely flat plot of 16,000 sq ft (1,500 m²). This resulte in two decisions being taken: firstly, to build the house on virtually one level and, secondly, to leave a large square courtyard in front of the main facade that acts like an anteroom to the dwelling as a whole.

Although it is part of the plot, the courtyard designed as a separate area from the house. As in other projects by Gutiérrez Cortina Architects, there is a desire to keep a certain distance between some areas and others so th a change of activity implies a journey.

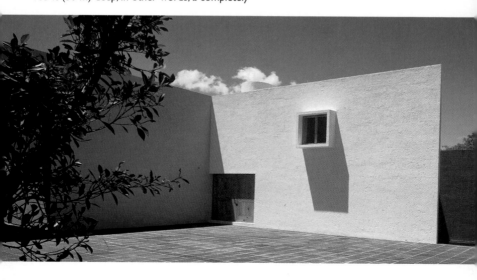

Detail of the large
window overlooking
the yard.
The cross-shape framing
is taken from one of the
windows of the Luis
Barragán house
in Tacubaya.

Openings in the roof allo
in natural light in the for
of controlled geometric ra

Stampfel Residence

Location: *Düsseldorf, Germany*
Year of construction: *1995*
Architects: *Wolfgang Döring, Michael Dahmen,*
Elmar Joeressen
Associates: *Bernhard Korte (landscaping)*
Photography: *Dieter Leistner, Frank Springer*

Right-hand pag
The yard was designed b
Bernhard Korte. The Japane
fishpond, the side wall of th
house, the garage wall, and th
row of concrete pillars mark out
perfectly rectangular are

The influence of the German masters of the modern movement (Walter Gropius, Marcel Breuer, Bruno Taut) can be seen in the geometric rigor, type of finish selected, and composition of the openings.

However, this house is organized on almost perfect symmetry, something that is not common in modern architecture, but more akin to the Beaux Arts tradition. In any case, here symmetry is neither a method of composition nor an instrument to build an attractive balanced facade, but a way of laying out spaces i the simplest and most immediate way possible.

The Japanese fishpond, adjacent to the house, and the yard with rows of abstract pillars and trees are not designed as outside spaces but as extensions of the dwelling itself.

Inside the house there is no entrance hall, because it is outside: the space between the yar gate and the house door acts as an anteroom.

The palisade that surrounds the plot hides the interior from view. From the street, all that can be seen are blocks of blurred colors through the translucent glass of the first-floor terrace.

Döring offers an austere geometric architecture with the intention of revealing other situations that are all too frequently stifled by an accumulation of spectacular images.

Although it has a floor area of 3,000 sq ft (275 m²), the Stampfel Residence is designed for just one couple. The house is built on a basis of load-bearing walls made of special concrete blocks. These have high thermal inertia in line with German energy-saving awareness.

Right-hand page Pictures belonging to the owners' modern art collection hang on virtually all the walls of the house

House Bielicky

Location: *Düsseldorf, Germany*
Year of construction: *1995*
Architects: *Wolfgang Döring, Michael Dahmen,*
Elmar Joeressen
Associates: *Georg Döring*
Photography: *Manos Meisen*

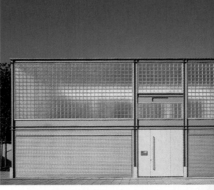

Here we have an austere style with no
concessions; with details taken from modern
tradition (tubular metal handrails, narrow
balconies, continuous windows, white walls).
The shape of the building is a perfect prism:
nothing projects beyond the plane of the walls.

A wall cuts the home in two lengthwise,
acting as a connecting element, supporting the
staircase, and separating the small rooms from
the larger, double-height areas. The break is
almost total as it coincides with a skylight in
the roof, the stairwell, and a long narrow
opening in the floor slab over the hall.

But the main thing this house reveals is
Döring's interest in the skin of the building.
The wall overlooking the street is hermetically
sealed. On the first floor, the gates of the
house's two garages and the pedestrian access
consist of a sheet of metal that occupies the
whole of the frontage. The front is closed off on
the second floor by a wall of translucent glass.

The living room is a large, double-height space,
with hardly any furniture, that could be used as
a concert hall. It is the real focal point of the
house, because although it is in a corner of
the building, it forms part of a larger area that
includes the paved terrace behind the
large windows.

The steel frame unit, with sheet
metal and glass block walls, houses
two garages and, on the upper
floor, a terrace. It acts as an
insulating chamber separating the
street from the private interior. In
fact the building has two entrances:
one in the wall to the street and
the other at the end of the corridor
crossing the glazed area.

The layout of the house
is designed for a family of
five: a married couple and
three children. It has four
bedrooms, three singles
and one double, all on the
upper floor.

The members of the Bielicky family
are great music lovers, as well as
being interested in contemporary art.
Therefore, the living room is ready to
be converted into a mini-concert hall.
The ceiling in particular is made from
a material specially designed to
absorb sound.

Casa Bergadà

Location: *L'Ametlla del Vallès, Barcelona, Spain*
Year of construction: *1996*
Architect: *Tonet Sunyer i Vives*
Builder: *Estructuras MABAI*
Promotor: *Lurdes Bergadà*
Associates: *Eva Morral, Daniela Hartman (design),*
Eduard Doce (structural engineer),
Francesc Belart (quantity surveyor)
Photography: *Joan Mundó*

Tonet Sunyer's first task on this project was earth-moving in order to produce two virtually flat levels, one approximately 10 ft (3 m) higher than the other, to coincide with the two floors of the house. So, the house sits astride the artificial slope. The floor slab between the first and second floors has been built using flat hollow brick arches over each of the center lines: an indigenous technique known as Catalan vaulting. Tonet Sunyer included this traditional solution to satisfy the owner, who wanted the house to resemble a farm.

On the first floor, the two main areas are occupied by the living room and the main entrance from the yard. A double space over the living room connects this area to the floor above. The staircase runs behind a large bookcase.

The two side areas are designed to accommodate the service area on one side and the master bedroom on the other. The former consists of the kitchen, pantry, one bedroom, bathroom and, facing the yard, the dining room.

One of the most important aspects of the project is the decor. Every room offers an authentic collection of modern yet simple furniture and tasteful details.

The facade is made up of a series of horizontal bands, the first of these being the sliding timber window shades and glazing on the first floor. The second is a strip of brick that forms the handrail to the second-floor terrace. Finally, there is a sliding window located just below the roof. The composition is reminiscent of some of the prairie houses of Frank Lloyd Wright.

The upper floor (wi
independent access from t
outside) is for the children.
is totally symmetrical, with
minimalist appearance: a lar
closet parallel to the doubl
height area separates t
communal area from t
bedroom

In addition to being the roo
where the bed is, the mast
bedroom also includes a dressin
room, a large bathroom
and a private pati

Casa López Bueno

Location: *Hinojos, Spain*
Year of construction: *1996*
Architect: *Antonio González Cordón*
Photography: *Hisao Suzuki, Fernando Alba*

This project involved the construction of a permanently occupied country house located in an isolated natural setting within the confines of the Doñana National Park. The layout had to provide a satisfactory solution for a conventional family home, extended with a series of out-buildings designed to be used as workshops, and for various other uses.

The design gives special consideration to the characteristics of the location: the quality of the surroundings in agricultural countryside with extensive, spacious views; and the rigor of the Andalusian climate, particularly significant in this case, as the most interesting views over the land coincide with one of the most inclement directions, the southwest.

The questions posed are answered by two simple architectural features: an inner courtyard that acts as a link between the residential area and the additional outbuildings, and a covered porch enclosed by screens that joins the rooms of the house and the exterior.

The building adopts a U-shape configuration. The two main arms consist of the living rooms of the house and the additional areas, the kitchen delimits the courtyard and provides direct access from the outside.

In this house, Antonio González demonstrates that reinterpreting traditional architecture can tame existing climatic extremes and create contemporary, comfortable, and elegant domestic areas.

Right-hand p
The area between the house a
the outside takes on the rc
assigned by traditio
typology: extension of
enclosed residential area ir
the setting, meticulou
protected against sunlight fr
the west by horizontal slate
screens around the perime

The courtyard is a mechanism between the two basic buildings of the unit. In this way it gets away from the traditional courtyard that used to be built as the nerve center of a house.

The inside of the house enjoys magnificent views of the local countryside. It does not suffer from direct exposure to the sun because the porches temper the sun's rays.

House in Bouscat

Location: *Le Bouscat, France*
Year of construction: *1998*
Architects: *Brochet Lajus & Pueyo Architectes*
Photography: *Philippe Ruault*

The roof of the house exten
into a pergola of metal stri
that offers protection fro
direct sunligh

The location of the house is in response to the desire to make use of the whole plot. The building does not have clearly defined boundaries and should not be seen as an independent item but as a house set in a yard.

The main south-facing wall acts as a porous, permeable boundary. It consists of identical glass panels that can open to provide movement between the inside and the outside and offer controlled natural ventilation. Lighting and privacy are achieved by adjusting the wooden screens. Space and light within the building are controlled in a similar way: by sliding partitions that can be moved or folded according to the desire of the user.

The house is split into areas that lead from one to the other in an orderly fashion. This spatial rhythm is punctuated by the vertical divisions that specify certain views and associate each inside room with a particular area of the yard. Inside the house the floor is divided by folding screens and the outside is split into thre areas: the first, closely linked to the house, contains the terraces and landscaped areas adjoining the building; the second consists of th swimming pool and pond area; and the third of trees, shrubs, and the lawn.

The flexibility of the building is based on contraptions that can change the rooms, from being light and opening onto the yard to being intimate and introverted. The house is based on rigid geometric system that produces a home with a rich diversity of environments.

In this unique space, contained within the dividing walls, the strategically placed trees act as exterior "furniture." The bench in the yard is echoed in the red sofa in the living room.

The furniture set against one of the dividing walls designates the use of the rooms. It is a closet for kitchen utensils, and becomes a bookshelf, and then a television unit. In the bedroom it turns into window shades identical to those of the main facade.

Casa en Bosques de Las Lomas

Location: *Bosques de Las Lomas, Mexico DF*
Year of construction: *1995*
Architects: *Bosco Gutiérrez Cortina, Fernando*
Cárdenas González, Emilio Guerrero
y Ramos, Alejandro Medina Macías
Associates: *Roberto Stark (structural engineer)*
Photography: *Alberto Moreno Guzmán*

The return of local architecture and traditional techniques is often confused with triviality, a picturesque image, and resorting to kitsch. This was the mistake made by the postmodernist movement, resulting in its speedy decline.

The juxtaposition of the modern and the traditional can be seen in very few places. One of them is Mexico. From Luis Barragán onwards, Mexico has had its own architectural language.

This house designed by Gutiérrez Cortina Arquitectos is on a demarcated plot 57 ft (17.5 m) wide by 115 ft (35 m) deep, the last 33 ft (10 m) of which are a back yard. The plot slopes sharply. The difference in level between the street and the end of the plot is 30 ft (9 m). This means that the house is built on a series of stepped terraces.

The house is arranged around three private courtyards surrounded by walls. The front one is a terrace that forms the roof of the garage. The rear one is more private and links to the master bedroom and family room on the upper floor. The third is a central courtyard, partly covered by a pergola and glass and partly enclosed by a concrete wall.

In many places a dramatic
effect is sought. The access
stairs, for example, become
narrower as they ascend,
leading into the atrium.
Only the pergola can be seen
from its entrance, along with
a blue freestanding tube
surrounded by carmine walls.

Right-hand page
To reach the atrium you
have to climb the stairs
that lead from the
entrance level to the main
floor and act as a large
linking space between the
various rooms

The main floor contain
communal areas of the
house, the lounge-dine
(open to the rear courty
and atrium), the library
and all services: kitchen
laundry room, drying a
utility room etc. ... Th
second floor contains th
bedrooms and a family

School House

Location: *Hayama, Japan*
Year of construction: *1998*
Architect: *Kengo Kuma*
Photography: *Mitsumasa Fujitsuka*

Traditional home styles are changing with the appearance of new technologies. Materials, building methods, and especially the IT revolution are contributing to a new way of understanding the home. Communication over the Internet allows people to work from home. The concept of the family is also changing.

Kengo Kuma's School House assimilates these requirements and creates a place of learning for artists as well as a residence. Both uses exist side by side in a building of clean lines whose main purpose is to blend with the surrounding forest, incorporating the more conceptual parameters of nature.

As in his previous works, Kengo Kuma attempts to design with the less tangible elements of architecture: light, water, air, countryside. New relationships are created between the user and the object, which is no longer a fixed or rigid concept, but one that has been transformed into a collection of journeys and sensations.

The first floor houses the communal services: kitchen, dining room, and living room, while the upper floor accommodates the bedrooms. The special feature of this conventional layout is flexibility: the rooms are similar in size and it is easy to appreciate that changing their function would not involve drastic alterations to the plans. Their own particular characteristics would continue to be enjoyed.

e interiors are
nimalist and designed
h great sensitivity to
ht and views.

t-hand page:
day, the house looks
e a solid block but by
ht the facade allows
mpses of the different
vironments it contains.

e gaps between the pine
ts can be adjusted to
ry the amount of light
tering each room,
difying the intimacy
d atmosphere.

Casa en Teià

Location: *Teià, Spain*
Year of construction: *1997*
Architect: *Mario Corea*
Photography: *Jordi Miralles*

Set facing the Mediterranean in the small town of Teià, the house seems to capture the luminosity and setting of the Catalan coast.

The neatly designed house, with plain materials and little embellishment, allows light and the linking of space to be the protagonists of a rational base that is produced from simple shapes, a predominance of right angles, and verticality. The references to Mediterranean architecture are juxtaposed with modern materials and comfort solutions: the uniform white commonly achieved with white limestone is replaced on the outside by travertine as the predominant material, and on the inside by plastered walls. The traditional clay paving is replaced by a red timber floating floor in all rooms, emphasizing spatial continuity.

The sloping plot allows the house to be developed on three levels. It is designed with a flowing section on the first floor in such a way that continuity in the various spaces is transmitted on both the horizontal and the vertical plane. The communal area of the house is connected with the yard and the swimming pool by the extension of timber decking from the inside to the outside.

The Casa en Teià as a whole is a juxtaposition of architectural references filtered by two clear desires: the dominance of the coastal setting and the predominance of elegance in its design.

The outside areas of the
building have been designed
in detail, forming a
harmonic whole. The yard is
also part of the minimalist
gamble, with orthogonal
composition and the
decking superimposed on the
lawn and pool.

Right-hand pa
The inside is governed by
minimalist attitude that prevails
the use of materials and t
application of simple shapes. The u
of travertine and red timber for t
floors and furniture is highlighted
two dissonant elements: the firepla
and an ocher wall in the ma
entran

Kappe Tamuri Residence

Location: *Topanga, California, United States*
Year of construction: *1997*
Builder: *Finn Kappe*
Architects: *Finn Kappe, Maureen Tamuri*
Associates: *Reiss, Brown, Ekmekji; Woods*
Engineering (structural),
Richard Reiss (civil engineer),
Finn Kappe (lighting)
Photography: *David Hewitt/Anne Garrison*
Architectural Photography

This two-floor house located on one side of the Topanga Canyon, a semi-rural area near Los Angeles, is the home and studio of the architects who designed it.

Although Kappe admits that the idea that gave rise to the project is a picture of a truck pulling a trailer, it is clear that one of the main attractions of the house is its interpretation of the countryside and topography. Without a doubt the sharp angular shapes that are combined within the sinuous design are reminiscent of the formation of the Topanga Canyon itself.

The house is raised on piles. The steel framework is nearly always visible. For Kappe it is important for the skeleton of the building to be intelligible, and the construction methods used confirm what is suggested by the apparent shapes. But the logic of the structure must not dominate the project, and therefore Kappe disassociates himself from architecture that rewards risk and technical innovation, as well as that which is only concerned with formal discoveries.

The architects were also interested in prefabricated and industrial materials such as corrugated sheet metal, which was immediately available and easy to adopt to any type of structure.

The project combines divergent interests and in the end becomes a vehicle for experimenting with architecture. With this project Kappe and Tamuri demonstrate that the biggest error is the fear of making a mistake and the only valid gamble is taking a risk.

Left-hand page:
nn Kappe combined his
ork as an architect and
esigner with that of
rector of works and
ntractor. In this way, his
vn house has become an
ample of resolving details,
electing materials and
uilding systems.

The rear of the house is more closed
off to protect it against the noise of
the highways to the north of the plot
and prevent it being overlooked from
neighboring houses to the west.

Following pages:
One of the obsessions of this couple,
both owners and architects, during
the building process, was to achieve
a flowing inner space. The succession
of architectural elements – walls,
beams, pillars, handrails – is linked
like the notes of a melody.

House Collserola

Location: *Barcelona, Spain*
Year of construction: *1995*
Architect: *Joan Rodón*
Associate: *Sac Groc (builder)*
Photography: *Eugeni Pons*

The house is arranged on three levels that follow the line of the hillside, by means of a series of concrete retaining walls. The other main material is timber, used both in the exterior cladding and interior floors.

Of the three floors inside the house, the first two – which intercommunicate through a double-height space between the living room and the study – contain most of the rooms comprising the basic layout of the project. Color plays a dual role: firstly, it is used to structure the planes of the various stepped walls that lead from the house and via the various terraces to the garage and street level; and, secondly, it esthetically configures the building, providing strong measures of expressiveness. Sometimes, color is also used to achieve shape. One of the outside staircases, made of exposed concrete, is magnificently highlighted by the deep blue of the wall against which it is placed so that it takes on an even more airborne appearance. The same effect is achieved by alternating warm and cold colors: if we look at the house from different angles, we see a preponderance of yellows and reds that brilliantly bring out the shapes, or blues and whites that remind us of the house's proximity to the Mediterranean.

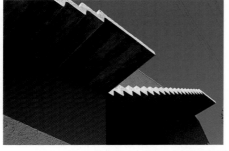

The superimposition of floors is one of the structure's major successes.

Vegetation helps to integrate the house into its surroundings.

Natural light penetrates the
building both in the
morning and evening.

Concrete, timber, and color
are blended beautifully.

The house is perfectly suited
to its surroundings.

The kitchen, with wood and stainless-steel fittings, is located in a continuous space on the lower level.

The location in the Sierra de Collserola offers magnificent views of the city of Barcelona.

The master bedroom is shaped like a cube into which the main openings are cut.

Treat Studio House

Location: *San Diego, California, United States*
Year of construction: *1995*
Client: *Robert Treat*
Architect: *Jeanne McCallum Architect*
Builder: *Bruce Hanson*
Associate: *David Smith (engineer)*
Photography: *David Heawitt/Anne Garrison*

Right-hand pa
All the walls are finished
brightly-colored stucco, creating
kind of three-dimensional pictur
The only exception is the offi
cabin, made of corrugated she
metal, that forms a separa
elemer

The existing house is a small building, a single-floor dwelling with symmetrically laid-out rooms.

Jeanne McCallum's design includes and enhances the old building. The studio has been built as an annex on the western boundary of the back yard. In this way the layout of the two buildings produces a secluded, protected courtyard around a tree, an outside living area that, given the benign San Diego climate, becomes the nerve center of the house. A timber deck has been added to the house and the walls have been stuccoed in intense colors in line with the owner's preference.

One of the fundamental requirements for the building, as an artist's workshop or studio, was to provide an abundance of diffused light from the north, thus avoiding reflections. To achieve this Jeanne McCallum built the outer walls with a combination of blind and glazed surfaces.

The practical windows are built into the solid elements or the glazed surfaces, where they stand out against the timber uprights that run a the way to the roof.

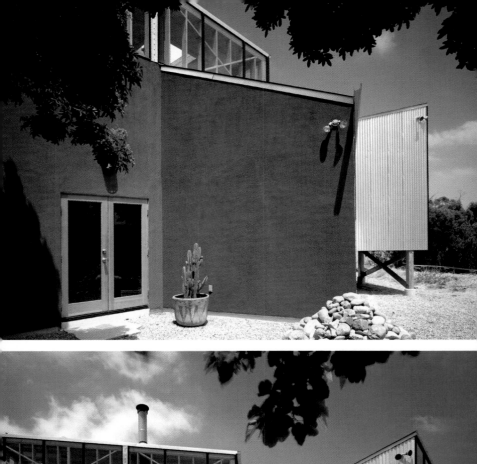

Left-hand page:
General view of the studio
from the rear garden,
with the railroad in the
foreground.

Light and space were
essential requirements for
the workshop.

View from the attic.
Timber is virtually the sole
material used internally.

View from the timber
staircase leading up to
the attic.
The framework and ribs of
the vertical walls have been
left visible.

Weiss/Churchill Residence

Location: *San Diego, California, United States*
Year of construction: *1993*
Architect: *Jeanne McCallum Architect*
Associates: *Mary Wilkinson, Roger Hill,*
John Baez
Photography: *Efteling*

Located below street level, the studio house sits on a downward sloping plot and is set out on four levels. A spectacular entrance across an arched bridge to a steel, timber, and glass tower takes you from one world to another. Once inside, the impression of space in movement – wide and flowing in its accentuated dimensions – culminates in the transparency of a glass wall, looking out over the hilly countryside. From the rear of the house, the same wall reveals the interior and its timber structure.

The new section is built in a trapezoidal shape in the west wing of the existing building. From the access pavilion, a timber staircase fixed to the wall, which joins all floors and dominates the whole of the interior space, descends to the first floor. This accommodates the kitchen and dining room projecting into the inner space. The mezzanine level contains a small studio. At the bottom end, the studio living area has huge glass walls opening onto the countryside on one side and a view of the interior space on the other. In one of these glass walls, a large square represents a mirror for the creative expression of the clients.

The elements that give shape to
the space are a mixture of natural
and industrial materials such as
metal, concrete blocks, timber,
and glass. The bridge is made of
timber with tubular metal
handrails supported at both ends
by concrete-block walls.

View of the dining room with
the kitchen in the background.

In the central area of the house, a spine of timber columns forms the supporting structure of the roof; timber columns are also to be found in the glazed perimeter wall. Use has been made of the *balloon frame* technique, typical of North American architecture. The floor slab is made of double timber beams covered with timber floorboards.

Wierich House

Location: *Recklinghausen, Germany*
Year of construction: *1997*
Architects: *Döring, Dahmen, Joeressen*
Photography: *Stefan Thurmann, Gruner & Jahr*

The Wierich house is situated in the northern part of the Ruhr and occupies a quarter of the 17,200 sq ft (1,600 m²) plot. The project is the product of clear, emphatic decisions that do not impose rigidity on the development but order it in such a way that any deviation is transformed into a delight for the residents. The first of these decisions was to concentrate the functional aspects of the building in one rectangular body that breaks with the orthogonal to produce a southwest facing living room and dining room.

The structure is also consistent with the nature of the project. The main body is of reinforced concrete, providing a constructional solution that offsets the thrust of the uneven terrain. The additional triangle that contains the living room and dining room is of steel with a facade built entirely of glass, allowing natural light to fill these rooms. The first floor contains the main area of the complex service arrangements. The living and service areas are separated by the stairwell and the elevator.

While meeting all the functional requirements, the Wierich house also addresses considerations of an esthetic nature. Residents are offered an architectural walkway on the upper floor. Beginning at the top of the stairs, the cohesive element of the building, this runs along the balcony and gallery, both of which look on to the internal areas and the garden.

The exterior spaces were created by Bernhard Korte who designed metal cubicles combined with porches and orthogonal plant-covered surfaces. The design of the garden is consistent with the care taken throughout the house, and the external living areas constitute the culminating point of this well-appointed dwelling.

The entrance to the house
combines materials that
are to be found in the
living room and other
interior spaces: concrete
and glass with a metal
framework.

At street level we find the
cornerstone of the house: a
greenhouse for collecting and
growing orchids. This, together
with the swimming pool,
sauna, and water purification
plant, requires a special
installation. These are located
in the lower basement.

The first floor of the building comprises the largest section of a functional complex. The living rooms and service areas are separated by the stairwell and elevator shaft. This vertical link connects the various levels of the house, from the wine cellar and garage to the upper floor, and acts as a light shaft as it is fully glazed at both ends.

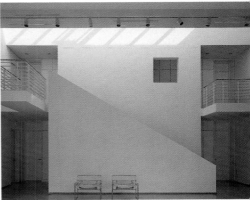

Apart from fulfilling all functional requirements, the Wierich House offers esthetic enjoyment to its inhabitants and includes an architectural stroll on the upper level. The journey begins at the top of the stairs, the cohesive center of the house, and runs through the balcony and gallery, both of which have views of the inside and outside.

Casa en Sant Jaume Sesoliveres

Location: *Igualada, Spain*
Year of construction: *1996*
Architect: *Jaume Riba*
Photography: *Eugeni Pons*

Right-hand page
South wall facing the yard

A basic theme developed in this typically modern design is the ambiguous relationship between the inside and the outside; the border between the two is diffuse. The inside is not an enclosed space, but open and linked with the patio and yard. In this sense, flow is more highly valued than a static conception of space. To achieve this, global solutions have been sought and particular attention has been given to the continuity of materials. The same criterion was valid for the whole work: the concrete of the roof is extended into the exterior projections, with walls leaving the interior and crossing glass divisions, and similar treatment is given to the internal and external floors.

The interior is continuous and unitary. The various rooms with their different functions are separated by large sliding doors; this gives flexibility to the layout and enables the space to be allocated as and when it is needed.

The sharpness in the definition of the rooms has been achieved to a large extent by a high level of automation: a rotating bookshelf houses all the books, a side access closet conceals the washing fixtures, a sliding panel and sliding window provide access to a kitchen table, and for the outer door a pneumatic mechanism has made it possible to use wall-height runners. Virtually the whole of the construction is in white concrete.

Detail of pond and yard.

The swimming pool is located on the north part of the plot. It is a major structure consisting of a curved wall that houses the changing rooms and clothes drying area as well as the rectangular pool.

View of the dining room.

The washbowl is designed as a freestanding unit built into the wall.

View of the living room located in the east wing.

The children's room. A sliding window offers views of the yard.

Right-hand pa
The kitchen, like t
surfaces in the bathroo
and laundry areas,
finished in white ceram

Casa en Igualada

Location: *Igualada, Spain*
Year of construction: *1996*
Architect: *Pep Zazurca*
Photography: *Eugeni Pons*

Pep Zazurca experiments with structures, materials, and finishes more closely related to industrial buildings than to domestic architectur. The house is organized around a rectangular ba with a metal pillar framework and a galvanized sheet-steel roof supported by curved latticewo roof trusses that cover a span of approximately 33 ft (10 m), providing extensive diaphanous interiors. The whole of the steel structure was constructed in the workshop and then taken to the site by mobile crane for erection. This enab the framework of the building to be completed just a few days. On the other hand, the side wal that enclose the house were hand-built in brick. The window openings are similar in design to those of old industrial buildings. The brick is lef bare on the inside while the outside has been c in steel. The main facade, built of timber, galvanized sheeting, and glass, is completely independent of the rest of the building. The architect does not follow any specific rules of composition but simply transfers the cross section of the house to the outside.

In some ways, he is trying to reproduce an image of those industrial buildings that were converted into homes: large spaces with no divisions or pillars. However, this is no salvaged building but one that has been built with a spec domestic purpose in mind.

This project is an attempt to recall known images in an attitude similar to postmodernism.

The plot slopes fairly sharply, so that although the main facade has two floors, the rear wall has only one. The first floor houses the garage, utility room, guest bedroom, shower room, and games room or gymnasium, and is directly accessible from the side yard.

A circular studio, clad in galvanized steel sheet, has been built on one of the sides of the building. Its shape is obviously reminiscent of an industrial storage tank.

...etails of sheet-steel
...nish of the side walls.

On the upper floor, a large area overlooking the main ...cade accommodates all the ...ouse's day-to-day ...nctions: living room, ...ining room, kitchen, ...orkplace…

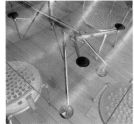

Rezek House

Location: *Los Angeles, California, United States*
Year of construction: *1991*
Architect: *Michael W. Folonis*
Photography: *Julie Phipps*

The Rezek House is located in a quiet, residential street in west Los Angeles, California. Near it, there are just two small houses located on both sides of a landscaped area in the middle of a privileged spot that still offers the large plots common 50 years ago.

Ron Rezek, the owner of the house, was also its designer. The idea of building and designing his own family home with the features of an art gallery was what inspired him. The yard also played a very important role in this project as Rezek claimed that there was close communication between architecture and the natural environment: exteriors with a lot of green vegetation brighten up the views from inside the house.

The Rezek House starts from a simple buildin plan based on a virtually rectangular base. A semicircular annex projects from the wall to th right of the main entrance. This is a counterpoi because it breaks the straight lines and angles that characterize the layout of this building. On the inside, this fully-glazed annex becomes an open family area that connects to the kitchen, dining room, and bathroom.

All rooms in the building ope
onto the outside via glaze
doors and large window

Immediately opposite the ma
entrance, attached to the wall, is
staircase that splits, right and le
into two branches fixed to the sam
wall, leading up to the upper floc

Right-hand pag
The living room has an origin
timber vault. Thanks to its excelle
acoustics, jazz concerts and ope
recitals are often held in

View of the dining room, with a set of black and white pictures.

White is the predominant color of most walls. The stairs lead to the upper floor that houses the bedrooms and main bathroom.

The kitchen area enjoys plenty of natural light. We can also see one of the many works of art that make the house an art gallery as well as a home.

Villa Chalkiades

Location: *Mitilene, Lesbos, Greece*
Year of construction: *1989*
Architects: *Eleni Gigantes, Elia Zenghelis*
Associates: *Elia Veneris, Stavros Aliferis,*
               Dirk Alten
Photography: *Laure Thorel*

This construction of a residential villa on the Greek island of Lesbos is the result of an elaborate project by the architects Eleni Gigantes and Elia Zenghelis in which they paid particular attention to the placing of the building in relation to the surrounding countryside and to an understanding of light.

The various floors do not sit on top of each other naturally but twist and turn to provide their rooms with the outlook desired. To achieve a solid, esthetic external configuration, the architects opted for sharp lines and simple volumes, while the additional features such as terrace roofs and ornamental fittings take on more voluptuous curved shapes. The building gives the appearance of a heterogeneous set of planes, lines, and directions that nevertheless work perfectly with regard to the interior layout. The strategic placing of openings and annexes and the link with the surroundings have been achieved by skillful use of the physical plot and a proper interpretation of the existing space.

The location, with very obvious topographic and scenic characteristics, was a basic premise when the Villa Chalkiades was first planned.

The building was placed on the highest spot, the house being laid out on three levels. Without a shadow of a doubt, one of the most interesting factors in this design is the careful articulation between these floors.

The authentic visual power of the building lies in the layout of the top floor. In order to provide the whole with esthetic tension, as well as locating the rooms in relation to the best views of the outside, the upper floor takes an unexpected turn, with the result that its prismatic shape, of similar dimensions to all the other floors, seems to project out over the rest of the building.

The entrance manages to comb[...] representativeness and efficie[...] with the help of ornamer[...] elements such as the styli[...] door handle and the sculptu[...] irregular lar[...]

The connection to the
outside, on the major and
minor scale, is one of the
main attractions of this
house and can be seen from
the layout of galleries and
balconies as well as
the complementary
installations outside.

House in Turku

Location: *Turku, Finland*
Year of construction: *1988*
Architect: *Antti Katajamäki*
Associates: *Maria Pesonen, Esko Rautakorpi, Antti
Simola, Ulla Ingman,
Mattias Ingman*
Photography: *Rautaruukki Oy*

Due to its initial experimental nature, the building was designed as an independent construction, standing alone. Therefore, topographical, typological, and scenic factors, s important to the architectural process, had n influence on its construction. The house grow without taking into account any external requirements, other than those of its own esthetic and functional development. But its design also has to take into account the form or conceptual excesses that prevent a house from being integrated into specific surroundin Because this is a detached, single-family villa, t becomes a minor risk, especially because of t adaptability of the design to an open plot and the moderate size of the building.

The spatial configuration of the house is in response to a simple design based on function needs. Dividing the space into two adjacent modules with different formal characteristics was put forward as the most appropriate solution for the layout of the residential and service areas. The use of steel and advanced erection techniques also proved very appropriate in that they were suited to the various construction requirements.

The main part of the building, which is 16 ft (5 m) high and faces west, consisted of a prisr with a regular base and a semicircular roof th gives it a very dynamic appearance. Connecte to the main part of the building, on the oppos side, is a shorter construction of a tubular design, whose length is determined by practic and spatial needs.

The way in which
spacious interi
treated responds tc
opposition of appear
and content.
objectives of Katajar
are to a large extent r
akin to mass produc
processes than to tho
interior des

Suburban House

Location: *California, United States*
Year of construction: *1995*
Architects: *McKay & Lyons*
Photography: *Undine Pröhl*

This house is arranged very methodically in strips that run lengthwise across the plot, leaving free space for the yard. These parallel strips, perceptible on the facade, vary in width, height, and alignment. These setbacks and projections give the appearance of different areas in the form of courtyards, halls, or porches in the yard. The layout also produces a subtle interplay on the facades as the floor slabs can be seen at different heights, even though they are flush.

The strictly formal nature of the house could seem rigid but the building is not dependent on the strips. It houses all the functional requirements without the appearance of dead or unusable space due to its geometry. Flexibility is also apparent in the generation of spaces that can be used for different activities.

The house lighting was studied in great detail. Because of the length of the plot and the particular layout of the wall openings, natural light filters in. The offset of some floor slabs enables sunlight to penetrate into specific areas, creating shafts of light in corridors and on staircases.

The ever-present sharp angles and whiteness of virtually all surfaces does not create a chilly atmosphere. Inside, the building is warm and comfortable. The yard also introduces a touch of nature into the house; a small pond, stepping stones, and palm trees provide the house with a woodland setting in contrast to the city.

The house is a combination [of]
geometric planes without [any]
curves. This formal rigidity d[oes]
not detract from the buildi[ng]
which features flexi[ble]
comfortable environme[nt]

House in Harmisch

Location: *Harmisch, Austria*
Year of construction: *1988*
Architects: *Michael Szyszkowitz, Karla Kowalski*
Photography: *Andreas Lichtblau*

The creative work of Szyszkowitz and Kowalski usually involves the construction of strange homes or residential centers with a spectacular, innovative focus that has established their names. Their preferred style has often been associated with the idea of a Graz school of architecture. Szyszkowitz was born in Graz and his language is deliberately opposed to the excessive sterility and rigidity of 1960s methodology. This reaction translates into an organization in which the layout of the shapes goes beyond the image of the building. Their work tries to instill an idea of Baroque splendor by means of spaces halfway between dimorphism and expressionist content. With these premises, the individual's dialogue with the structure is as important as the structure's dialogue with its surroundings.

Designed for the descendants of an established local family, the house is set on a plot that was affected by the war. The existing building was badly damaged and restoration would have bee very expensive and not suitable for its new purpose. The new building is not a depiction of conventional luxury, but rather an interpretatio of the culture and lifestyle of the owners. This involved the need to establish harmony betwee the architecture and the countryside and to create a generous, peaceful atmosphere – but a the same time include something of the extraordinary and unexpected. The owners' bri was perfectly in line with the designers' theori which were simply to develop their innovative ideas within a specific physical environment.

The layout of the hou
meets two criteria: on t
one hand, the restrictio
of the site, both immedia
and overall; on the othe
the particular typologic
morphology favored l
the designe

ide, the various rooms
tch their surroundings
fectly. The northern
l of the house
ommodates the more
blic areas: garages,
eption, and hall; while
southern end houses
more conventional
idential rooms:
lrooms, study, kitchen,
l bathrooms.

Wolf House

Location: *Ridgway, Colorado, United States*
Year of construction: *1989*
Architects: *Sottsass Associati*
Associates: *Johanna Grawunder, Lichtdesign,*
Michael Barber
Photography: *Santi Caleca*

To experiment, investigate, and discover new
architectural values and apply them to all their
designs is one of the fundamental objectives of
the Sottsass partnership. It creates new trends
and shapes, giving this morphology content and
concepts that allow intercommunication
between the building and the individual. This
process pursues innovation and is based on
intuitive notions that are always supported by
the security guaranteed by technique and years
of experience.

The project covers the design of a single family
residence, with an adjacent guest house, interior
design, and landscaping. Integrating the house
into the landscape is one of their fundamental
aims. The layout of courtyards and plants
becomes a composite element of the typological
structure of the building.

The land is undulating, a feature that is used to
benefit the integration of the house into its
surroundings. The house is aligned north–south,
molding itself to the gentle slope of the land in
order to capture the best views of the Sheffels
mountains. The building relates to its
surroundings in two ways: on the one hand, on a
larger referential scale, the architecture is a new
element within the natural framework affirming
its independence with colors and shapes, while
at the same time subordinating itself to the
grandeur and magnitude of the environment,
seeking optimal views; on the other, on a more
immediate scale, the building has gardens and
plants that are used as architectural
components, helping the house to display itself
in the best light.

401

The development is laid out with two detached buildings, the main house and the guest house. The former is more complex in configuration. It is organized horizontally and split into two sections connected by a glazed gallery that acts as entrance and living room.

The strong and highly insulating metal framework and glazing ar ideal materials for trapping ligh and providing views as well a establishing links between th two sections of the house. Th shades of color used on th outside contrast with the soft discreet paintwork of th whole of the inside

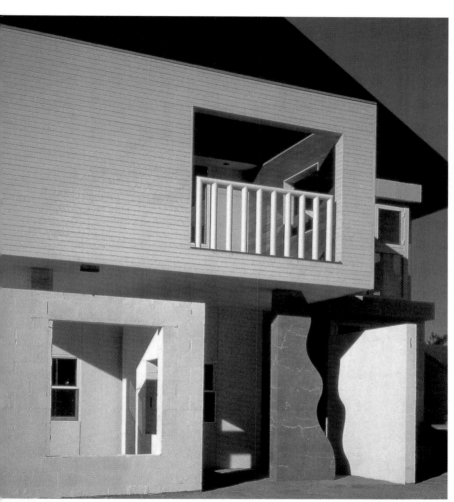

Casa Hidalgo

Location: *Alella, Barcelona, Spain*
Year of construction: *1988*
Architects: *Jordi Garcés, Enric Sòria*
Photography: *Lluis Casals*

The Casa Hidalgo has a floor area of 4,850 sq ft (450 m²) and sits on a plot that runs east to west and is bounded at the side by a steep slope running down to the road. Due to its elevated location, the building is well placed for sun and enjoys magnificent panoramic views to the sea.

Taking advantage of the topographical characteristics of the plot, Garcés and Sòria produced a highly creative design based on simple geometric lines. In this way, the single-family home is structured on an abstract set of three cube-shape buildings and three large windows that are interrelated by the variable rhythm of their relative positions. From the outside, the structure appears gigantic, sober, and uniform, since all its walls have been plastered and look like smooth gray surfaces.

The external geometric rigidity is diluted on the inside, where space is continuous and fluid; however, as the windows on the main facades are contained within their corresponding planes the original triple cube composition that structures the architectural reality of the Casa Hidalgo is apparent inside the house.

Nevertheless, the inside of this unusual house contains all the conventional requirements and services of a contemporary home.

In the three cubes, the main facade facing the sea
contains enormous rectangular metal-framed
windows divided into large panels. These windows
run from the ground to the ceiling of the upper
floor in a single sweep, establishing themselves as
the main features of the configuration of the
building due to their very size.

side, plastered and
ainted brick walls
ternate, with a
redominance of light
lors that intensify the
vironmental
ansparency created by the
undant natural light that
e whole house enjoys.

Westchester House

Location: *New York, United States*
Year of construction: *1987*
Architects: *Richard Meier & Partners*
Photography: *Wolfgang Hoyt/Esto*

The hill on which this house stands offers a wide variety of views and a countryside interlaced with stone walls. The Westchester House stands out imposingly as an almost magical building set against exuberant vegetation and the blue of the sky. The house is almost completely white, the favorite color of the architect, Richard Meier, as it enhances the perception of the colors that exist in natural light and in nature itself. The play between light and shade and mass and volume can be fully appreciated, thanks to the contrast with the white surface.

This house does not face in one direction alone. Far from being located frontally, the facade consists of two rectangular units, one set back from the other in an east–west direction alongside a hallway that is accessed via a staircase parallel to the same line.

The brilliant white of the building is not only based on the traditional idea of a house, but also provides a strong extravert character that goes far beyond the simple function of a refuge, without detracting from the location of the home. The house is a structure that acts like a prism set in the natural countryside around it.

The design is simple and pure. Meier, thought of as the Palladio of the 20th century, has used a classic design combined with touches of modernism on the walls. The house, garage, and pool are located just below the highest point and are arranged around the east–west line that splits the house and at the same time acts as a dividing wall.

View of the first-floor
living room. The decor is
functional and the use of
the color white, glass,
and timber contributes
to creating a
luminous interior.

View of the front door
with its metal frame
and original awning
painted blue.

House in Germany

Location: *Germany*
Year of construction: *1997*
Architect: *David Chipperfield Architects*
Photography: *Stefan Müller*

The house is situated in a residential area. Access to the plot from the street is at the lowest point of the plot. The first outside area we encounter has an exposed brick staircase on one side that runs across the plot, opening onto the rear yard and leaving behind the side wall of the building with the main entrance.

The three-floor house demonstrates a conscientious study of its section. The floor that absorbs the slope of the plot, the lower floor, is characterized by its careful location on the plot and by the treatment of the inside and outside. The two upper floors, in contrast, are arranged around a courtyard facing the rear yard, to the south, and with access from the middle floor.

Chipperfield planned this project as a progression of spaces. The house is the result of combining a series of rooms, each individually designed both compositionally and spatially.

For Chipperfield, the materials are the determining elements of this type of project. Specifically, in this dwelling, the sought-after texture was found in handmade bricks.

In this project the architect combines exquisite attention to the location and well-being of the inhabitants with various mental mechanisms such as abstraction. To summarize, a worthy professional design perpetuates central European traditions – Mies and Mendelsohn to name but two – of late 19th and 20th century domestic design.

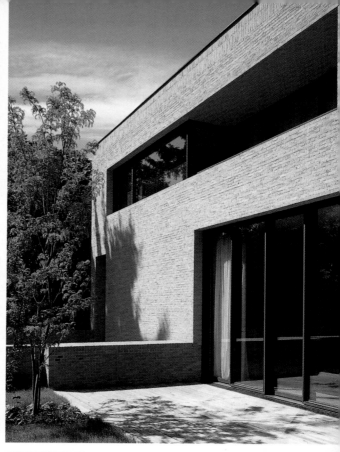

The esthetics of the house are established by the contrast between the glazed areas and the roughness of the brick. This deliberate clash between rough materials and completely smooth textures is a reproach to current trends for perfect finishes.

House in Glencoe

Location: *Glencoe, Illinois, United States*
Year of construction: *1989*
Architects: *Architectonica Architects*
Photography: *Tim Hursley*

The criterion pursued by the firm of architects in the design of this single-family home was that it had to comply with three fundamental conditions. These were, firstly, laying out the various rooms on a single floor; secondly, taking advantage of and letting oneself be seduced by the spectacular nature of the location; and, finally, having sufficient space to accommodate a very extensive art collection. The architects, Laurinda Spear and Bernardo Fort-Brescia, added a particularly personal and suggestive interpretation of modern architecture to this set of requirements.

This single family home is built in the town of Glencoe, Illinois, very close to Chicago, on a plot that is about 65 ft (20 m) above the level of Lake Michigan, on a flat piece of land laid to grass with a few scattered majestic oaks. These trees could not be destroyed and so the whole building had to be built around them out of respect for the environment and the topographic features of the site. Its unusual location, with at least three fronts, means that it enjoys magnificent vistas of the lake and its spectacular beauty from any of its rooms.

This single family home is a studio, the prime function of which is to provide comfort and pleasure, without concerning itself with symmetry or equilibrium of the different rooms which make up the end product. Things are designed so they appear to be completely relaxed by chance – as can be seen from the layout of the windows with amazing views, and their irregular but harmonious configuration.

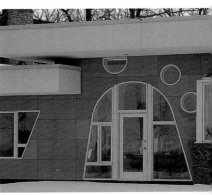

The main door is located on the south side, cut in a granite wall that symbolically guides visitors inside.

The various openings take on unbelievable and varied shapes. Sometimes the same door is subdivided into different irregular shapes, maintaining a pleasant harmony.

View of the east terrace adjoining the lounge.

Right-hand page
Detail of one of the large windows

Partial view of the covered pool, more than 65 ft (20 m) long

View of the dining room that forms a single space with the lounge, with contemporary sculptures and paintings on display

Extension of Tait-Doulgeris House

Location: *Paddington, Australia*
Year of construction: *1999*
Architects: *Buzacott & Ocolisan Associates*
Photography: *Patrick Birgham Hall*

The brief for this project was to remodel an old two-floor house located on a plot 25 ft (7.5 m) wide by 80 ft (25 m) deep.

The remodeling was designed to leave extensive open spaces, two bedrooms, a den, and a north-facing swimming pool to the rear of the house. The width of the plot offered great flexibility in the design of the service area that appears to lean against one of the sides, creating diaphanous open spaces.

The first floor is split by a wood-veneered unit that separates the lounge-diner from the service areas. These rooms open onto the rear patio of the house, which contains a swimming pool along one side. The threshold of the window between the kitchen and the pool becomes an informal area for sitting or dining.

The upper floor again uses the same method for dividing the space, a timber unit laid lengthwise and parallel to the staircase. It serves as a closet for both bedrooms and the dressing room. The bathroom faces onto the swimming pool. The den on the upper floor opens onto the terrace with excellent side views of the city and the Harbor Bridge itself.

The architecture is generally simple, contained and uses few materials.

The vertical partitions become hollow walls with lacquered or timber surfaces. These walls are of differing heights and incorporate door-like openings.

Casa en La Punta

Location: *Bosques de las Lomas, Mexico*
Year of construction: *1998*
Architects: *Alfonso López Baz, Javier Calleja*
Associates: *Raul Pulido, Octavio Cardozo*
Photography: *Héctor Velazco*

Surrounded by many houses of different styles, this house that apparently shines with modesty — as it should, due to its esthetically refined values — seems to have organized and harmonized the surrounding urban chaos.

Virtually windowless, in order to offer a visually immaculate appearance, this latest project of the LBC Group sits on a plot 7 ft (2 m) above street level. The architects use this position to place a courtyard around the house that provides privacy and controlled views.

Deliberately geometric and carefully detailed, the house simply reveals large panels of stony skin from which buildings of various shapes grow. Impeccably designed semicircular and flat roofs, with aluminum awnings that protect the walls from continuous sunlight, provide shade an irregularly-shaped pool and terrace that offers views of the different parts of the buildi

The layout comprises two floors above the platform plus a basement garage that is achieve as a result of the incline of the street in which the house is located. The yard surrounds all rooms, with the intention of providing privacy and creating its own environment.

The range of light colors used gives a feeling serenity and simplicity that reminds us that the most important people are without doubt the inhabitants of the house themselves.

A landscaped area surrounds the
building and acts as a barrier
between the bustle of the city
and the desired tranquility of the
house. In this way the house is
protected from its urban
surroundings.

Left-hand page:
The facade stands out for its
refined sobriety. It combines
windowless panels with glazed
areas and sheet-metal roofs that
protect against direct sunlight.

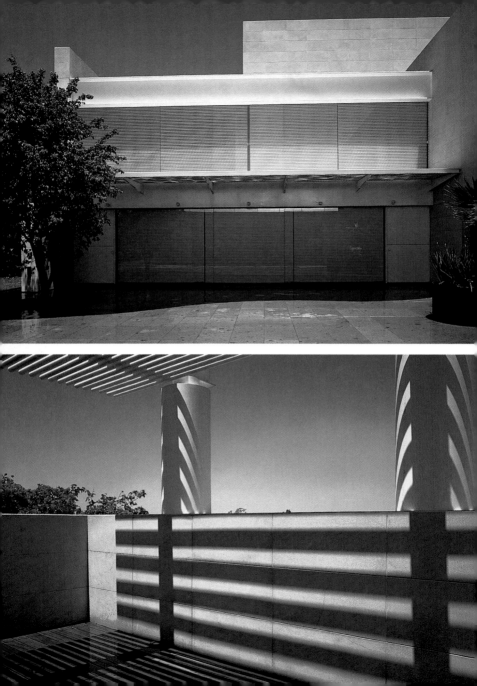

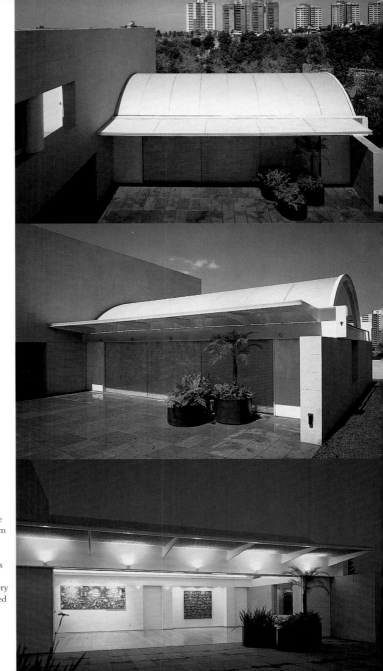

The interior features the same materials as the exterior: glass, concrete, and aluminum.

The vaulted roofs enhance the rooms and create warm light effects.

The terraces and balconies allow open-air activities. These outside areas of every shape and size usually need some kind of sun protection: pergolas, shades, or awnings.

Ásendi House

Location: *Reykjavik, Iceland*
Year of construction: *1997*
Architects: *Studio Granda*
Photography: *Sigurgeir Sigurjónsson*

This project consists of extending a 1970s house. The client wanted bedrooms, a bathroom, a breakfast bar, a storage area, and a den.

The existing house has a single floor and a garage on the side and is located on a corner. Studio Granda decided to convert the garage into a small storeroom and a work area. This significantly reduced the size of the extension. The extension was located above the garage and connected to the house via a new entrance hall.

The facade and shape of the extension copy that of the original house and try to restrict the impact of the alterations carried out during the 1980s. The corner is emphasized by the construction of an upper floor that distinguishe the space and balances the scale and proportio of the openings.

The entrance and the new parking space that uses primary materials – basalt, teak, granite, and ceramic tiles – is landscaped. A simple combination of finishes creates a warm, elegant whole that continues inside.

Over the main entrance is a piece by the artis Lilja Pálmadóttir, which was specially commissioned for the building.

The parking area is not
covered but provides vehicle
parking close to the house.
The area is made distinctive
in appearance by giving it a
change of paving.

Light playing on the
courtyard produces many
different effects that are
made visible by the
glazed surfaces and
other finishes.

Glass House in Almelo

Location: *Almelo, Netherlands*
Year of construction: *1997*
Architect: *Dirk Jan Postel*
Photography: *Jordi Miralles*

The design is based on a repeated module, the size of a single bedroom, that determines both the structure and layout of the rooms and the placing of all openings. This frugal container adapts easily to the project, which is sited conventionally with hardly any variation, even on the outside.

Facing the street, and on the side walls, a screen-printed sheet of glass, fitted as a ventilated outer layer, covers the whole of the building, concealing the size and position of the openings. Only a small porch at the entrance and the garage door interrupt the continuity of the cladding. During the day, the sheet of glass reflects the surroundings like a mirror; at night the interior lighting reveals the whole house.

This box, silent and cold to the street, changes in the yard, where large windows that also match the structural module allow a smooth transition between the inside and the outside. A glass urn of exquisite purity acts as a winter garden and as a symbol of this desire for opposites. The rest of the wall is covered with light timber sheets laid as a ventilated facade that completes the more attractive face of the house. That attractiveness is repeated in the birch cladding inside.

The Glass House is an example of efficient work with a minimum of effort, condensing all the promise in the clear, forceful decisions that produce a building which is cold and refined on the outside, yet warm and comfortable on the inside.

The staircase that can be seen from the street connects to the upper floor, where the bedrooms are situated.

The materials used on the outside and inside are limited. In contrast with the external glazed skin, all the interior walls are timber. All the doors in the house are translucent glass.

HOUSES BY THE SEA

A seaside location implies the coexistence of a whole range of factors that make it possible for urban areas or centers with exceptional settings and weather to spring up. Mere proximity to a large expanse of water, the advantage enjoyed by all the single-family homes presented in this section, has a significant impact on the climate. Seas and oceans are capable of moderating extreme temperatures since their thermal inertia is greater than that of air. They are therefore able to restrain both very hot and very cold air, and land located leeward of a marine environment will be warmer in winter and cooler in summer. This can be verified on a day-to-day basis and also by the season. People who live in warm climates live around their houses rather than inside them. They spend much of their time in the open air and seek the protection of the hearth only when they feel the need for intimacy or when they are forced to go inside by inclement weather. In hot, humid climates, typical of coastal locations, people spend an even greater part of their life outdoors, where they can, than people who live in arid areas, because they have the advantage of pleasant breezes.

The architecture characteristic of places with a hot dry climate or cold climate demonstrates marked differences from warmer and more humid seaside locations.

Although each location has to be considered from an independent and particular viewpoint because of the geographic and social diversity characteristic of the coast, there is a set of features and general factors that are amply exemplified in the various projects presented here.

It is worth looking more deeply into some of these factors as they are representative of the coastal homes described. The number of times they appear and the clear role they play demonstrate this.

Gables or projections are fixed constructions which are located at the top of the walls of many of these buildings; they project horizontally, protecting the walls and particularly the windows from sunlight and rain. They are usually opaque and their size basically depends on the angle of incidence of the sun. The best ones admit sunlight in winter but keep it out in summer. Gables located on the south side of the house are the most effective.

Screens are rigid, opaque, and normally fixed elements on walls to create shade from the sun over a specific glazed area. They can be adjusted to suit the angle of the sun.

Shutters are practical, moveable units, consisting of slats, that can be placed in front of an opening to shut out direct sunlight completely but allow ventilation, a certain amount of light, and views of the outside. As they are adjustable, they can be set to provide the desired protection and ventilation at any given time. Awnings or outside drapes are flexible, mobile items, upright or sloping, that can be used to shade part of a wall or opening.

Colored and/or reflecting glass can be used to glaze an opening as it also affords protection, letting in some light and a view of the outside, but no ventilation. It is useful in situations where ventilation is not important and sunlight not too strong. Verandas are covered areas on the side of a house that can be open to the outside or enclosed with glass.

Porches are another architectural feature very common to seaside houses. They are covered areas added to a building at first-floor level and open to the outside. They form a link between the inside and the outside and illuminate the outside areas around them. The use of courtyards is also common. These areas are surrounded by one or more walls but open to the outside from above.

This analysis of the architectural characteristics of coastal areas, where in many cases the weather is warm and humid, makes it clear that there are features and elements that are commonly used in this very specific habitat. Each and every one of the single-family homes in this section beautifully exemplifies the extent to which the environment influences human

development and how the climate and physical surroundings can determine the design and construction of homes designed by and for the individual. For these houses the effect of the sun and protection against adverse weather conditions, together with the beauty of nature, have been the principal factors influencing the architecture.

Casa en Na Xemena

Location: *Ibiza, Spain*
Year of construction: *1997*
Architect: *Ramon Esteve*
Associates: *Juan A. Ferrero, Antonio Calvo*
Photography: *Ramon Esteve*

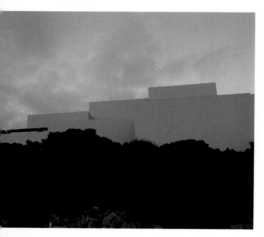

The magnitude of all the component parts of this timeless landscape instills in us respect for such equilibrium, sensitivity for the grandeur, and dialogue between the image of the territory and the building: that is what is lasting, attractive and extraordinary in the world of architecture.

From the preparation of the initial plans, the selection of materials and colors, the buildings and building elements constitute a natural fluidity, without being constrained by a rigid geometric format, while at the same time maintaining a rational base. The house is sited in such a way that it can continue to grow as determined by the guidelines of the original nucleus. The combination of various buildings that form the interior rooms is laid out as a sequence of spaces whose measurements vary proportionally in all three dimensions, increasing in size as they go.

The architectural structure is set on a rocky base, appearing as a compact and simple whole and following the shape of the cliff. From the outside the layout of the terraces and swimming pool, slightly offset, creates a visual perspective that completes the rounded geometry of the house itself. It seeks a harmonious relationship with its surroundings, with no strident overtones, like a smooth and logical progression between the land and the countryside. The various floor levels in the design act as a dynamic feature, providing areas such as the terrace and swimming pool with their own identity, facing the sea, enjoying the changing light of the Mediterranean throughout the day.

The austere geometry of the wa[...]
is enhanced by the stairs leadi[...]
to the house and terraces. T[...]
impression given is of [...]
enclosure sculpted out of the lan[...]
surrounded by the water of t[...]
swimming pool and bench[...]
made out of old railroad ti[...]

Minute square openings scatt[...]
weak light on the outside pavi[...]
during the nigh[...]

Right-hand pag[...]
View of the outside stairca[...]
during constructio[...]

In the master bedroom, the service areas are arranged in a corner of the room. The tub is built into the floor and gives a direct view of the outside.

The outside walls are perforated to capture light following a natural order marked by the interior configuration.

Teak boarding runs from the lounge, the ceiling, and wall of the dining room to the smooth cement paving. An inside staircase made of teak planks set into the wall connects the lounge with the study located above the dining room, from which the roof terraces can be accessed.

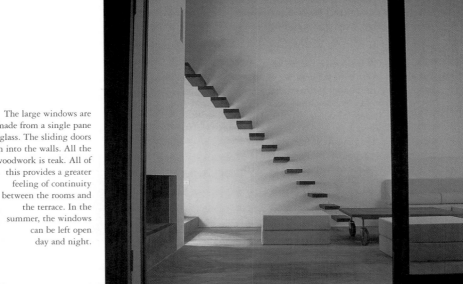

The large windows are made from a single pane of glass. The sliding doors run into the walls. All the woodwork is teak. All of this provides a greater feeling of continuity between the rooms and the terrace. In the summer, the windows can be left open day and night.

Casa en Los Vilos

Location: *Los Vilos, Chile*
Year of construction: *1996*
Architect: *Cristián Boza*
Builder: *Pablo Epulez*
Associates: *Paola Durruty (project),*
               Ricardo Aránguiz (structural engineer)
Photography: *Cristian Boza*

Setting and topography always affect architecture, but there are some cases where they do it radically and it is difficult to discern whether we are talking about a building or a landscape. This house, designed by the Chilean architect Cristián Boza at the top of some cliffs near Los Vilos, belongs to the style of architecture that is built into its surroundings and after a while it is hard to believe that it has not always been there.

Boza first builds a path that runs down from the highest part of the plot, between the rocks, to the edge of the cliff, in a succession of stepped terraces and platforms. Along this narrow path run all the rooms of the house. The bedrooms overlook the path on one side and the cliff on the other. The succession of doors and windows at differing levels in the curved wall of the outside passageway gives the impression of a narrow village street, rather than a single house.

At the end of the house, on the edge of the cliff, a large 26 ft (8 m) tall area houses the living room, dining room, and, in the attic, the master bedroom that can be completely opened or closed by a system of sliding wooden doors.

There are various levels, runs, and remarkable views: this is not a question of building somewhere new but of placing yourself in an existing landscape, slightly modifying a corner of the coastline so that you can sleep and dine in it, and await dusk in the shade of a wall, contemplating the ocean.

The roof of the house is flat and acts as an enormous terrace that ca be accessed from the upper section of the plot and from the path.

The Chilean architect designed into the surroundings of the hous a series of landscaped happenings: vantage points, staircases, pergolas, bridges, gazebos…

All the walls are masonry: rock and cement. The internal partition walls are horizontally-laid eucalyptus planks and all the fittings are bronze.

There is no difference in the finish of the outside and the inside. Thus, whether you are standing in the living room or the bedroom you have the feeling of being immersed in the landscape.

House in Susman Bay

Location: *Galveston, Texas, United States*
Year of construction: *1995*
Builder: *Philip J. Douglas, Inc.*
Architect: *Natalye Appel*
Associates: *Matrix Structural Engineers,*
Peter J. Hurley (structural engineer)
Photography: *Undine Pröhl*

The owners are a couple from Houston who wanted to build a weekend house to which they could invite their family, friends, and customers for a few days' rest and relaxation.

This is why the design combines substantial areas for parties and gatherings of large numbers of people, with private areas where you can get away from it all and relax. This division is very clearly reflected in the final design of the house. However, the concept at the heart of the project is to build the house as if it were a simple building close to the beach.

Due to the high water table, practically at ground level, the house is raised on a platform supported by piles so that, apart from a small storeroom, the whole of the first floor is open and used as parking space.

The house consists of two enclosed rectangular buildings located at both ends and joined by a large double-height covered area that houses the enormous living room-dining room-bar-kitchen, with huge windows overlooking the bay. The roof of each section has a different slope that makes it easily recognizable from the road and the central glazed strip identifies the main door to the house.

The gray-painted timber that covers the walls is also used on the living-room walls, which makes the room look as if it were intended to be an outside porch.

efi-hand page:

he lake forms part of the ard. Therefore there is no ool, only a small sectioned-ff area for very small hildren. The house has its wn jetty on which a timber ergola has been built.

wo outside staircases at ach end of the building ad to the upper floor, here the actual entrance to ne house is located.

FISH

Formally, Natalye Appel captures the esthetics of the old local cottages. This bond with indigenous architecture involves the breakdown of the building into different sections in order to reproduce the scale of the windows, roofs, balconies, and staircases of the traditional buildings.

Views of the large central room. Halogen lamps hanging from the ceiling provide lighting. The air-conditioning pipes are left visible.

House in Capistrano Beach

Location: *Capistrano Beach, California, United States*
Year of construction: *1995*
Builder: *Philip J. Douglas, Inc.*
Architect: *Rob Wellington Quigley*
Photography: *Undine Pröhl*

The proximity of the beach means that the architecture changes. With it, a sensual, fun world, often disconcerting, explodes and architecture becomes direct, without preconceptions, based on the first models of modernity, but with its rigidity smoothed by more spontaneous gestures.

The buildings near the beach reveal this changeable, ephemeral, and random nature and demonstrate the intense feeling of displacement and temporariness that impregnates the landscape in the same way that the unordered proliferation of mobile units translates the absence of any peremptory urge.

The house is composed of juxtapositions, tensions, fragmentations integrated into a difficult end unit that nevertheless manages to travel through its spaces.

The east- and west-facing walls form parallel planes that enclose the house. On the north and south faces, these rigid planes become blurred and empty out in some places to reveal the interior, making it seem as though the sea filters through the openings and domestic life escapes onto the sand. The lines used for these two walls curve gently, revealing the effect that erosion has on the landscape.

Clearly influenced by its special location, the architecture of this home has a hedonistic side, demonstrated in a series of areas and finishes primarily designed to be enjoyed by the senses. As we approach the beach, the materials change and the design becomes mobile, less rigid, and more uninhibited.

The range of materials used is extensive and changes as we move from the street to the beach: exposed concrete, glass, asphalt-covered timber, fabric roofs, plants.

is interesting to see how
e entry develops. From the
reet we can see the
fferent sections of the
ilding, which blurs the
oundary between one house
d the next.

Following pages:
This home is a sensitive sequence
of rooms of very different sizes,
different ways of obtaining light,
and contrasted styles. The simul-
taneous perception of a large
number of elements causes
conflict and doubt in the observer,
enriching his or her perception.
The first floor is for daily life and
the upper floor contains the
bedroom area, bathroom, den, and
guest apartment.

Water and Glass House

Location: *Shizuoka, Japan*
Year of construction: *1995*
Architect: *Kengo Kuma*
Photography: *Futjitsuka Mitsumasa*

The origin of this house is, on the one hand, a critique of predefined shapes, converted into clichés of what a villa should be, and on the other a reflection on the act of seeing and being seen. The central idea of the Water and Glass House is a study of the different ways of seeing – in this case nature. There is a series of filters and frames located between nature and the onlooker, through which the outside world is visible. In this way, these materials demonstrate their transparency. There is no object to look at; they are translucent skins that reproduce images and construct an intermediate space between nature and the one who observes it.

The house is not an object but an assortment of spaces resulting from the superimposition of different transparencies pierced by the countryside. Features such as the sheet of water located on the upper floor of the house that merges with the sea in the distance, or the roof of metal strips that filters the light, are treated as abstract frames or filters and not as obstacles.

All this lies beneath a general impression of calm that involves equilibrium and an objective use of materials.

The life that goes on within the building is more important to Kuma than the form of the architecture. In this sense, the flow and movement inside the house must create the greatest possible interest. On the other hand, nature, or the landscape, is part of the life that goes on in this house; in fact nature takes on meaning when it comes into contact with architecture and the latter gives it a framework. The design permits an open relationship with the outside world; there is no clear differentiation between inside and outside.

The staircase is light and translucent, with glass treads and a metal frame.

The space that crosses the bridge, on entering the house, receives light from overhead.

The glazed areas and pillars seem to float on water.

Right-hand page:
In order to understand the architecture of Kengo Kuma, all you need are images of the landscape and daybreak as seen from the Water and Glass House.

Villa Nautilus

Location: *Acapulco, Mexico*
Year of construction: *1998*
Architects: *Migdal Architects*
Photography: *Alberto Moreno*

Located in the city of Acapulco, Villa Nautilus is the outcome of concepts that interested Migdal Arquitectos regarding the location and design of the house: topography, climate, function, views, and tectonics among other things.

The steep slope of the land means that the building is the cohesive factor of the site as it reinterprets the existing topography by the placing of a series of buildings that adapt to the immediate surroundings.

There is no primacy of areas: habitable areas combine with walkways and stairs. In this rich combination of environments, the service areas occupy a specific position: facing west in order to block the sunlight and acting as an environmental filter, moderating the extremes of weather and especially the high temperatures that can be reached in these latitudes.

The villa is designed on a logical and rational basis, as evidenced by its esthetic harmony, structural discipline, and design layout governed by consistent internal rules. Given these characteristics, you might think that the design of the building could turn out somewhat rigid, but the house surprises us with its richness and splendor. Migdal Arquitectos have produced a varied catalogue of environments that, apart from seeking the physical and spiritual comfort of the inhabitants, surprises with many esthetic and perceptive sensations.

-hand page:

 details are the result of
 ciculous study. Part of the
 erior lighting, for example,
 sists of tubes of light along
 baseboards that form the
 nsition from the inside to the
 side. The surface finishes and
 ings complete an overall
 earance that is luxurious but
 er excessive or ostentatious.

The various floors rotate slightly so as to cover a wide range of views of the magnificent bay. Spectators can enjoy the varying aspects of the countryside depending on which floor they are standing. The house rotates towards the north and the sun protection parapets get smaller as it turns. The tectonic nature of the project is inherent in the structural desire that generated it. To solve the building problems that arose as a result of building on a cliff, it was decided to support the rooms with load-bearing walls, solid floor slabs, and beam and arched slabs.

Edmonds Residence

Location: *Horseshoe Bay, Texas, United States*
Year of construction: *1993*
Builder: *Frank Morris Constructions Co. Ltd.*
Architect: *Morris Jerome Neal*
Associate: *V. Vives*
Photography: *Paul Bardagjy*

The large walled courtyard connects exclusively with the master bedroom.

Neal defines his architecture as both modern and vernacular. In other words, although his architecture is clearly modern in its treatment of space and the technical solutions used, it frequently uses images and a method of integration with the surroundings that is typical of traditional houses.

The house is located in Horseshoe Bay, Texas, in a leafy setting on a slight slope from which the golf course can be seen.

The home enjoys an excellent site but, at the same time, it is obliged to conserve this space. As in all Neal's work, harmonious integration between architecture and its surroundings is the starting point of the project.

In this case, the Texan architect has decided to set out the rooms on a single floor so that the building does not extend beyond the treetops. Neal has not designed any clear, recognizable shape, with a precise outline, but has set out the various areas of the house in a zigzag line blending with the undulations of the land and the space between the trees.

Each of the three main wings of the house has its own individual hip roof, while the areas that link them have a concrete slab roof. The end result is closer to a collection of small scattered pavilions than to a single building.

The linear nature of the house means that it does not have four walls but just two: one in front (access) and one at the back (yard). Each of them is designed differently since the direction in which they face, the views, and the level of acceptable privacy in each case are almost opposite. It could be said that this is a schizophrenic house, with two completely different and opposing personalities.

Around the three hip roofs, Neal designed a narrow sliding window to give the impression that they are not attached to the walls.

The terrace fireplace can be used as a barbecue.

Carmichael Residence

Location: *Lake Vista, Texas, United States*
Year of construction: *1996*
Builder: *Frank Morris Constructions*
Architect: *Morris Jerome Neal*
Associate: *V. Vives*
Photography: *Paul Bardagjy*

View of the main facade facing the lake.

Detail of access to the third floor at the top of the stairs.

Nighttime view of the front facade. In contrast with the large windows and lake-facing terraces, the openings are few and small on this wall.

M. J. Neal describes this house on the banks Lake Vista in Texas as a watchtower. Without a doubt the architectural richness and complexi of the house are more than that, but what is certain is that the architect based the design that idea. The spirit, essence, and possibly the reason why the Carmichael family decided to build their home on this site and not elsewhe is the opportunity it gives them to go out on terrace and lay in the sun facing a magnificent panorama of Lake Vista.

Despite being just a short distance from the shore, the house is surrounded by trees that have been retained. In this way a dual effect is achieved: on the one hand the building is camouflaged by the foliage so that its impact the landscape (a landscape which they love an therefore do not wish to damage) is minimize and, on the other, the views of the lake are never the same because each one is varied an enriched by the trees.

However, this decision brings with it the obligation to raise the house well above grou level so that the main rooms can enjoy the views. The living room, dining room, kitchen, a bedrooms are therefore on the third floor, 20 (6 m) above ground level.

The house is based on two rectangular bloc of three floors, set at an angle but not touchi in the style of Malevich.

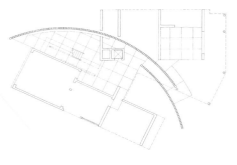

Second floor.

Third floor.

Detail of hall leading
to the living room. A
skylight illuminates the
wall in an intense yellow.

The kitchen is completely open to the living room, which is why maximum care has been taken with details and finishes.

View of the master bathroom. An amazing view over the lake can be enjoyed from the tub.

House in Sintra

Location: *Sintra, Portugal*
Year of construction: *1995*
Architect: *Frederico Valsassina*

Right-hand pa
The bedroom shutters
designed not only
protection against the s
but also as a security syste

One of the main virtues of the Valsassina project is its perfect communion with the landscape. The house is completely on one leve However, the floor is not always on the same level but adjusts to the site. Located in a pine grove, one of the initial requirements was that no tree should be cut down unnecessarily. The house has an irregular perimeter with many indents. To a certain extent, it spreads like an c slick in an organic manner from a combination of small modules. In some places part of the garden is surrounded by the house, forming an internal courtyard, while in others a room disappears between the pine trees.

Despite this spatial complexity, the construction is very simple. Everything is based on a network of pillars. There are no curved walls or diagonals; the house has a stepped line with clear references to Utzon and Coderch.

There is a clear distinction between the yard wall and the front wall. The entrance is in the center of the house and the yard and swimmin pool can be clearly seen from the hall as the corridor at this point is very narrow. On one side are the communal rooms and on the othe the bedrooms. All the major rooms of the hou (living room, dining room, and bedrooms) overlook the yard, while the kitchen and bathroom, garage, and guest bedroom overlook the front of the house.

Just as important as the built areas are the landscaping of the yard, the extensive paved terrace, and the swimming pool.

Frederico Valsassina respected the topography wherever possible, adapting to the different levels. He used a dip in the ground for building the swimming pool. He also planted more pines, jacarandas, and local flora.

The hall allows views through the house, from the pool to the pine grove and from the entrance to the yard.

Frederico Valsassina used traditional materials and building methods such as white walls and masonry, and ceramic floors.

489

Casa Boenders

Location: *Ibiza, Spain*
Year of construction: *1988*
Architects: *José Antonio Martínez Lapeña,*
    Elías Torres Tur

The architects commissioned to design this house decided to create a single space in which the house and the garden, the interior and exterior, work and play, entertainment and recreation, would live harmoniously side by side.

This single-story family home was built on the island of Ibiza (Spain) in the middle of a luxuriant pine wood on a gently sloping, south-facing hillside offering magnificent views over the sea and San Antonio Bay. The architecture of the building is perfectly suited to the topography of the site.

An irregular floor forms the base on which this single-story family house is built. The architects' firm intention not to create any kind of pre-established artificial and unnecessary separation is the reason why there is only one floor. It houses the lounges, dining room, a very functional kitchen, and the study – these rooms make up the family rooms – as well as the master bedroom or night area. All these rooms are arranged around a series of inner courtyar and open-air nooks. The yard, covering a very large area, includes a swimming pool with a pat at one end that is ideal as a solarium.

The outside is contained within a complex, intricate system of walls, shades, pergolas, and s on that make it habitable and turn the various corners of the garden into new additional roor for the house.

From the outside, the building's architecture i essentially straight lines, broken only by the pyramid effect created by the stone steps that surround the house and a few cylindrical pillars rising out of the swimming pool.

The basic aim of the pr
is to create a uniform w
without interruption or
sudden changes of scene
The fragile materials w
which the external
architectural elements l
been built (timber at o
end of the pool, mosaic
laid on the terrace, and
metal, among others)
reinforce this concept a
very effectively break th
assumed boundaries be
the yard and the outside
the building, thus achie
real spatial continuity.

oth inside and outside, e predominant color is hite. On the inside the floors are tiled and the ceilings are timber beamed. The furniture has been designed for mfort. Cushions, sofas, and drapes throughout the house are all in light colors.

House in Manhattan Beach

Location: *Los Angeles, United States*
Year of construction: *1989*
Architect: *Ray Kappe*
Photography: *Reiner Blunck*

Ray Kappe sought to build a weekend house primarily to provide entertainment, sun, water, and rest. To achieve this he designed a system of small outside terraces that, together with the extensive flat roof, creates a close relationship between the house, the ocean and the public beach areas.

This house is located opposite Manhattan Beach and faces the sea. The plot on which it is built is slightly sloping, a feature to which the house adapts. This topographic peculiarity is responsible for the magnificent sea views and the privilege of being able to see the sun rising and setting every day of the year.

The building consists of three contrasting floors raised on a completely irregular base. The first floor contains the guest rooms and a den with a gigantic television screen. The middle floor, also the access floor, includes the main entrance that is reached via an outside staircase, the living room, bar, dining room, kitchen, ironing room, washroom, small wine store, utility room and large garage. It is therefore the area where the majority of family life takes place. The top floor houses the master bedroom, bathroom, and a shower/changing room with direct access to the swimming pool. In addition to the main staircase, a small elevator serves all floors. A winding staircase at the rear of the house is the only access to the roof, which houses the oval pool, a glass-covered walkway, and areas for both sunbathing and enjoying fabulous views over the sea.

The kitchen with its characteristic
curved lines and shapes.

The semicircular shape of the bar
and living room helps to create a
relationship between the owners
of the house and their guests.

The laminated glass mai
staircase, together with th
handrail and wall in the sam
material, create a gloss
surface that increases th
penetration of dim ligh
into the hous

Casa en la isla

Location: *Ibiza, Spain*
Year of construction: *1990*
Architect: *Francisco de la Guardia*
Photography: *Ferrán Freixa*

Using traditional materials from the island of Ibiza, Francisco de la Guardia has created a home where the intimacy of the individual is respected and where enjoying this wonderful landscape is not only a privilege but an absolutely palpable reality.

This house is located in Ibiza, in the middle of the Mediterranean, on a high hillock enjoying magnificent views over the sea. The whole building has been designed to fit the slope of the plot, so that all the rooms are at varying levels.

The house is designed on three levels. The upper level contains the vehicle access and main entrance to the house. It consists of a large hall with two spacious patios that provide access to the four main areas of the house: the lounge and dining room area, kitchen and bathroom area, study and library, and the bedrooms – as well as a guest suite, the service entrance, service room and wine store. The north wing houses a suite consisting of double bedroom and bathroom, kitchen, and office-diner leading out onto the main terrace that surrounds the whole building and gives access to a sauna and shower room. This recreation area also houses the large swimming pool that is the main feature of the rear of the house.

The architect has created two large patios to act as sun traps, so the rest of the square windows covering the walls are relatively small.

Left-hand page
The building materials ar
local. Load-bearing wall
and partition walls ar
plastered inside and out
the floors and walls of th
bathrooms have been line
in local white marble. Th
woodwork of all doors an
sliding units, outsid
shutters, and closets i
natural Austrian pine

There is a close connection
between the outside and
inside of the house, where
the inner courtyards create
the clearest link: the glass
walls reflect the colors of
the yard; the plants thus
become a major feature.
Tiled floors are another
repeated theme.

Detached House in Ibiza

Location: *Ibiza, Spain*
Year of construction: *1988*
Architects: *Enrique Álvarez-Sala, Carlos Rubio,*
           Ignacio Vicens y Hualde
Photography: *Francesc Tur*

This detached house stands next to the sea, echoing the traditional, deeply-rooted white architecture of times gone by. Its clear, emphatic though restrained shape contrasts sharply and quite dramatically with the beautiful yet sparse natural surroundings.

This building stands on the island of Ibiza, in the middle of the Mediterranean Sea, on the highest part of a hillside, with a pinewood in the background and most of its grounds facing the sea. The southern aspect of the house results in magnificent views over D'Alt Vila and the port of Ibiza town.

The single-story construction has a rectangular base and is structured around two axes, perpendicular to each other, to which the various parts that make up the design are attached. These axial lines are emphasized by the colored walls that extend into the garden, organizing it into different areas. A retaining wall is used as a big terrace similar to those already present, so that it constitutes the garage and at the same time defines the basic height of the site. All the main rooms come out into the external space, contained behind the frontage, with the latter becoming a patio-yard clearly delimited by the swimming pool wall.

In addition to the main house, there is a summerhouse for guests, completely independent from the rest of the house.

The chairs are different in
every room, where they fulfil a
decorative and functional role.

View of the living room.
The unusual circular
roof can be seen.

View of the swimming pool from the
porch. The rectilinear and symmetrical
geometry of the room is conducive to
relaxation and convivial conversation.

The bright exterior colors are reflected inside the house in the pictures that decorate the walls on one side and in some items of furniture painted yellow, red, and blue, in contrast with the whole. The various pieces of furniture have been carefully selected and draw attention to the modern and innovative character of the house.

House in East Quogue

Location: *New York, United States*
Year of construction: *1987*
Architect: *Robert Stern*
Photography: *Peter Aaron*

In this work Robert Stern exemplifies simplicity and the use of materials typical of a very pure and genuine architecture that seems to have disappeared from modern civilization.

This charming, detached house is found near East Quogue, in New York State, on the shores of the Atlantic Ocean, on a plot of ground with all the characteristics of a coastal area. It is small in size and the most outstanding feature is possibly the fact that it has been built right on the edge of a dune. Separated only by a strip of sand from a peaceful beach, the land on which the house is built has an irregular and undulating surface, where only some sparse brushwood grows. The architect's intention was to make maximum use of this plot, adapting the construction to the latter's topography, so that the beautiful view can be enjoyed as much as possible.

This construction is built on a rectangular base and is two stories high on its north side and only one on its south side. It also has an attic under the roof. The hazardous position of this house right on the edge of the dune made it possible to tuck away three small guest rooms that follow the slope behind the dune.

The different types of window are similar in their configuration, combining and contrasting to show their constructional richness: squares within semicircles, rectangles, circles inside a square or an eyelid shape.

The overhang extends to the main floor, just below the level of the dune, with an attractive porch from which you can watch the sun set across the bay. This floor is intended for family life, and includes a large living room, dining room, and kitchen. The first floor, in the lowest part of the site, contains the bedrooms, except the master bedroom, and bathrooms.

Right-hand pa
The roofs, which are sharp
inclined, are clad with sla
that combine at the high
points with reddish tiles. T
walls comprising doors a
windows are painted white a
stand out from dark
backgrounds, as do t
balustrades that run arou
the terraces and balconi

The master bedroom is located in the attic, the highest part of the building, and is lit by a very bold classical arched window.

Tones of white and cream have been used for the walls. The floors are covered with terracotta tiles and carpets that create a warm and welcoming atmosphere. The furniture is rustic, made of mahogany.

House in Bells Beach

Location: *Bells Beach, Australia*
Year of construction: *1990*
Architect: *Robert Robertson*
Photography: *Reiner Blunk*

This detached house is located in the southern part of Victoria. The plot is right on the edge of the Australian continent, close to the ocean and the summer sea breezes, right in line with the coast, on a slightly sloping and fairly irregular raised hummock. The view is simply incredible since the waves on this part of the coast, with their blue-green color, acquire a singular beauty when contrasted with the intense green of the surrounding vegetation.

The structure of this work of architecture consists of three pavilions arranged in parallel with the beach, connected to each other via a low section containing the staff quarters and a pergola. The result is a unit spread out over a single story on a slightly irregular base. The house consists of a central living area that includes a pantry-style kitchen, an exclusive area for the parents in the extreme north, and another for the children on the opposite side. The corrugated iron roofs chosen by Robert Robertson for this home are intended to imitate the movement of the ocean waters as they swell up and break on the three pavilions: the two lateral ones seem to roll down toward the Pacific; the middle one, on the other hand, goes in the opposite direction towards the hill.

The interior of the house gives something of the impression of a large and finely appointed tent. In fact, the inside of the house seems to be all floors and ceilings, the walls are cancelled out and the difference between the inside and the outside blurs. Everything about the house seems to recall the custom of living in enormous spaces where life was simple, free, and natural.

The material used in m[...]
of the house is red ce[...]
wood, while most of t[...]
wall surface consists [...]
glass windows. The wa[...]
are painted white and t[...]
furniture is rather sparse [...]
order to respect t[...]
transparency and clari[...]
of the spac[...]

House in Noosa Heads

Location: *Noosa Heads, Australia*
Year of construction: *1989*
Architect: *Geoffrey Pie*
Photography: *Reiner Blunk*

This detached house built by the architect Geoffrey Pie was designed as a refuge, close to the beach, for a client who was confined to a wheelchair. This fact naturally dictated the structure and the distribution of the various spaces throughout the house.

This residence is situated in Noosa Heads, Queensland, Australia, a beautiful summer seaside resort, on the high part of a mountain covered in the thick intense green vegetation where koala bears live. The plot with its irregular surface has a pronounced slope down to the ocean that stretches out to the horizon, offering a beautiful view. The topographical peculiarities of the plot do not pose any problems because this building has been arranged to follow the chosen plot exactly.

This construction has been built to follow a very irregular design that stands two stories high and consists of three independent areas; the intermediate section, roofed and transparent, acts as a linkway. One of the other sections forms the house and the third the garage (occupying both stories) and office.

Geoffrey Pie's main aim in designing this detached house was undoubtedly to take advantage of the sunny aspect, the sea breeze and the beautiful views, without sacrificing the private nature of the bedrooms and rest areas.

As the owner is highly sensitive to cold, the whole design of the property ensures that maximum natural light comes in; big windows open out to the exterior and onto the terrace.

Thanks to the stepped structure
of the frontage looking out over
the sea, most of the living
spaces on the top floor have
direct access to a terrace where
there is a rectangular
swimming pool, wall-to-wall
with the owner's suite.

Right-hand pag
A folding canvas ro
provides areas of shade
avoid any occasional ove
exposure to the sun whi
still allowing the pleasa
ever-present sea bree
to be enjoye

The door and windo
frames are in dark-gre
aluminum, to compleme
the vegetation, surroundi
reinforced glass. T
interior walls have be
painted white. T
staircases are terraco
tiled, as are some of t
rooms. Other floors a
made of forest woods a
some are carpete
Beechwood has been us
on the terraces and th
corresponding balustrad

House in Jutland

Location: *Jutland, Denmark*
Year of construction: *1990*
Architects: *Torsten Thorup, Claus Bonderup*
Photography: *Bent Rej*

The architects Torsten Thorup and Claus Bonderup felt that it was very important for this detached house to form part of a rigid unit surrounded by a simple yet dramatic landscape, which is then incorporated into the whole. It is in the interior of the house that its real spirit and remarkable individuality will be developed.

This house was built on the west coast of the Jutland peninsula (Denmark), away from the front line of the sea towards the interior, lost between sand dunes. The irregular and undulating land on which it is built is completely covered with thick vegetation that hides most of the building, allowing it to escape inquisitive eyes. Its exceptional position and curious configuration allow it to enjoy some incredible views over the North Sea.

The structure of this residence consists of a series of independent square areas, of different sizes, that create a complex and intricate sequence. The whole house is contained within one story, the tower being the only element that juts out from the building.

The construction of the various living areas has been inspired by the simple lines of a cube and a circle, as in the case of the living room, which is based on a square. The height of the room corresponds perfectly with its other measurements, giving equilibrium and balance to the whole. At the same time the traditional vision of a city has dominated this architectural work, forming its essential basis. All the streets, market places, and squares with their different measurements and characters are there.

The powerful light from
the sea floods into the
rooms, and views of the
sky and the sand dune
environment can also
be enjoyed.

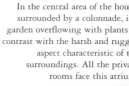

In the central area of the hou
surrounded by a colonnade, i
garden overflowing with plants
contrast with the harsh and rugg
aspect characteristic of t
surroundings. All the priva
rooms face this atriu

e roofs of the two circular
as that house the summer
ing room and a studio create
aulted area, like an original
pola, virtually spherical, with
ar geodesic echoes. Their chief
ment is the vegetation that
ablishes a clear bond with the
tural outside world, making it
her like a winter garden.

House in Mallorca

Location: *Mallorca, Spain*
Year of construction: *1990*
Architect: *Pere Nicolau*
Photography: *Francesc Tur*

Mindful of the sea, the pines, the slope of the mountain, popular culture, and contemporary architecture – the signs of a special language emerge from this house, which is an example of what Pere Nicolau's conscience and professionalism offer as an alternative to the systematic destruction of the Mallorcan coastline.

This detached house is situated in the Marmassem cove in the port of Andratx, at the top of a very pronounced slope with a thick pinewood as the most immediate environment. It has been placed in the landscape with subtlety and respect, carefully following the slope of the plot by using terraces.

On a foundation that is only slightly irregular and starting from a remit to meet the needs of normal family life, a profound bond with the sea, and rather stressed austerity, Nicolau sorted the daily activities of this house on three floors.

The first or entrance floor has a living room that connects with the roofed terrace next to the sea, which can be seen between the crowns of the pines, the splendid dining-living room, the kitchen, and a library; this level also includes the garage and the staff area. The upper floor contains the four bedrooms and three bathrooms, one of which is incorporated in the dressing room of the master suite. These rooms all have open terraces looking over the trees to the sea; they have been designed to act as suntraps. Finally, in the basement, next to the swimming pool, there is the leisure section: the rooms connected with washing and bathing, the children's rooms, and sports areas.

Outside, whatever is not glass or exposed stone is white. The walls, the pillars, and the shutters are this color, to contrast with the blue of the sea, the green of the pines, th ocher of the quarry stone and the sky.

side, the white walls
mbine with the clear
nes of the earthenware
oors, the wood of the
ilings, and the staircase
at links different levels.

House in Long Island

Location: *Long Island, New York, United States*
Year of construction: *1989*
Architect: *Steven Haas*
Photography: *Peter Aaron*

Some years ago, Steven Haas bought an abandoned property of around 320,000 sq ft (30,000 m²), demolished the house that was there and subdivided it into six independent plots. This spectacular house occupies the plot with the most splendid views, and is based on a very simple concept: water and a place to live, merely separated by a transparent glass wall.

The surface of the plot is rugged and uneven, although there is also a sandy beach on one of its sides and dense colorful vegetation to complete and soften the immediate environment. The building has been perfectly adapted to the topographical peculiarities of the location, which offer many possibilities.

The axonometric planes of this house reveal a set of curvilinear spaces within the rectangular shape that defines its base. To the side of the front entrance of the building, one of the most private areas, are a cricket pitch and a badminton court overlooked by a 100-year-old beech.

The house is on two distinct levels: the first floor contains all the socializing areas, and the second floor is the more intimate night-time area.

Access is from the rear, through an entrance next to the garage, which has space for a number of vehicles.

Facing the sea, on the south side, is the most important part of the first floor: an enormous room that unifies the living room with a fireside nook and an area for watching television, the dining room, and the kitchen, only separated from the rest by a kind of counter. Behind the living room is a study library, the only room that has solid walls for insulation.

The house makes a big impact because of the amount of glass: it seems to move and reflect the surrounding countryside.

There are very few rooms with clear boundaries inside the house. This includes the covered swimming pool, which seems to flow through the windows and doors that go from the ground to the ceiling.

The interior decor, chosen by the architect himself, is not at all overstated, but protects the clarity and transparency of the rooms.

Spielberg Residence

Location: *East Hampton, New York, United States*
Year of construction: *1990*
Architects: *Robert Siegel, Charles Gwathmey*
Photography: *Steven Brooke*

This building is located in East Hampton, Long Island, New York, at the top of a steeply-sloping dune. The architects were not intimidated by the very uneven plot, but instead used it as a pedestal for the house, defined, on the landward side, by a stretch of grass and, on the slope down to the Atlantic Ocean, by the sharp profile of another dune covered in pine trees. These trees, planted years ago, were transplanted in accordance with a new landscaping scheme.

The remit for this project included a main residence, a guest house, a tennis court, and a swimming pool. The entrance driveway, defined by a cypress hedge to the west and an artificial hedge on the east side, extends for almost 330 ft (100 m) along an axis that leads it perfectly to a small wood of pear trees, from the edge of which there are clear views of the Atlantic Ocean. To see the house, with its slightly west-facing aspect, you must come very close; when finally glimpsed, the building is hidden by an imposing construction. This is a single guest house with a kitchen, dining room, living room, and several bedrooms. Immediately behind this is the tennis court, then a small staff house and storage area. An entrance patio leads to the main residence which has three floors on the north facade. On the one hand the latter anchors the construction to the ground and, on the other, establishes a wall to separate it from the dune and the ocean.

The simple and discreet
appearance of the building
(a discretion that is
reflected in the relatively
small number of rooms, in
the fairly small dimensions
of the grounds, and in the
fact that the house is not
right on the sea-front) is
its principal charm

Think-Tank

Location: *Skibbereen, Ireland*
Year of construction: *1998*
Architect: *Philip Gumuchdjian*
Photography: *Philip Gumuchdjian, Sandro Michahelles*

The architecture of this house reflects a wide range of references: structures of boats with living accommodation, granaries, cattle sheds, mountain huts, and, in a more abstract way, a European perspective on Japanese pavilions. All these references are brought together, or essentially come down to the building, dividing up into a simple expression of framework, roof, and outer covering. The dominant element of the design is the projecting structure of the roof that provides protection against the pronounced rainfall which affects the region, as well as a certain feeling of withdrawal from it.

A marked hierarchy of architectural elements (roof, structure, and glass faces) was fundamental in suggesting that it should be interpreted as a pre-existing closed structure, as a "unit" found on the site: a simple atemporal object. The effect of transparency was emphasized with perforated screens to keep the building as open as possible whilst still providing a framework for views and suggesting intimacy and protection.

The construction materials were chosen so as to juxtapose stable elements, such as glass and stainless steel, with materials more likely to undergo substantial modifications or significant erosion, such as the roof boarding, fillets, and platform based on cedarwood, as well as the Iroko wood structure.

In contrast to the intense colors and the reflections issuing from the site (the green of the fields, the silver-blue of the river, dramatic grays and blues of the sky), the silvery tone of the building changes all the time, darkening whenever the structure and the roof get wet, and then fading under the effects of the sun.

...e interaction with the forces of nature is
...ect and total.

...e contrast of more stable materials (for
...ample stainless steel) with changing
...es (for example the wood platforms) is a
...sic dialogue for the construction and
...ucture of the house.

...t-hand page:
...e recurring image of this project as
...elemental hut finds a subdued and
...gant contemporary interpretation in the
...in living space.

...e setting of the Think-Tank speaks of
...lation and introspection.

e care and attention paid to the
nstructional details during the
sign process, and its subsequent
cution, make simplicity a
ue and the language of the
terials rich and complex.

With a minimal surface area
the interior space manages
to free itself from separative
elements that would
fragment the perception
of the landscape.

Baggy House

Location: *North Devon, Great Britain*
Year of construction: *1998*
Architects: *Hudson & Featherstone*
Photography: *Jo Reld, John Peck, Tim Brotherton*

The principal characteristic of the site of this house is the contrast between the very open views toward the south and the east, and those to the north, where the plot rises up toward Middleborough Hill. The first designs produced preliminary ideas of a house with two faces: a rather opaque one to contrast with the other more transparent one facing the sun, the sea, and the mountains.

The north facade protects the private rooms from an old adjacent stable. This is the solid side that can be seen on arrival, hiding the views of the sea, and ensuring interior privacy. Opacity is obtained by using low, compact shapes, covered with tiles, small windows, and a large chimney marking the entrance. After passing through the main door you reach a low entrance hall dominated by a granite column and the stairs at the back, bathed in natural light, that lead to the rooms on the upper level, whose southerly aspect offers marvelous views. Glass screens frame these views and in summer they can be moved aside in order to convert the living room into a pavilion open to the ocean. This is the heart of the house from which the remaining space flows out, and it is the link between the opaque zone and the transparent one.

Decisions about the shape and construction of the building were fundamental, therefore considerations about the surroundings and the actual structure reflect this: the thick walls on the north side have insulation on the outer face that provides a high thermal mass; while the light wood, steel, and glass construction of the walls on the south facade benefit from solar radiation incorporating means to obtain natural light and passive ventilation for the rooms in the house.

The concrete diving board, the waterfall, and the stairs were constructed *in situ* and slip neatly into the pink wall that emerges from the water. Wooden platforms and a tiled bridge have been positioned in the swimming pool in order to define and separate its different sections.

The garden-pool is situated in an existing rock garden, in the lowest and most protected part of the premises. From the main house and the gardens located higher up, the swimming pool appears as a pink wall that slips into the horizon, contrasting with a dry stone wall at its main boundary. The wall protects the swimming pool from being seen directly from the outside; the pool can only be glimpsed from the access driveway.

Right-hand pa
A sequence of prefabricated pieces
concrete form the floor that leads to t
hidden garde

The prominent position of the buildi
and the nature conservation area
which it stands affected the desi
process. The plan obeyed some v
clear guidelines: a detached house wi
six bedrooms and provision for gues
taking maximum advantage of the si

K-S House

Location: *Malibu, California, United States*
Year of construction: *1999*
Architect: *Edward R.Niles Architect*
Photography: *Edward R.Niles*

The prevalent idea in this Californian house overlooking the Pacific Ocean is the play between fullness and emptiness. It consists of various sections displaying pure geometry and contrasted materials, arranged symmetrically along an axis that materializes in a single glass gallery running round the whole building.

The rhythm produced by the sequences alternating between transparency and opacity culminates in the single bedroom in the house: an opaque body that stands out obliquely, like a funnel, over the landscape. A glazed volume which juts out over this on its broadest face opens it up toward the views and connects it with the exterior. Two translucent, symmetrical volumes precede the bedroom, each with a bathroom and a dressing room. A wide glass gallery separates them from the rest of the house, as though protecting a sacred intimacy.

The whole building is a succession of containers arranged along a "street." Access is from the end opposite the bedroom, where two garages are arranged symmetrically on either side of the gallery, or from the patio. Two pairs of closed sections that contain living and staff areas lead to a large unitary space shared by the kitchen, the dining room, and the living room. This is where the interior space flows into and integrates with the exterior; as if the kitchen, the dining room and the living room were actually on the patio and the patio shared this interior space.

The solid cubic elements are for evening activities and have minimum transparency, in contrast with the web of steel beams in the external gallery and the rooms in which daytime activities take place.

This play between fullness and emptiness, containers of different materials, rhythms, and transparencies, is produced on a horizontal platform, on the same level, on which the building is positioned. This same floor runs through the interior and the exterior; only the closed volumes have carpet, indicating a degree of intimacy and seclusion, a feeling of being inside and enclosed.

Right-hand pa
The geometry used throughout the proje
is very simple: right angles and cub
sections are combined in strict orde
without allowing curves or asymmetr
The glazed roofs of the gallery allow t
volumes to be seen in full, thus reinforci
the three-dimensional quality of objec
They are boxes detached from each oth
around which daily activities take place
the fluid space that connects the

Tsirigakis House

Location: *Mikonos, Greece*
Year of construction: *1998*
Architect: *Xavier Barba*
Photography: *Eugeni Pons*

This retirement home is located on the hills of Mikonos, far away from the tourists. The threat of earthquakes required a reinforced concrete construction. The house also had to be able to protect itself against the strong winds from the Aegean Sea. The walls extend to protect the swimming pool and surround the entrance patio. In order to reinforce the building's link with the landscape, most of the surfaces are clad with local stone, making limited use of the smooth whitewashed stucco so typical of the architecture of the Greek islands.

The new construction merges in the distance into dry, rocky walls, with the cupola and the characteristic chimneys barely visible over the bathroom. A roof made of wood and interwoven branches rests on stone pillars to shade the terrace overlooking the port.

The 2,150 sq ft (200 m²) interior has a living-dining room, a master suite, and three guest bedrooms on the main floor, as well as a two-bedroom flat for the family's son and guests underneath. Natural light gently illuminates the interior, surrounded by white walls, arches and columns, traditional wood beam ceilings, and floors in a light brown color. A series of stairs and a thick wall separate the dining room from the living room. Generally speaking, all the details in this house have been designed to maximize contact with nature.

One of the typical aspects of this house
is the whitewashed stucco that enfolds
the gentle, rounded forms, as well as
the dry stone walls that are used in
most of the construction and facade.

Casa González

Location: *Los Yesos, Granada, Spain*
Year of construction: *1998*
Architect: *Javier Terrados*
Photography: *Fernando Alda*

The plot on which this house stands is close to the sea, in Los Yesos, a village to the south of Granada in Spain. It is a diaphanous summer house open to the exterior so that its inhabitants can spend as much time as possible in the open air. The clients wanted to recall and retain the memories of what had been their summer activity for so long: taking holidays in a caravan.

So, this idea became the ruling image that shaped the project in its design and construction stage. Making the most of the slope, an extended volume was arranged perpendicular to this, closed off on the side of the mountain and open toward the sea. It is supported on the upper level of the plot and rises above the lower level. In this way the whole of the ground floor becomes a veranda, an open space protected from excessive exposure to the sun. The idea of lightness was important, and so a metal structure was chosen, with big windows between very slender pillars which seem to disappear into the shade of the veranda.

On the second floor two bedrooms with their respective bathrooms share a terrace with magnificent views. In the front by the sea, where the rooms are much more open to the outside, is the living-dining room and a second broad and partially-roofed terrace. The wall sections on the whole of the facade overlooking the sea have been designed in a modular way using aluminum structures that support the sliding windows, the window shades and the guard-rails of the living-dining room.

From the main entrance of the house, on the side of the mountain, only the two upper levels which are subtly separated from the ground can be seen: a thin line of sea appears emphasizing the volumes and conveying a feeling of light, movement, and air.

The views and the proximity to the sea are the criteria in accordance with which the bedrooms in the house are organized. First of all, on the side facing the mountain, where the volumes are more enclosed, there is a strip of bathrooms and storage rooms. Then comes the entrance at one end of the house.

Only the two upper levels are visible from the house's main entrance, which is on the side facing the mountain. These appear to be separated from the ground. A thin line of sea highlights the volumes and conveys lightness, movement and airiness.

The house has a succession of platforms facing the sea that shelter the areas open to the air, while allowing them to enjoy the best views. Each of these has a skylight in a different area, so that light can pass through, creating a staggered connection between the various levels of the house. The doors and windows between the terrace and the living room give the rooms privacy, without depriving them of their fine view.

Casa Reutter

Location: *Cantagua, Chile*
Year of construction: *1999*
Architect: *Mathias Klotz*
Photography: *Alberto Piovano*

The Casa Reutter stands on a wooded plot with a gentle slope, close to the Cachagua beach, 90 miles (140 km) from Santiago de Chile. The house consists of two twin horizontal volumes that appear to float, pierced by a third vertical stone body acting as a support. In this way the house is detached from the ground and rises up between the pines, where it enjoys an exceptional view over the Pacific Ocean. The copse protects it from the sun and gives extra privacy to the glazed areas and terraces.

The two sections differ in size and are made different materials: the larger one is made of wood whereas the other is clad in corrugated copper. As though it were "a house within a house," the larger section contains part of the metal section. Together they produce an effect horizontality that is further accentuated by a bridge leading to the roof of the house. This functions as a terrace and from there you can make your way to the terrace in front of the living room. The only room on the top floor is studio contained in the concrete body, clearly visible above the terrace.

The living room, dining room, and part of the kitchen form a whole. Only the fireplace and some very lightweight shelves separate it from the bedroom area, contained in the copper section. The facade looking out to the sea and the one facing the bedrooms are fully glazed. In this way new links are established between the inside and the outside.

These two boxes combine perfectly: one houses the private area of the house – more enclosed and compact – and the other, light and transparent, contains the areas intended for family life, opening toward the pinewood.

It was very important to achieve a balance and mutual understanding
with the natural environment for this beach house. The possibilities of
the plot – the slope, the views, and the trees – were used to maximum
advantage. The materials used for the external cladding were specially
chosen, taking into account the desire for harmony.

Separated by a few yards from the north facade (the sunniest)
a wooden framework acts as a semi-transparent screen, filtering
the sunlight, and protecting the privacy of the living room and
the dining room.

Some elements, such as the big wooden roof terrace and the bridge
that provides the link with the ground, are clear nautical references
reflecting the surroundings. Large volumes, pure forms, clear lines,
and natural materials dominate this work. Having found a way of
communicating with the plot, this building blends in perfectly.

Casa Gontovnik

Location: *Barranquilla, Puerto Colombia, Colombia*
Year of construction: *1996*
Architects: *Guillermo Arias, Luís Cuartas*
Photography: *Andrés Lejona*

The volumes of this deceptively simple house have been designed to resolve the plot-related complications inherent in the project. In spite of its magnificent geographical situation, sea views are difficult to achieve because of the proportions and topography of the site. The plot, measuring 52 ft (16 m) wide by 180 ft (55 m) long, lies between two other properties and slopes up from the street to the top of a rocky cliff. The volume has therefore been split into levels, almost as if it were climbing up the cliff itself, in order to obtain spectacular views over the Caribbean Sea. This ruling principle generates three main bodies. The first, on street level, is where the garages, guest rooms, and children's rooms are found. The second intermediate level, through which access to the house is gained, contains the corridors, a staff area, and the dining room, arranged around a central patio. This patio not only contributes to the natural cooling system, but also becomes the light source for the project. Interior spaces draw their light from here, while remaining secluded from the immediate neighbors. Finally, the third volume, located at the top of the cliff, contains the living room and the master bedroom that look over the steep cliff. This bedroom leads onto the roof, designed as a terrace-garden. Maximum space has been obtained by making the most of the difference in levels between the volumes of the house. The central corridor that runs along one side of the house, has become one of the most spacious aspects of the project.

It was on the basis of this same architectural objective that a solution was found not only for the awkward dialogue with the setting, but also for the ambivalence of the layout.

On the other hand, this is a project that, in itself, reveals the ability of architecture to produce ideal living environments without having recourse to sophisticated systems or costly materials.

Careful thought was given to the points at which light would enter the house. The living areas have large glazed spaces protected by shades with wooden slats, deflecting the direct incidence of the sun's rays. In the service areas, such as the bathrooms, the size of the windows was reduced to limit the entry of light and to preserve privacy.

The success of an architectural project whose objective is to produce a home depends, among other factors, on the relationship with its setting. In this case, the layout of the house was also intended to fulfill the requirements of both a permanent residence and a home for seaside vacations.

Left-hand page:
A small veranda was set on the terrace, defined by a pergola and a small swimming pool. These volumetric tricks are completed by a wooden roof that spreads over the swimming pool, right to the edge of the cliff.

House in Japan

Location: *Tokyo, Japan*
Year of construction: *1998*
Architects: *Legorreta Architects*
Photography: *Katsuhida Kida*

This is a house used as a second residence or place of relaxation by a Japanese professor of music. For this reason the rooms were designed to give priority to aspects of seclusion and tranquillity, as well as to establish a direct connection with the sea. The architecture has been kept simple in order to emphasize the marvelous views.

The entrance to the house is intentionally concealed, with a hint of mystery: a feature shared by Japanese and Mexican culture. From here, there is an entrance tower leading to a blue arched corridor, from which you can go down into the main area, containing the living room and dining room, or into either of the two bedrooms. The main feature of this central area is a large window opening onto the sea.

Stone and water, as well as a small separate patio, have been used to suggest unexpected cultural juxtapositions. The stone-based interior flooring, the washbasins, the wood, and other special items were produced in Mexico and exported to Japan, the aim being to give all the rooms a special character. Cultural interplay therefore had an important role in the process of designing and building this house.

Special care was taken with the relationship between the interior and the exterior. Consequently, the terraces became an integral part both of the interior and the surrounding landscape. A swimming pool runs round the entire house, ensuring that water is an ever-present aspect of the design. The exterior consists of pure white plane surfaces, with a succession of volumes firmly set in an orderly arrangement, following the slope of the plot.

The use of color to enhance the value of the plane surface, and the ever-present overflowing water features are reminders of Barragán, who is also inspired by the ancient traditions of Arab gardens. The architectural language used is further reinforced by a series of fleeting allusions and references that carry additional significance.

t-hand page:
ne building looks westward across
e bay to the Pacific Ocean, and the
ain view is the union between the
y and the infinite sea. An imposing
nge of mountains surrounds the bay
d a group of nearby houses is
attered across the rocky hills.
cuated on top of a small artificial
omontory, this house is separated
om its closest neighbors to the
uth by a narrow road that drops
ruptly toward the sea.

Steel House

Location: *Byron Bay, Australia*
Year of construction: *1997*
Architects: *Grose & Bradley*
Photography: *Anthony Browell*

The house is located on a hillock with a southerly aspect, looking towards Byron Bay, the most easterly point of Australia, and towards the Gold Coast to the north. As this is a house standing amid a varied landscape, the main view draws the attention to the rising sun. In a way, the architecture of this building owes its characteristics to this crucial requirement.

The desire to live in the open air in this overwhelming landscape was another of the important arguments controlling the way that this work was conceived and designed: on a primitive platform set in the natural world.

The form of the house also reflects this to a certain degree, since it is a minimal structure, following rural tradition, with its own mechanisms for controlling the environment. In order to achieve the feeling of living in the midst of a natural environment, the facades are mainly flat with practical fixed windows whose shades protect against the early rays of the sun.

In winter, the warm morning sun penetrates right inside the "platform," while in summer the ephemeral shadows of the window shades not only physically but also figuratively refresh the interior, by creating a feeling of freshness.

The building retains its original galvanized steel structure, with a rough, untreated appearance, and zinc panels have been used on the walls. These materials and their finishes have given the building the appearance of a harsh artificial object; this being the only possible way of creating a building in such a powerful landscape.

This house has been constructed as a simple volumetric unit that rises out of a powerful and extreme landscape.

The modular structure
and the presence of the
metal slab create a clear
and concise volumetry.

Right-hand page:
Views of the central
living area, designed as a
semi-external room.

Casa Ugarte

Location: *Maitencillo Sur, Chile*
Year of construction: *1995*
Architect: *Mathias Klotz*
Photography: *Alberto Piovano*

This project involved a small weekend house located close to the Maitencillo Sur cliff, 90 miles (140 km) to the north of Santiago de Chile.

Lightness and luminosity are the overwhelming impressions evoked by its elemental structure. The construction makes use of local building traditions: the finish of the unpolished wood is rough and rudimentary. The key to the design of this house is the precarious nature of the basic shelter or hut, as a simplified construction in contrast to the immensity of the Pacific Ocean. Its presence as an object that is ideal yet abstract at the same time has a strong impact on the landscape, transforming it and giving it a new interpretation.

The house consists of two separate parts, connected by a passage that forms the main entrance and extends into the interior. The bedrooms and bathrooms are located in the smaller area, while the other section contains the kitchen, dining room, and living room on the first floor, and a den on the second floor.

The terraces have been designed as semi-constructed spaces, as hollow or empty areas of both buildings, protected from the strong south winds. The larger section of the house is bored right through at its south end, in turn generating a feeling of continuity with the living room and creating the impression of a much larger interior.

The Casa Ugarte is made entirely of wood, both outside and in. The facades have been clad with superimposed slats, and the interior is wood-paneled. To create variety between sections each part of the house has a different surface finish.

The stairs and the
fireplace hearth are
inserted and
independent units.

The house consists of two
separate parts, connected
by a passage leading off
to the interior spaces.

House in Corfu

Location: *Corfu, Greece*
Year of construction: *1998*
Architect: *Xavier Barba*
Photography: *Eugeni Pons*

This project involved constructing a summerhouse and swimming pool for Lord Jacob Rothschild, to act as a complementary leisure and relaxation area for a house already in existence, situated on a spectacular promontory in Corfu, with views over the waters to Albania.

Right from the start the need to preserve the natural conditions was an imperative. An ideal site for this was finally found in a Venetian marble quarry tucked away from sight. After a degree of initial work involving removing some rocks and cleaning the area, the craggy sides were used as a natural course for the waterfall that flowed out of the swimming pool.

The summerhouse sought its inspiration in the villas built by the Romans on similar sites. Its interior houses a heated swimming pool, and the white pergola with open sides shelters a dining and relaxation area, with a kitchen, changing rooms, and bathrooms to the rear. Classical statues, reliefs, and a Byzantine mosaic were incorporated in the exterior space, open to the sea. There is also a series of terraces with low stone walls and a water feature resembling an ancient fountain. Olive trees and cypresses complete this idyllic scene. On one side an entrance in the style of a ruin was designed. The emphasis on horizontal dimensions and the absence of a prominent constructed body, as well as the reliance on the design of the external spaces as a fundamental basis, stand out as the basic guiding principles of this project. In other words, the sensitive handling of the surroundings and the magnificent use made of these in retaining their mysterious essence are the most important characteristics of the work.

The construction consists of an extension, in the form of an outdoor dining room/pavilion, swimming pool, and relaxation area, for one of the Rothschild family's summer homes.

The house's bond with water is obvious.

Casa en Calella de Palafrugell

Location: *Calella de Palafrugell, Gerona, Spain*
Year of construction: *1998*
Architects: *Josep Maria Bosch Reig, Lluis Jubert,*
            Eugenia Santacana
Photography: *Eugeni Pons*

This house, located outside the town center of Calella de Palafrugell on the Costa Brava, on the shores of the Mediterranean, was originally built in 1965 by the architect Josep Maria Bosch Reig as a second home for two families.

The dwelling consists of volumes arranged on a steeply sloping plot that the architect has used to create broad terraces at different levels, closely associated with the interior of the house and enjoying excellent views.

Initially, one of the houses consisted of a first floor and a small guest apartment, with independent access, on the second floor, both floors being connected by an internal staircase. The other house takes up the rest of the second floor while its own guest apartment is on the first floor.

The renovations carried out by the architects Lluis Jubert and Eugenia Santacana seek to maintain the original character of the house, simply by modifying the layout of each house to suit the new requirements of both families.

Part of the layout of each house has been maintained on the first floor with the rest on the second floor. The guest area has been converted into bedrooms and bathrooms, each having a share in the landscaped areas without sacrificing their extensive views.

The landscaped areas have been extended to run to the sea. Each space is associated with the exterior in a different way, thus providing an infinity of visual effects.

The main materials used in the new design are revealed in the interior jatova wood floor, the iroko wood external platform, the new window frames in white aluminum with adjustable window shades to regulate the rays of the sun, the white plaster walls, and the new transparent glass balustrades, allowing uninterrupted views over the water.

Partial views of the house on one of the boundaries of the broad, steep plot and views of the exterior.

Taken as a whole, the project consisted of carefully redesigning the interior of a preexisting building and improving the standard of its interiors (quality materials, orderly arrangement, and fluidity of the spaces), as well as remedying constructional defects that had arisen after years of exposure to the marine environment.

The bareness of the spaces as well as the finishing touches based on a simple and sophisticated design are distinctive characteristics of this interior renovation project.

HOUSES IN THE COUNTRY

The birth of the country house was closely associated with economic and rural activities. It met the need for people to have somewhere to live close to their place of work, all the more so at a time when there was no transport infrastructure. This also explains the existence of temporary dwellings in cultivated areas far away from the main residential area and nearby villages. Originally the rural house incorporated a set of spaces, interior and exterior, whose economic function was clearly defined: corrals, henhouses, storerooms, tool rooms, among others, formed an integral part of the house. The rural property was considered to be an economic unit, to which the fields, woods, pastures, and small temporary dwellings belonged, together with the streams or pools of water that surrounded it. So, taken in its broadest sense, it was a business, small or large, with a dual aim: to meet the primary needs of the family on the one hand, and to play a part in the market economy as a supplier within a more general framework. This view of the country world explains how the rural economy developed and how social relations traditionally operated within country life. One of the common aspects defining these buildings is the phenomenon of dispersion,

influenced by three main factors: the search for water, the need to be in contact with the woods, and the topographical characteristics. It is clear that the intrinsic purpose of this type of construction was determined by work in the fields. Its function was to offer shelter to ranchers and farmers, as well as to provide sufficient space to hold the cattle, for storage and for the production of handmade goods.

Although this explains the history behind the house in the country and allows us to understand the current situation, the houses presented in the different projects making up this chapter appear to be defined by principles that differ considerably from those that originally determined their existence. This type of dwelling has now become a place to which its inhabitants escape, in search of repose and the advantages and charms of a life in direct contact with nature, a world that has now disappeared completely from the big cities. Before reaching this point, these agricultural residences have traveled along a path of continuous development. We can establish a parallelism or contrast, depending on the analysis, between the purpose of these second homes throughout history. For the emerging middle class, the originators of commercial relations and interchange, the house in the country represented a change in their activity; but the aristocracy, with much free time and the financial means to enjoy it, used them as a retreat where they could relax and enjoy themselves in all kinds of ways, thus adding a new dimension. Finally, in the present day, people escaping the confines of class have transformed these residences into leisure and relaxation homes. Sometimes a relatively specific activity is carried out here but, basically, their purpose is to relieve the stress of a professional lifestyle, in a place where people can devote themselves absolutely to their family and personal relationships, and attain spiritual peace. These are the conditions under which people are now returning to seek and above all enjoy a state of freedom and vacation. However, for this liberation to be total there must be a degree of continuity, a new lifestyle in which the second home or residence becomes an essential factor. Many people are now looking for a vacation or weekend house where they can relax outside their social circle. Engrossed in a demanding job, people nowadays, particularly if they work in the city, find it difficult to find time for their personal or family life, without this involving enormous effort. Given that a certain amount of leisure time is absolutely essential for a person's good general

equilibrium, the summer home is viewed as being a means of making a complete break from everyday life. This is why the houses built in the country that are covered in this chapter have evolved from their original function in years gone by.

The projects include, on the one hand, the adaptation and reconversion of an old mansion, to meet the typical needs and requirements of modern life, and, on the other hand, a completely new construction. Although there are various examples of rebuilding in this chapter, most of the projects were constructed over the last ten years.

Möbius House

Location: *Het Gooi, Holland*
Year of construction: *1998*
Architects: *Van Berkel & Bos / UN Studio*
Photography: *Christian Richters, Ingmar Swalue*

The Möbius house offers a new perspective on the house: its spaces follow on from one another without establishing any clear limits between rooms. These limits are not merely physical, but also include those relating to the functionality or temporality of the activities taking place in the house. Van Berkel & Bos have produced a theoretical manifesto that takes material form in this house.

The building seamlessly incorporates plan, movement, and structure in a fluid way. The house connects all the activities that take place in the home so that work, socializing, family life, and individual activities have their place in this spiral arrangement.

The concept of movement also extends to the organization of the two basic materials used in the building: concrete and glass, used interchangeably. Concrete is used for furniture and glass for the facades and some of the interior partitions.

In the Möbius house residential typology has been used as a privileged field of experimentation for observing domestic aspirations as the century drew to a close. In this way the project is a clear materialization of the theories developed by this Dutch team. It has constructed an amazing building, incorporating environments that associate form, function, and time, yet without sacrificing a warm and sophisticated ambience.

The plan of the building includes two enclosed linear routes that converge on the corridor areas, demonstrating how two people can live together yet remain independent, meeting in set places that will be the communal areas of the house. The idea of two entities following their own trajectory yet sharing certain points, and even changing roles at times, has been developed extensively in order to take over the material form and construction of the building.

UN Studio asked a specialist to portray the spaces being used as though being lived in by an onlooker. The house cannot be perceived as a whole if it is considered as a mere construction. The way it is used and its organization are an integral part of the project.

The basic materials used in the construction are concrete and glass. They have exchanged roles in various situations: glass becomes part of the facades and the interior partitions, and concrete has been used for some of the furniture.

P House

Location: *Gramastetten, Austria*
Year of construction: *1998*
Architects: *Pauhof Architects*
Photography: *Matteo Piazza*

The project involved a process o
stylistic reduction within a huma
habitat, that could only b
understood as the result of anothe
extremely delicate and emotionall
traumatic process

This detached house situated in Gramastetten,
designed by the architects Michael Hofstätter
and Wolfgang Pauzenberg, lies in the Austrian
countryside, amid rolling fields dotted with trees
against Mediterranean-style hills.

The radical reduction of geometrical forms
seems to have allowed this house to approach
the purest simplicity of style. An infinity of
possible viewpoints, however, reveals an
extremely complicated design.

The house can be interpreted as a volume
formed by two blocks: a clean, ethereal one
without any visible means of support, clad with
aluminum panels, above another larger, rougher,
and more weighty block, made of concrete. A
traditional residential layout is split between these
two boxes: the first houses the bedrooms, the
second the living rooms and the staff quarters. The
bedrooms in the upper block open toward the
east and west, while the lower block is south
facing. The play of opposites defines a project that
shuns the typological and linguistic associations of
Austrian rural architecture. These are the
bureaucratic shackles that architects and owners
endured and only survived thanks to their tenacity.

The choice of materials; the subtle control of
joints, textures and details; the way the house
has been positioned in the countryside; and the
permeability between the interior and the
exterior are the major achievements of the P
House. They eventually won the O Ölandes-
kulturpreis, a cultural prize awarded in
recognition of the detailed work that went into
this home and the way in which the building has
remained true to the original project.

The two parts are presented in their raw state and also avoid physical contact between each other. The metal box is supported on a central pillar and a wall containing the staircase. It is propped up on its edges by slender metal supports. There is also a space between the lower box and the ground, to which the latter is anchored by a concrete wall that, together with the pergola, define the exterior space and protect the privacy of its inhabitants.

623

In contrast with the sedateness of the facades, the interior of the house is warm and welcoming. The materials and textures have been chosen to give the rooms a comfortable ambience. The windows and the gap between the two floors allow the low-level entry of light.

Lineal House

Location: *Millerton, New York, United States*
Year of construction: *1996*
Architect: *Peter Gluck*
Associate: *Suki Dixon (project director)*
Photography: *Paul Warchol*

This project involved the conversion of a house on the roadside. The construction dated back to the early 19th century and needed extension to meet the needs of a family with four children.

The initial approach to the project consisted of re-establishing a more open relationship between the house and its natural surroundings.

The construction became lighter, with an air of relative fragility. The roof consisted of a metal sheet and the walls became transparent.

The new wing was built away from the road, seeking a more private and peaceful immediate environment, facing the lake and protected by the coppice. Two contextual elements had to be taken into consideration: firstly, the countryside and, secondly, the vernacular architecture.

Although the difference between the two constructions is quite obvious, or perhaps because of this, both forms or languages are perfectly integrated.

The extension consists of a linear volume on two floors, with two transparent glass facades. A conventional glued plywood structure supports a few A-frames, also made of wood. The house corridor is the width of a room and is arranged so that all the rooms have good views toward the waterfall in one direction and, in the other direction, toward the new rock garden.

The usual problem of the relationship between old and new has been resolved by a connection between the two buildings, acting as a link.

Left-hand page:

The two roofs are clearly separate. The space that separates them seeks to emphasize the inevitable difference between old and new, yet, because of their proximity, shows the inevitable relationship established between the two parts. The situation and geometry of the simple new roof, in the form of a metal sheet, evokes the language of the old rural forms.

The linear layout also allows a high degree of privacy. There are two bedrooms in the new wing, a den, and a living room, as well as a staff area. The idea was to have an independent space for the children and another one for guests.

A lightweight metal staircase, lacquered gray, separates the spaces of the old house from those in the extension.

Residence in Lake Weyba

Location: *Noosa Heads, Australia*
Year of construction: *1996*
Architect: *Gabriel Poole*
Associates: *Elisabeth Poole (design), Rod Bligh-*
Bligh Tanner (structure), Barry
Hamlet (aluminum)
Photography: *Peter Hyatt*

The building gentl
touches the ground and
has the appearance of
delicate artifact

Architects really cannot base their work on information coming directly from tradition. Gabriel Poole is very aware that investigating and using new technology to construct his house allows costs to be cut and does not go against harmonious coexistence with the Lake Weyba landscape. Quite the contrary. The lightness achieved by using a fine metal structure means that the house merges gently with the land, evoking ephemeral constructions such as the architecture of pavilions, tents, or verandas.

Space is an absolute vacuum that must be measured and defined, in which certain new forms must be produced. Poole organizes the living space into three pavilions, differentiated in accordance with the layout of a home. The roof is the obvious, explicit part of the house. Its polycarbonate cladding, its pitch, edges, and points of interaction clearly demonstrate the way in which its inhabitants confront the elements. When seen from inside the roof structure is also a clearly intelligible constructional theme. The roof is the top of the house. And since it is placed between its occupants and the sky, it becomes a substitute for the latter in the world of those who live in it.

The purpose of the
material is to define the
building. Its surfaces
must be bound up with
whatever is going on
inside it.

Located at one end, the
entrance pavilion contains
the kitchen, office, dining
room, and living room-
den. The surface area
these occupy can be
doubled by extending the
vinyl and steel panels,
creating a veranda area.

The bathroom area is found in the second pavilion, with a shower and washroom area. The color of certain surfaces contrasts with the monochrome fiber-cement walls, and the light and the views of nature from the interior are conducive to relaxation and meditation. The third pavilion is taken up by the master bedroom.

Left-hand page:
Poole gathers together many aspects typical of traditional Japanese space, such as horizontality, the possibility of opening up to the landscape by incorporating it in domestic life, spatial continuity, and the use of natural light.

The kitchen and living room are open yet protected by an extendable roof. The total surface area of the house is 1,800 sq ft (170 m²). The total cost was approximately 150,000 dollars.

Stremmel Residence

Location: *Reno, Nevada, United States*
Year of construction: *1995*
Architect: *Mark Mack*
Photography: *Undine Pröhl*

Some recent examples from the international scene are revealing a trend toward restraint in preference to exuberance, reduction rather than redundancy, unity as opposed to dispersion, and local simplicity instead of crosscultural ambitions.

Mark Mack is an architect who gives priority to simplicity and clarity of approach, and amazes by the forcefulness of the volumes, colors, and textures he uses.

He built the Stremmel Residence in a desert area on the outskirts of Reno. When we look at the result we realize that fine architecture does not require grand gestures. His work reveals an obvious confidence in his professional skills, rather than technological ostentation or resources.

To a certain extent the Stremmel Residence reproduces the organizational layout of the old patio houses, whose rooms surround an empty central space where a swimming pool or water feature is located. The need to mark out a living area in contrast to the immensity of the desert was the deciding factor in placing the home on a concrete platform. Mack is aware that creating a microcosm juxtaposed with the predominant aridity is difficult and restricts the inhabitable space to specific limits. Within this parallelepiped of air, he works by differentiating and cloning volumes, mindful of the interconnection between them, creating a fluid, floating space that is both interior and exterior, thus giving meaning to the whole project.

Mack's architecture is protective, substantial, and habitable, on a personal scale. The wall proclaims strength and autonomy, and is full of importance and dignity.

The water feature and the lawn mark the area within which the architecture intervenes, separating it from the aridity of the desert.

Detached houses are
privileged experimental are[a]
for observing the domesti[c]
aspirations of our times at clos[e]
hand. They expose, in fu[ll]
light, the side that contain[s]
the dreams, emotions, an[d]
aspirations of their inhabitant[s]
and the creative capabilities [of]
the architect[s]

The interior spaces amaze
with their simplicity,
clarity of approach, and
economy of means.

Casa en Celaya

Location: *Celaya, Guanajuato, Mexico*
Year of construction: *1994*
Architects: *Alfonso López Baz, Javier Calleja Ariño*
Associates: *Guillermo Flores, Octavio Cardoza, Arturo*
Hérnandez (structure)
Photography: *Fernando Cordero*

This elegant pavilion stands on a gentle slope in the middle of the landscaped plain of the San Rafael ranch, on the outskirts of the town of Celaya. The ranch is an equestrian center, with jumping course and indoor and outdoor schools, as well as stables for 30 horses.

The pavilion visually dominates the main jumping course, close to an area densely covered by age-old trees, and at first sight seems to be a metaphor for the white poles that divide the fields and stand out in sharp contrast to the green farmland.

The layout consists of two sections or pavilions, joined yet separated at the same time by a smooth stretch of water that meets both practical and esthetic requirements, sending out multiple reflections while increasing the humidity and the feeling of coolness in a dry climate where temperatures often reach 104°F (40°C).

The pavilions are joined by walkways of natural wood. These cross the water and their arched roofs rise to a considerable height in the central part, without sacrificing the domestic character of the layout.

The two pavilions are completely independent. At the front of them only walls, staff quarters, and chimneys are to be seen. Although the two buildings have extremely large windows, in both cases these are incorporated in the facades overlooking the equestrian schools, in an east-west direction.

The vaulted roof is completely smooth, without light sources or ventilation grilles. All the closets are built into the walls, so that the room remains uncluttered, containing only tables and chairs. The glass panels merge into each other without any intermediate frameworks. Access is through a single door located in one corner.

Second Residence in Nou de Gaià

Location: *Nou de Gaià, Tarragona, Spain*
Year of construction: *1993*
Architects: *Pepita Teixidor y Xavier Sust*
Associates: *Nicole Grumser y Silvia Álvarez;*
Inmaculada Casado (master builder);
Ferran Bermejo (structure);
Construcciones Serramia (builder)
Photography: *Lluís Casals*

Right-hand pag
Entrance from t
yard to the librar

One of the main objectives of this construction was to capture light and air from the outside in those parts of the house shaded by the mountain. The roof was the ideal flat area on which to locate the largest window in the house in order to achieve this.

The building was a nicely situated property in the center of a small town near Tarragona, consisting of two floors, one circular and facing south with extensive views over the town, the fields, and, in the distance, the sea.

The interior space was laid out on a fairly open plan, with only the kitchen and bathroom partitioned off. It incorporated an interior patio that, together with the staircase, allowed light

from the skylight to reach the first floor. The latter is a mixture of a light source and architecture: achieved by extending one slope o the roof, it provides lighting for the dual-level staircase, and, through a transparent false ceiling the washroom on the second floor.

Outside elements such as the staircase arch and the crenellations around the edge of the plot were restored. One significant aspect is a dual exterior staircase allowing access to the second floor, forming an arch over the main entrance on the first floor.

The austere combination was
sufficiently attractive to make
maintaining the external appearance as
far as possible the aim of the
renovations, without this adversely
affecting the project. One of the main
objectives was to capture light and air
from the outside in those areas that
were screened by the mountain,
without this having too much effect on
the walls, made of a mixture of clay
and rubble, whose vulnerable condition
suggested that it was possible they
might collapse.

The pool strives to play
the role of the moon when
contemplated from the
upper areas of the house.

The first floor comprises the main
entrance, the dining room/living
room, library, kitchen, and a
washroom. On the second floor are
the large master bedroom, two
dens, the dressing room, and the
bathroom. The floors are of stone
and ceramic tiles on the first floor
and parquet on the second.

Aktion Poliphile

Location: *Wieshaden, Germany*
Year of construction: *1992*
Cliente: *Galerie Z.B., Frankfurt*
Architects: *Studio Granda*
Photography: *Norbert Miguletz*

It is very difficult, if not impossible, to define the Aktion Poliphile project, undertaken by Studio Granda, in a single word. Actually two would be sufficient, although three are really needed for its minimal description: symbolism, beauty, and utility. In a sense, providing a definition means making a selection and, for greater accuracy, retaining the word that in itse contains the whole meaning of the object. Not one of the words "symbol," "esthetics," or "practicality" is sufficient in itself to define Aktion Poliphile. Its constant interaction and interdependence, causes and effect at the same time, form an indissoluble unit that does not have, or need, a word to define it.

The project comprises two houses built on t fertile land of north Wiesbaden in Germany: th Saturn house and the Delia house. Saturn symbolizes the idea of the paradox of time, tha creates only to go on to destroy what it has created. Saturn's descendant, Delia, is the symb of the pure goodness of youth, energy, and health. Delia represents modern times. Her dar side, judiciously concealed, reflects the somber, sad, and torpid coldness of the neighboring Saturn, the two houses forming their own private planetary system.

Saturn is solid and impenetrable. Its roof is lead, and the walls, without any characteristic features or details, are plastered dark red. No one passes through its protective wall, through its windowless faces, blind to the street.

Coming from the northern woods, Delia sits neatly in the extended palm of her ancestor. The house's cedarwood walls are bleached by the sun.

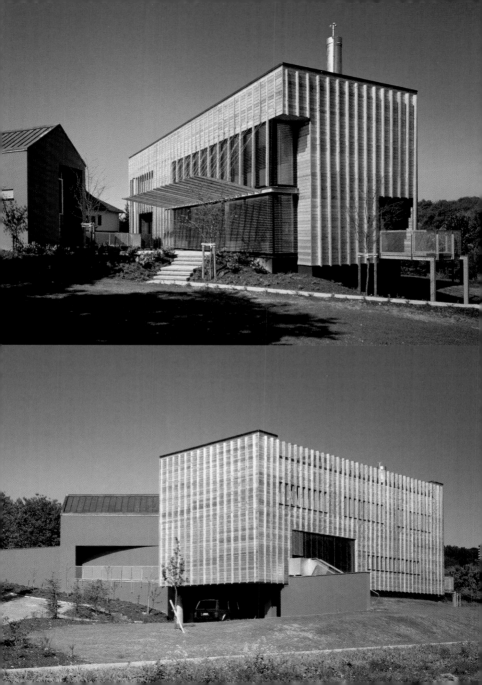

View of the climbing
plant, trained by strips
wood held down with
iron cables.

Detail of the finish of t
walls of the Delia house
formed by the
juxtaposition of strips o
cedarwood arranged
horizontally.

A bridge links the Satu
house with the Delia
house, at the point whe
the wall from the entra
to the boundary ends,
descending to ground
level to connect them.

A garden on the flat roof of
the Delia house offers a secret
refuge with extensive views
over the long valley.

Following pages:
General view of the staircase
joining the first floor with the
second floor in the Delia house.

Detail of the kitchen in the
Delia house, protected by
frosted-glass sliding doors.

A beam provides a finishing touch
to the low wall of the stairwell.

The black floor tiles and iron
details combine with the
omnipresent wood and white
interior walls of Delia.

Foster House in Germany

Location: *Germany*
Year of construction: *1994*
Architects: *Sir Norman Foster & Partners*
Associates: *Ken Shuttleworth, Mark Braun, Dieter*
Mülller, Rob Watson, Alison Holroyd;
Ove Arup & Partners, Boll and Partner
Photography: *Dennis Gilbert*

The layout of the house extends over two interconnecting floors and gives access to the entrance level by means of an internal ramp that runs parallel to the retaining wall. Two exterior staircases flank the constructed space, providing the alternative accesses required by the plan – the one used for the staff quarters and the one directly connecting with the owner's private den – linking together the various floors with the terrace on the lower level and the yard. A concrete foundation slab brings the volume of the house into contact with the natural earth.

A fundamental aspect of the composition of the house is the imposing metal canopy, supported by sections, taking in the whole of the building.

The first floor contains the shared areas of the house and the master bedroom, rooms that extend toward the outside terrace through the large glazed panels of the facade. The distribution of the shared areas was determined by the client's layout requirements, which placed great emphasis on the kitchen and dining room areas.

The connections from all levels to the outside allow the children to gain direct access to the yard, and provide peaceful areas next to the parents' den and a private entrance to the staff quarters. This assortment of interior and exterior passageways allows a rare feeling of community that, at the same time, respects the individual privacy of each of the inhabitants.

Previous pages:
The dining room opens onto the terrace, by sliding back the glazed faces on the facade.

A sloping corridor connects the different levels in the house with the main entrance.

The kitchen opens onto a double-height dining room.

A double space connects the small den on the top floor with the master bedroom.

Bedroom area within the master suite, from which the staircase ascends to the den.

Right-hand page:
The double space over the dining room is emphasized by the vertical glazed face that follows the ramp as it descends.

Casa Gaspar

Location: *Zahora, Cádiz, Spain*
Year of construction: *1991*
Architect: *Alberto Campo Baeza*
Associates: *Diego Corrales (master builder),*
Manuel C. (builder),
Mármoles Chacón (flooring)

An austere square house enclosed by white plane surfaces, the only continuous light being low and horizontal, and four symmetrically arranged lemon trees, two on the front patio and two more on the rear patio, producing spectacular effects as well as guaranteeing the symmetry of the composition: these are the simple yet major features of the work of the Cádiz architect Campo Baeza.

The building, which the architect named *Hortus Conclusus* is typical of isolated houses in the Andalusian countryside. Aiming for total privacy, this house is located on a flat plot in the middle of a field of orange trees: a square of 60 x 60 ft (18 x 18 m) defined by four adobe walls 11 ft (3.5 m) high and divided into three equal proportional parts, with the central part roofed. Transversally the division produces three proportional parts: the surface area of the central area is twice that of the two lateral areas and the services area is to the side of this. The roof over the central area is 15 ft (4.5 m) high.

The entrance to the house is through the front patio; the swimming pool is located on the rear patio, and the living room occupies the space between the patios. The house, which covers 1200 sq ft (120 m²), includes two bedrooms opening onto the exterior areas.

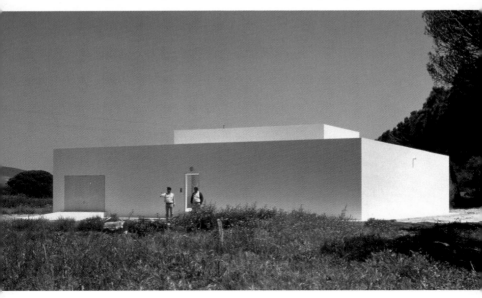

Rear patio.

Front patio.
The symmetry of the
composition is clearly
emphasized by the four
lemon trees producing
spectacular effects.

Right-hand page:
Another view of the continuous
sequence of spaces.

Rear patio with the pool.

Interior – exterior continuity: where the
low adobe walls intersect with the high
walls, four glass windows open up.

Byrne Residence

Location: *Arizona, United States*
Year of construction: *1997*
Architect: *William Bruder*
Photography: *Bill Timmerman*

William P. Bruder has once again found a way of dealing with the difficulties of placing a new construction within an existing landscape. The awesome desert stretching out in front of the Byrne Residence is one of the main aspects of this project that manages to reconcile wide open spaces with generous amounts of private space.

The natural unevenness of the plot is overcome by constructing the house on two levels. The entrance, for both people and cars, is on the first floor. The succession of walls takes us all the way around the building: first from outside to inside, and then, at the other end of the house, to another open space.

The corridors and passageways are concentrated against the walls. Most of the rooms, on the other hand, open onto the desert landscape. On the main floor this applies to the kitchen, the dining room, the living room, the large terrace, and the double bedroom with its own bathroom, dressing-room, and terrace. The ground floor also faces south-east. However, unlike the first floor, its north-east face is set into the ground.

In contrast with the dominant presence of the walls, the materials used on the exterior – such as copper or galvanized metal – change color to reflect the surrounding countryside.

In short, with an outstanding effort to adapt to a quite exceptional environment, William P. Bruder has created a house successfully balancing his personal language with clear sculptural connotations.

The construction does not
clash with this desert
setting. Built on a slope, its
situation on the upper part
of the plot lends the house
enjoyable views.
One of the most difficult
pre-existing factors to be
overcome was the site on
which the house is built: the
Arizona desert. To adapt to
this, Bruder establishes a
parallelism between the
construction and the rocky
walls of the canyons.

The materials used on the
exterior change color to reflect
the surrounding countryside.
The cladding, in copper or
galvanized metal, is in
chromatic harmony with
the land.

Right-hand page:
None of the transition areas such
as corridors, entrance, and
staircases, is closed in. They
retain a direct relationship
with the exterior.

The interior contains a range of
different areas, some of which are
extravert, full of light, and closely
associated with the exterior. Others
are darker and more intimate areas
designated for the more
private rooms.

The house is positioned on the
upper part of the plot. The way in
which the structural walls are built
to follow the curves of the changes
allows all the rooms to enjoy
splendid panoramic views.

Villa M

Location: *Zedelgem, Belgium*
Year of construction: *1994*
Architect: *Stéphane Beel*
Associates: *Dirk Hendriks, Paul van Eygen, Hans
        Verstuyft, Harm Wassink, Hans Lust, Philippe
        Viérin (design), SCES (structure), R.Boydens
        (installations)*
Photography: *Lieve Blancquart*

The site of the Villa M i
clearing in the wood of abc
2½ acres (1 hectar
completely flat. The plot
actually the garden of the c
mansion next door, separat
by brick wa

This house is very long (200 ft. long by 23 ft. wide (60 m x 7 m), parallel with one of the existing walls. Therefore, it is a familiar element in the yard, one more wall, a wall you can live in.

The various areas are arranged throughout the house in a sequential way, separated by architectural silences that may be small patios or even free-standing areas housing the services. The purpose of these gaps is to distance the adjoining rooms. In this way, although there are no doors to interrupt the spatial continuity, the bedrooms are separated from the rest of the living space, the kitchen isolated from the dining room, and the dining room from the living room.

The rear facade has hardly any openings, apart from a continuous window allowing light into the individual bedrooms and the entrance door.

The front facade, on the other hand, has lots o openings and terraces. Both are clad with vertical red cedarwood laths. The roofs are made of anodized aluminum sheets.

A house that initially seems illogical in terms its dimensions and proportion, when analyzed i greater depth reveals innumerable possible relationships, both within the house and between the interior and the exterior.

Combining the wish for neutrality with an unusual design, associating the house with the surroundings in an independent alliance: these two ideas were present from the outset and were maintained as constant references throughout the design process.

The house is not constructed on ground level, but is slightly elevated. This strip between the ground and the floor of the house is open, so that it creates a dark line, as if the house were suspended in the air.

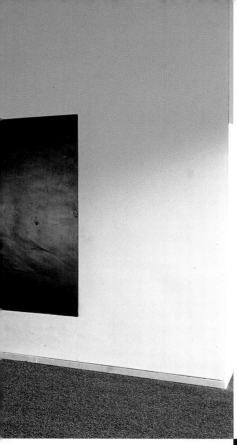

From the yard, as the light fades, the interior of the house appears like a stage setting. Through the enormous glass doors and windows people can be seen moving through the rooms as though they were characters in a play being staged on a wooden dais. From the inside the large glass areas frame the countryside, ruffled by the slight movement of leaves in the wind.

House with Three Patios

Location: *Brasschaat, Belgium*
Year of construction: *1993*
Architect: *Xaveer de Geyter*
Associates: *Piet Crevits, Alain De Backer*
            (design team), Jeroen Thomas
            (structure), Yves Brunier (landscape)
Photography: *Hans Welerman*

In volumetric terms this house is a square block slotted into the dune, and through it, but also projecting slightly above it, toward the street. The entrance drive runs up the small hill until it levels out on the horizontal plane of the roof, establishing a point of union between the natural topography of the site and the elemental cubic geometry of the house. A fence runs alongside the road that makes its way through the pines up toward the roof. The roof then becomes an access floor.

The layout of the house has been designed by breaking up the rectangular block into strips parallel to the street. Although compositional relationships can be found between the various strips, each one of them is characterized by its own organization. Occupying the strip half-buried in the dune, the children's apartment consists of a den connected to two bedrooms that share a bathroom. Bedrooms and den open onto their corresponding private patios, supported by the rear retaining wall.

The way in which the materials, and in particular the flooring, have been arranged clearly reflects the functional organization, in strips, of the interior of the house. To emphasize this layout the same material has been used for each section, as can be seen in the floors of the trapezoidal terrace and the living room, both made of wood, but laid in different directions.

Each element in the house evokes numerous architectural references (Le Corbusier, Zen gardens, neoplastic compositions...).

Bom Jesus House

Location: *Braga, Portugal*
Year of construction: *1994*
Architect: *Eduardo Souto de Moura*
Photography: *Luis Ferreira Alves*

The simplicity of the design and language used
in the Bom Jesus House, on the outskirts of
Braga, is a clear example of how to respond in
an appropriate way, yet simply and subtly, to pre-
existing physical factors, to cultural tradition
and native craftsmanship, and to particular
design requirements.

The composition of this detached house
incorporates two buildings, combining two
different layouts and constructional systems,
bringing the two houses together in one single
project. A wall of natural stone, following the
irregular mountain plot, extends along the
house. A cube of concrete and glass that sits on
the platform defined by the stone wall
symbolizes the meeting between old and new.
This composition, based on a theme of duality,
integrates with the plot to create a succession
of interior and exterior spaces, between which
physical and visual communication is established.

The staff areas, utility areas, and garage are
concentrated on the first floor. On the second
floor the bedrooms, living room, and dining
room extend for the full length of the southeast
facade, accompanying the precise rhythm kept by
the natural-colored aluminum framework that
also determines the rhythm of the structure.
The use of materials in their natural state – such
as the granite of the lower part, the varnished
beechwood doors and interior fittings, the
bubinga wood floor on the first floor, and the
Alentejo tiled floors on the first floor – are
characteristics that reappear in all Souto de
Moura's projects.

The stone cube that forms the lower part of the house indicates a desire to reflect the colors of the walls surrounding the property.

A prism rises above the roof, providing zenithal lighting to the bathrooms and the second floor.

Left-hand page:
A broad wood-floored terrace balcony stretches in front of the glass south-east facade on the second floor of the house.

The stone wall forms a terrace that encloses the land, creating a landscaped upper platform in direct contact with the rooms in the house.

In the house, materials in their natural state are combined with others such as glass or aluminum.

Detail of the staircase in the double-height entrance space.

Detail of the support for the metal and wood staircase in the entrance hall.

The aluminum framework of the double-height entrance to the house separates interior and exterior at the point where the granite wall penetrates it.

Right-hand page
Spatial continuity is produced in the communal interior areas of the house and this is extended to the exterior by means of the large glass facades

Casa Amat

Location: *Alella, Barcelona, Spain*
Year of construction: *1993*
Architect: *Antoni de Moragas*
Photography: *Lluís Casals*

The plot on which the house has been built is almost square and virtually flat, even though it is not level with the neighboring house. This difference in height facilitated the construction of a basement on the plot. It has been used to provide a parking area, with access from the street located to the east, as well as a series of rooms intended for various purposes and some service areas.

Inside, the organization of the house stems from a completely regular volume: it is a box with two floors going from one side of the plot to the other, from east to west. A tunnel crosses the building and joins the yard in the north part with the one in the south part: two different spaces used alternately throughout the year, one for winter and the other for summer.

The two master bedrooms with private bathroom and dressing room are located on the second floor, as well as two double bedrooms arranged symmetrically with the latter, each with bathroom and dressing room. They all look over a wide, open veranda, although they also have north-facing windows, looking toward the rear of the house.

The roof is made of copper and describes a gentle curve that is almost imperceptible when the house is viewed from the front, but is much more evident on the lateral facades.

The walls are made of stuccoed and painted brick on the first floor and are wood-paneled on the second floor. The window frames of both the sliding windows and the fixed ones are made of galvanized steel.

The yard decking is made of wood specially suitable for outdoor use and is slightly higher than the level of the lawn.

Two views of the
east facade.

Views of the veranda that provides protection from excessive light. The light filtering through the fence sketches different colors and textures on the walls. The colors of these walls are warm, going from ocher to yellow and red.

Views of the kitchen from the veranda.

General view of the living
room, dining room, and its
furniture: two large French
windows provide access to
the yard and the veranda.

Due to its width, the
hall leading to the
single flight of stairs is
positioned transversely
within the area.

House in Lochau

Location: *Lochau, Austria*
Year of construction: *1996*
Architects: *Carlo Baumschlager, Dietmar Eberle*
Photography: *Eduard Hueber*

The architect's job centers on the process of creating the building: communication with the client in order to find the solutions that best satisfy their needs, buildings in harmony with the site, and consideration of the various professions involved in the construction. These elements come together in an architecture that is sensitive, functional, and elegant.

The house in Lochau is located on an enormous plot owned by the client's family, whose aim, with this project, was to ensure that other buildings did not affect their splendid views over the adjacent lake.

The first floor contains the garage, and also provides a multifunctional space for domestic or DIY tasks, utility areas, and a guest bathroom.

The second floor contains the living area and the bedrooms. The kitchen and bathroom are alongside. This level is intended to be a single room. The spaces flow into each other without any obvious physical partitions. In this way the functional areas do not impinge on a leisure space that enjoys the best views.

The double facade is one of the project's most interesting aspects. It emerged from the decision to use certain prefabricated constructional elements to facilitate work and keep costs down, and from the relationship that must be established between the building and the exterior space.

The double facade is one of
the project's most interesting
concepts: it consists of a glass
box covered with slats of
wood that regulate the entry
of light and the intimacy of
the rooms. These slats are
closer together on the first
floor. They are more spaced
out on the second floor and
move to and fro so that the
landscape and the light can
penetrate the interior.

Right-hand page:
The strategy of the
architects is to reduce
the project to a few
powerful decisions.
The constructional details
take a leading role since
they have been
carefully designed.

Details of the facade.

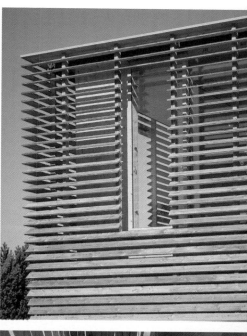

Can Cardenal

Location: *Batet de la Serra, Olot, Spain*
Year of construction: *1995*
Architects: *Aranda, Pigem, Vilalta arquitectes*
Photography: *Eugeni Pons*

Using opposition, contrast and paradox the project is woven together with the most delicate of threads. Undressed stone and granite, the first one rough and the second polished, opacity and transparency, old and new. Then and now. Sometimes one against the other, but, mainly, one with and for the other. Opposites that meet. A harmonious encounter that creates a fascinating dialogue of contrasts that find their point of connection and their complete meaning precisely in their contradiction.

The initial project consisted of constructing a small summer house for guests, attached to the main house on the Can Cardenal farm in Batet de la Serra (Olot).

The design consisted of a square-based summer house on two floors, attached to the east facade of the farm, extending the south-facing main facade in this direction. The point of union between the two constructions is a strip of translucent glass, functioning as an element of visual separation.

The material from which the walls of the summer house are built, and their finish, conveys a disturbing sense of unreality and magic. Polished pieces of green granite form a continuous, compact body, and at the same time create an amazing impression of transparency. The smooth and shiny texture of the walls, where the reflection of the trees produces ethereal images, is in sharp contrast to the roughness of the old stone walls.

The farm conveys the importance and sense of its own history and the new neighbor can certainly approach it without harming it, resemble it without copying it, and distance itself without forgetting it.

Detail of the solution
employed for the roof, where
the steel supports can be
seen, almost imperceptible
at first glance.

Right-hand page.
Interior view of the second
floor of the summer house.

The guest bedroom is found
on the first floor of the
summer house. The play of
light created by the facade is
continued inside the room

Country House in Worcester

This is an 18th-century farm, with wood facades painted white, four completely symmetrical windows, a double-shed roof, and a small veranda. It stands in a field surrounded by trees, only a short distance away from the large grain silos. The project doubled the size of the existing house, and included a covered swimming pool and an art gallery. So it was a transformation, not only of size, but also of functions.

This extension designed by Peter Gluck neither repeated nor imitated the style of the old white wooden house, but managed to absorb its atmosphere, its esthetics, and its close relationship with the countryside. Somehow the facade of the house had to maintain its pre-eminent position, so there was a clear purpose in producing an image full of allusions and reminiscences.

Combining two styles, Peter Gluck built a house that alternates between modernity and tradition, in a continuous dialogue. Gluck exploits the images of the buildings that traditionally surrounded farms: granaries and storehouses; yet he does so by means of modern technology and language, as well as new functions.

A small glass gallery connects the existing building with the new areas.

Location: *Worcester, New York, United States*
Year of construction: *1995*
Architect: *Peter Gluck*
Photography: *Paul Warchol*

Peter Gluck's project consisted of extending an old farm with wooden facades painted white, originally built in the 18th century.

The land around the pool was excavated. This was firstly in order to gain additional privacy, and secondly to ensure that the windows remained above ground level.

The covered pool was designed not only for swimming, but also as an area for leisure and relaxation, as an alternative to the living room, and closely linked with the yard.

General view of the living room, where the beam of wood holding up the double-shed roof can be seen.

Krummins-Hiller Residence

Location: *Noosa, Australia*
Architect: *John Mainwaring*
Photography: *Peter Hyatt*

A married couple decided to renovate an old farm known as Mount View, located near Noosa, on the coast of Queensland, a state in north Australia with a tropical climate.

Termites had destroyed a significant part of the structure, the roof, and the walls of the house, built almost entirely of wood in 1890. The stripping of some of those elements, that could not be used under any circumstances because of their degree of deterioration, transformed the image of the building. The views over both sides of the hill were multiplied and, by creating larger spaces, interesting visual relationships were discovered between rooms that had previously been separate.

The definitive renovation involved minimum changes to the external appearance of the house (basically replacing the wood roof with a metal sheet one) while inside the conversion had obvious repercussions. Most of the walls were taken down and replaced by sliding panel doors. The existing structure was reinforced with metal sections and all the finishes were improved.

The architect's intention was to produce an image of a rural community, formed by the later additions of buildings and constructions dispersed at random.

The architect took advantage of the fact that the project involved constructing and renovating various buildings in order to give the whole area the appearance of a rural community, in which the various parts were positioned on the plot without any strict order, following the trees and the topography. Somehow it is here that there is a better awareness of the setting, since it already formed part of the whole.

Mainwaring basically works with lightweight materials. Nevertheless there are some exceptions, such as the concrete structure painted red, housing the garage.

The openings on both facades, the wide windows, and the slatted walls were selected with the intention of providing ventilation in summer and allowing the house to become a greenhouse in winter.

View of the bridge connecting the existing summer house, constructed in the 19th century, with the new building designed by John Mainwaring.

"Following the renovations, the interiors have been opened up to provide airy, unobstructed views. The existing construction was completely inward-looking since it had been designed to provide protection from the local hunters and native tribes."
John Mainwaring.

First floor of the guest house.

Detail of one of the bathrooms.

S House

Location: *Ogumi, Japan*
Year of construction: *1996*
Architect: *Toyo Ito*
Photography: *Nacasa*

The structure is formed by two lines of pillars that support corrugated metal sheet roof below which closed and open spaces alternate

The clients were a pair of artists that wanted the project to include a workshop and a gallery, in addition to the domestic spaces.

The owners were very keen that many of the activities associated with their work should be fully visible to the neighbors or inquisitive people coming up to look at their residence. Their house workshop also had to be a cultural center and a place where they could display their own work.

Toyo Ito located the dwelling right on the edge of an artificial lake (constructed as a reservoir), alongside a mountain slope. At no time did he want to make it blend into the landscape, modify the topography, or adjust it to the slope. The house is positioned on an artificial rectangular platform, perfectly flat, resembling buildings on many other sites.

This does not mean that the house ignores its surroundings. On the contrary, it is in direct contact with the lake, the woods, the sun, and the air. However what is beyond doubt is that Toyo Ito wanted to convey the impression that the house did not belong to the setting, or form part of the landscape. It is certainly imbued with a taste for the ephemeral and nomadic and looks as though it could be dismantled at any time and taken away to another place.

The spaces are defined by prefabricated elements and unfinished materials. The astonishing thing about this house is its coherence. Unquestionably, it is a house that embodies a particular concept of life, in which work, art, and nature all have their place.

View from the lake. It can be seen that the open spaces allow a view right through the building. In this way the house does not constitute a visual barrier.

Left-hand page:
Detail of the facade. The walls are built from prefabricated elements.

View of the area dedicated to the workshop. Although it is an external space, some drapes hanging from the roof do allow a degree of intimacy at certain moments, and can provide protection against the rays of the sun.

View of the entrance hall. Many of the elements and materials used are industrial in origin. The pieces on display in the hall were produced by the owners of the house, a pair of artists.

View from the living room to the hall. One of the resources employed is the play of transparencies, typical of Toyo Ito.

View of the den on the second floor. The severity of the finishes is not only determined by esthetic considerations, but also has a practical function, since it lowered the cost of the work considerably.

Casa Sendín

Location: *Madrid, Spain*
Year of construction: *1994*
Architect: *Tonet Sunyer*
Photography: *Ángel Luís Baltanás*

Although from the exterior its double height is not evident, the volume to the rear of the south patio has two levels.
As you approach the house you become aware of the height created by the vertical union between the first floor and the basement.

The Casa Sendín took shape after deep consideration of the setting and provides an intelligent response to each determining factor of the surroundings.

The program comprised a detached house to act as a main residence and a graphics studio for the owner. The objective was therefore a project that had to include various functions and external landscaped spaces, while respecting the independence between its various components.

The living area is south-facing, protected from the sun during hot periods by a large exterior veranda formed by slats of wood. However, it was essential for this property to face two ways in order to enjoy the views of the mountains, so this became the theme of the construction.

The two patios of the house are arranged in front of the studio. Both provide abundant natural light, appearing to expand the basement and avoiding the impression of an underground setting. In this way the work place is never out of sight of those who live in the house. At the same time the users of the studio retain the privacy they need, provided by the rock gardens located on the patios.

There are several landscaped areas separating the pathways to the studio and to the house, arranged around the entrance to the plot. The south yard of the house acts as a filter for family privacy, clearly indicating the different entrances.

The house was the result of deep consideration of the setting, its location, and the climate. It provides a response to each factor of the surroundings, using the resources available and a sensible choice of materials.

The central part houses the living area and is located in order to make the most of the views toward the mountains. An exterior veranda, made of metal and wood slats, was designed in order to provide protection from the direct rays of the sun.

The interior spaces are characterized by abundant natural light. The materials used and the surface finishes give the house quality and comfort.

Four Horizons House

Location: *Watagan Forest, Hunter Valley, Australia*
Year of construction: *1998*
Architect: *Lindsay Johnston*
Associates: *Su Johnston, Robert White*
Photography: *Peter Hyatt, Michael Nicholson*

The Four Horizons house stands on a cliff, in the middle of a eucalyptus wood, the Watagan State Forest, recently designated as a National Park. The construction, located at a height of 1400 ft (430 m) above sea level, with spectacular views over the valley of the Hunter river, is 90 miles (150 km) north of Sydney.

The essential element of this project is the holistic design of the house. The site on which it is located, with its relative geographical isolation and the absence of any public utilities (water, electricity, drains, telephone) suggest that the architect and the client wanted to go beyond conducting an experiment in extreme conditions. If the house was not self-sufficient in terms of energy and services, it would be doomed to failure.

The water supply involved collecting and using rainfall. Solar energy is used to heat the water, to generate electricity, and to run a radio that combines telephone/fax/email. The setting of the house and the constructional solutions allow for natural air-conditioning. The waste generated is processed and then returned safely into the environment. Firewood is used for cooking as well as heating.

As a traditional Australian detached dwelling, this house is outstandingly economical in energy consumption. In Four Horizons the location, setting, selection of materials, constructional method, and careful management of resources and waste were all guided by an integral conception of the finished house.

The house is built in parallel with the cliffs in order to take advantage of the morning sun in winter and the cool summer breezes, turning its back on the prevailing wind. Outside, there is a series of solar panels, the generators, the garage and stable buildings, backing onto a closed yard forming a patio.

The Four Horizons house is exceptional because of its energy savings. Not counting the contributions of the sun and firewood, its net energy consumption is about a third of the average normal consumption.

Following pages:
The roofing system of the house takes the form of an overhanging double-shed roof, free-standing, using a typical Australian metal and galvanized corrugated metal sheet structure. This first roof is separated from the actual house in order to regulate the ventilation, the temperature, and the entry of light into the house, and also to provide a large area of shade where rainwater can be collected.
Under the main roof there are two living areas with curved metal secondary roofs. These cover firstly the communal areas with the living rooms, dining room, kitchen, and pantry, and, secondly, a den and the bedrooms with their respective bathrooms. These two areas of the house are separated by an open corridor providing improved thermal efficiency, as well as insulation against noise and activity.

House on the Prairie

Location: *United States*
Year of construction: *1995*
Architects: *Turner Brooks*
Photography: *Undine Pröhl*

This house in the country is on a magnificent prairie in Wisconsin. In order to enjoy the best views and solve the problems presented by the uneven plot, the house stands on a system of pillars that raise it up. The height of elevation is varied, and in this way, the building is leveled out without the need for any earth moving. At the highest point of the house, the views are enhanced by the construction of a veranda that resembles a periscope – a watchtower that characterizes the building and allows those staying there to enjoy the beautiful countryside.

This residence consists of three spaces, two of which are joined although clearly differentiated in terms of both form and finish. The house is built almost entirely of wood. The constructional details are real structural treasures. The points at which framework meets the facade, the combination of the two bodies making up the building and the doors and windows were the subject of careful consideration.

The entrance to the house is via a back road level with the site. On the other side of the plot, access to the extension on the more open and wooded side is gained via a staircase as a difference in level of approximately 5 ft (1.5 m) had to be compensated for. The lower level contains the communal areas: living room, dining room, and kitchen; while the upper area houses the bedrooms with their respective bathrooms.

The house interiors
combine wood and
plastered surfaces painted
white. The structure of
the house is clearly
evident and the beams
and pillars of wood have
been left exposed.

The house has two floors, but these have different levels, creating subtle effects. On the first floor, for example, two steps separate the dining room from the living area. In addition, a section of wrought metal has been removed in order to create a double height, providing a feeling of spaciousness.

Sevenig-Goergen House

Location: *Luxembourg*
Year of construction: *1999*
Architects: *Françoise Bruck, Thomas Weckerle*
Photography: *Lucas Roth, Thomas Weckerle*

The work to renovate and extend this semidetached house, built in 1910, consisted of adding a kitchen and bedroom on the first floor and a bathroom on the second floor.

The annex was built with a concrete slab providing a base for a wood structure comprising vertical panels. At certain points the design of the wooden construction was modified and adapted to incorporate a window, or to provide a link with the existing cornice.

The whole of the new section, combined with the choice of material and colors, clearly differentiates the annex from the existing house. The dialogue is established from a new interpretation of prevalent elements: the volumetry (the house), the theme of the exterior terraces, the composition of the facades (open closed surfaces), the proportions of the windows, and the level of the cornice.

The original house was left almost entirely intact. The interior design concept is based on accentuating certain original characteristics with small details. For example, the existing stairwell, that receives natural light, was painted saffron yellow. In this way it contrasts with the rest of the spaces painted white, and resembles an incandescent body with its own illumination. The service area, formed by lined stainless steel pipework, slots through the patio and constantly emits different reflections.

The translucent glass walls allow light from the surrounding bedrooms into its interior, transforming it into a monolith body, harmonizing with the weight of the interior walls.

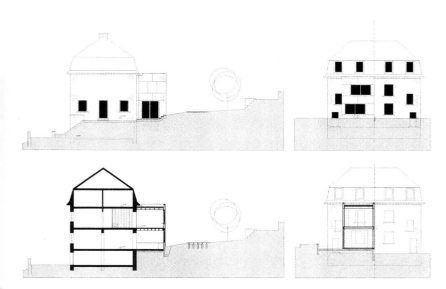

733

The renovations involved changing the windows. To avoid losing light some of the walls are translucent, creating ethereal, barely evident partitions. In the face of the abstract glass body, the everyday details of the house, such as the radiators, pipework, door frames, and so on are perceived in a different way.

Right-hand page:
The challenge of this project was to locate a bathroom in an area without any windows, that would act as a passage to the bedrooms. The wedge-shape construction optimizes the surface area of the bathroom and creates a spacious entrance, with interesting effects.

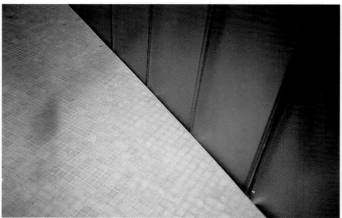

While the bathroom and the attached bedrooms give off a lot of light, the glass face dematerializes to become a fine, light membrane. The bathroom becomes a virtual space, like a bubble in space. The limits between it and the space surrounding it vanish. Inside, there is a contrast between the glass and the ceramic material used for the flooring. So, a dream atmosphere is created, defined by the light, the reflections, and the sound of water.

House in Viana do Castelo

Location: *Viana do Castelo, Portugal*
Year of construction: *1996*
Architect: *João Alvaro Rocha*
Photography: *Luis Ferreira Alves*

Standing on a small base, the building has been designed as a simple rectangular unit of one single story, with a basement in the central part. The base, the roof, and the side walls create a rectangular framework that, rather like a large window looking toward the sea, contains the various bodies of the rooms. Each of these opens to the outside by means of a system of wood shutters that, when closed, remain in line with the calm exterior in the same material.

Although the house slots neatly into this simple yet enormous frame, there is complexity inside, where areas combine and are differentiated by the zenithal light, or the differences in roof heights. Some areas of ambiguous use such as the veranda or the lattice gate are so transparent that they allow the other side of the construction to be seen. The enclosures of the house are distributed in a linear way along this large frame, with the washroom areas inside.

The use of color, the mobility of the rear facade, and the subtle play of levels between the land, the basement, and the main platform, give fluency and freedom to this uniform construction, apparently rigid and dictatorial.

The metaphor of the window is a figure continually pursued in this building, possibly because of the force this work possesses, emerging from the more emphatic simplicity of its architecture.

The interior is perceptively
influenced by the openings
onto the facade that create
numerous plays of light.

The finishes combine
stone surfaces, wood floors
and partitions, and
smooth plastering on the
walls and ceilings.

House in Ibiza

Location: *Ibiza, Spain*
Year of construction: *1998*
Architect: *Stéphane Bourgueois*
Photography: *Pere Planells*

This house in the Balearic Islands is midway between a traditional structure and a sophisticated contemporary house. The owner began with a classic project and designed most of the elements making up the building. The layout is based on a conventional plan: the first floor houses the daytime areas and a guest bedroom, and the second floor contains the master bedroom. The perceived division of the different spaces is achieved by means of walls or openings: they are changes of section that allow the room to be subdivided by creating different environments.

Special attention was paid to the finish on the surfaces, cutting down the list of materials, and using a restricted pallet of colors. The interior partitions are plastered and the floors are in continuous stone, with no paving stones even in the bathroom, where the floor of both the shower room and the washroom is made of polished stones.

The coherence of the project is partly achieved by the furniture that is almost entirely craftsman-made.

The living room has a
visual relationship with
the kitchen and with the
external spaces that
surround the house

The rustic furniture
contrasts with the more
refined forms but does not
clash with this similar yet
varied whole

House in San Bernabé

Location: *San Bernabé, Mexico*
Year of construction: *1990*
Architects: *Ada Dewes, Sergio Puente*
Photography: *Richard Bryant/Arcaid*

Standing like a Toltec pyramid in the Mexican countryside, this building is in keeping with the idiosyncrasy of the place. It is a family house situated some distance from the small town of San Bernabé, which belongs to Mexico City. The property is owned by the two architects that designed it: a German woman and a Mexican man. And it is precisely this blend of disparate cultures and origins that has produced this authentic Mexican temple with its lead-gray, sun-filled interior.

The pyramid-shape building recalls the temples erected here by the Aztecs and the surroundings have been captured in the architecture through the contrast that determines its axes. The inspiration for the design comes from its dominant natural features: an airy building, with beamed ceilings and directed views, opening transversely into the maguey yard.

The axis of the building opens upward through the glass roof in the center of the house, giving it the appearance of a greenhouse. The use of glass transforms the void between the main sections of the building into a defined space, linking exterior with interior. The main elevation, however, is sealed off at the central axis against the road, the urban environment, and the social world. The purpose of this is in fact to protect the interior.

The elevation through which you enter consists of a compact, concrete block, divided by a glass door that forms the axial structure. This central axis is clearly perceptible from the outside through the wooden staircase leading into the house, which crosses at right angles and extends into a loft.

Left-hand page:
An old reclaimed staircase
of fine wood stands in the
center and forms the
central point of the house,
providing a link between
interior and exterior,
upstairs and downstairs.

White gives the interior
extraordinary luminosity.
This *noncolor* constantly
expands and duplicates
the interior through the
interplay of glass and
cold colors.

Sperl House

Location: *Zerlach, Austria*
Year of construction: *1989*
Architect: *Ernst Giselbrecht*
Photography: *Ernst Giselbrecht*

This house in Zerlach (Austria) is owned by horse lovers. Prior to its construction, architect Ernst Giselbrecht gave careful thought to the landscape, trying to decipher the different meanings and values the countryside holds for city and country dwellers. The Austrian designer believed that these two interpretations must be reflected in architecture itself: *consuming* nature in contrast to *working* with it or *living* in it must be shown in the architectural references of the place. These two contrasting extremes must form part of the configuration and renovation of the landscape. Urban dwellers who spend their free time in the country, take on a very important and active role in the process.

The Sperl House was created as a weekend retreat, a place to which its owners, Ingebord and Gerfried Sperl – both keen riders – could come to relax and enjoy their leisure time. The house was built onto an existing structure that then became the stables. Located in a mountainous area, an ideal spot for riding, the house is constructed on sloping ground. Giselbrecht has overcome this obstacle by using supports tectonically adapted to cope with the irregularity of the slope on the west side. The shell of the house thus appears to float almost in counterpoint over the steep drop.

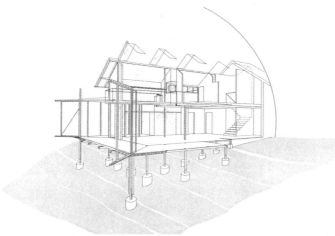

Drawing of the building.

Detail of the geometric beam and the structure of the columns at one of the corners of the main elevation.

Right-hand page: Wood is the principal material used inside the house.

Wachter House

Location: *Amberes, Belgium*
Year of construction: *1990*
Architect: *Jo Crepain*
Photography: *Richard Bryant/Arcaid*

Here Jo Crepain's creative efforts have been directed at a house in woodland belonging to a small town not far from the Belgian city of Amberes. The basic criterion for the design was the site itself, surrounded by attractive countryside, with three old beech trees, the dry bed of a stream, and a not very favorable position. The project involved more than 23 preliminary plans and finally produced a collage of different areas with clearly defined functions.

The plan of the house is in the form of three adjoining rectangles, one of which is divided in three. The building consists of four distinct parts: two identical blocks arranged side by side and separated by an internal patio, another unit perpendicular to these, and a fourth unit adjoining the third. The first two structures comprise the entrance and are symbolically linked by four columns. Together these form a virtual facade concealing the internal patio. Real access to the house is via the third structure, which is very narrow and long. The fourth unit is like an annex to the third and completes the facilities of the house.

Entrance to the building is at the end of the west elevation of the main section, while the linking stairs are positioned at the opposite end. Jo Crepain has transformed this long, slender space into an architectural journey extending for 144 ft (44 m) and leading the visitor through the modern paintings collection displayed on the walls.

The interior of the house is composed of large juxtaposed spaces, with double-height ceilings. The whiteness of the walls and the multiplicity of openings, both circular and rectangular, provide plenty of natural light, making the interior seem more spacious.

House in Le Vésinet

Location: *Le Vésinet, Paris, France*
Year of construction: *1989*
Architects: *Monica Donati, Bernard Dubor*
Photography: *Deidi Von Schaewen*

Initially, the idea of designing and creating your own house may seem to offer advantages, yet many architects find this a difficult task. In this case the basic requirement was to provide a large, well-lit space for the architect's studio. When a building serves the double function of living area and work space, it needs to be very spacious: this is essential if an uncomfortable overlap between the two functions is to be avoided. This house in the countryside at Le Vésinet, a town very close to Paris, is the result of just such a brief and is used all year round. Despite its location, access to the city is good and the owners do not feel isolated, which is very important for those in the liberal professions.

The house stands on a basically flat and rectangular piece of land with few topographical variations. It has been adapted to suit the long, narrow dimensions of the site and the location makes it quite secluded: the sides of the lot that adjoin the road are planted with leafy trees that act as a natural barrier; in the yard, the vegetation and thick branches of the trees provide shade and protection.

The building blends into the landscape and, like the land itself, is in the form of a quadrilateral, though longer and more narrow. The north elevation extends into space when it reaches the west end of the building. This forms a type of screen attached to the structure of the house that shields the front elevation.

The two sections of the house are linked by a double-height, semi-enclosed patio. This is one of the areas in which the building is opened to the exterior, through a large window filling the height and breadth of the face.

The main feature of the living room is the bookcase, fitted into the wall space and located just above the fireplace. A specially positioned light illuminates this feature, thus emphasizing its importance to the room as a whole.

Knipschild House

Location: *Napa Valley, California, United States*
Year of construction: *1987*
Architect: *Marc Mack*
Photography: *Reiner Blunck*

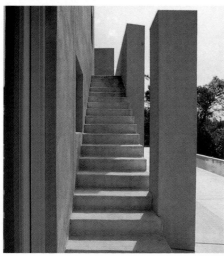

This 36,600 sq ft (3,400 m²) building stands on top of a small, oak-covered hillside, looking toward the retreat of the writer Jack London in the Valley of the Moon, Glen Ellen, California. From the bottom of the hill the house stands out clearly among the rich, green vegetation because of its solitary, strategic position and the materials from which it is built.

This house is part of a design development program by Batey and Mack for a series of basic standard plans characteristic of their buildings of this period: rectangular, square, cruciform, L, H, or U-shape and so on offering great flexibility to express a variety of characters and fulfil the needs of their different clients.

The plans are basically rectangular and are arranged in the form of the letter H.

The external space of the house is defined by the different meaning given to each of the elevations, by contrasting one that is open to the landscape and the light with another that is closed and compact.

The south elevation is symmetrical, pink, solid, and compact, concealing an open, spacious interior. It is structured around two apparently separate parts linked externally by a concrete structure with sky-blue columns and, internally, by a transverse corridor. Both areas have windows and glass doors allowing light into the interior and opening it up to the outside and to the landscape.

There is also a terrace with a pond. Built on a raised plinth, this marks the boundary between the environment created by mankind and that created by nature.

The materials used for the exterior are basically concrete and slate, with metal for the entrance: the structural system consists of interlinking faces on a stone block.

Right-hand page:
The interior is spacious and opens to the south, with all the first-floor rooms looking on to the pond. The two parts are linked by a transverse corridor and each is connected with the floor above.

Van Veelen House

Location: *Holland*
Year of construction: *1988*
Architects: *Cees Dam & Partners*
Photography: *Erik Hesmerg*

The Van Veelen House is built on a flat plot of land in the middle of a small wood. The materials and colors used allow it to blend into the landscape, becoming a continuation of it that is in harmony with nature. The building emerges gradually from its surroundings, without interference, with no sudden break in continuity. Surrounded by rich vegetation, it takes advantage of change in the ground level to produce fine, balanced lines, precise proportioning of space, and beautiful views of the surrounding wood. This house, with its pure geometric form, is a spectacular example of the work of the Dutch architect Cees Dam.

The Van Veelen House, like others by the same architect, shows clear differences between the front and rear elevations, which are interpreted in different ways. The house, designed to meet the needs of those living there, is surrounded by a thick wall that acts as protection against the outside and, like the house itself, is in harmony with its surroundings.

Built of concrete blocks, the front elevation with its thick wall and lack of glazed openings connecting it with the outside, is solid – the interpretation is a closed and private one. The rear elevation, however, is transparent, completely open, and in permanent dialogue with its surroundings. This side has a porched area with a circular roof, created by joining the squares and the outside wall extensions. This leads onto a large patio with a bench where you can sit and enjoy the sun and commune with nature. A link with the outside is created by extending the tiling of the patio into the house and sliding back the glass corner units.

Right-hand page:
The kitchen, designed by Cees Dam, is spacious, original and includes a dining area. The design is very sophisticated: the ceiling is completely white and the fittings and appliances are in black-veined imitation marble.

The living room has steel support columns positioned diagonally and a slightly angled fireplace dividing the room into two triangles. The glass partitions placed to the rear and the semicircular canopy over the space give it an unusual look. There are separate areas: the living area, the fireplace, and the library. All the furnishings in this room are designer pieces, including the fireplace.

Residence in Harding Township

Location: *Harding Township,*
New Jersey, United States
Year of construction: *1989*
Architects: *Richard Meier & Partners*
Photography: *Scott Francis – Esto*

This house is situated in a gently sloping meadow, with woodland to the northeast and stunning views to the south and east. From the center of the building, two axes extend perpendicularly outward toward the boundaries of the site, penetrating the landscape and giving the house a very special position in a place that remains difficult to define.

For New York architect Richard Meier, circles and squares are important elements of style. The latest owners of the property, a couple who are keen art collectors, also share the architect's love of geometry, which is apparent in his design.

The building is structured around a central, two-story cylinder, although its space is partially absorbed by the orthogonal structure adjoining it, within a square base. It is an excellent example of Meier's work, which characteristically includes the use of white to sharpen perception of the tones present in natural light and in nature itself. The white surfaces provide a contrast that enhances the interplay of light and shade, of mass and void. The white form is not only rooted in the traditional concept of the house, it is also an expression of strength and extroversion in relation to a site that goes beyond its internal function as a place of shelter.

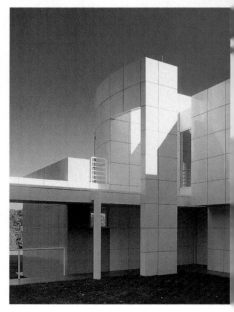

The interior is designed to house numerous works of art; any additional decorative elements have therefore been dispensed with. The exquisite living room occupies the entire rotunda. The tables are *Unikate* by Edgar and Joyce Andersen. The chimney rises solidly, like a sculpture against the landscape.

House in Sun Valley

Location: *Sun Valley, Idaho, United States*
Year of construction: *1988*
Architect: *Bart Prince*
Photography: *Deidi Von Schaewen*

The owner of this building – who already owned a house designed by Frank Lloyd Wright in Bliss, Idaho – wanted to build a summer residence in the Sun Valley area, with a view to selling it at some later point. The program therefore centered on the creation of a building that would be interesting and functional and go beyond the standard architectural designs, but that would also catch the eye of a wide variety of people, including those who would like to spend part of the year in the Sun Valley area.

It is a family house standing on an attractive 10 acre (4 hectare) site. Rather than contrasting with the undulating hills and mountains around it, the building blends perfectly into the natural framework of the surrounding valley. The terrain is sandy and somewhat uneven and rough, and the structure extends and stretches out across it, unconfined by any finite form. Two intertwining S-shape walls form three clearly differentiated areas, linked by a central axis. The result is a completely irregular two-story base: a basement and main floor. A ramp leads from the exterior to the upper part and an entrance enclosed beneath a low roof. A pair of curving cross beams, one vertical, the other horizontal, outline each of the gently twisting forms of the central space. The result is a completely irregular, two-story base.

Bart Prince wanted to ensure that every room would receive sunlight at some time of the year and therefore produced a more or less linear design. The glazed openings to the exterior are in a variety of forms, the curving walls and the original staggered skylight create strange and constant contrasts of light and shade and interesting chiaroscuro effects.

In the interior there is a striking combination of stone and carpeting as floor coverings in some areas. The walls alternate constantly between stone and light plaster.

Coombs House

Location: *California, United States*
Year of construction: *1993*
Architects: *Goldman Firth Architects*
Photography: *Undine Pröhl*

This Californian residence is located on top of a hill, giving it panoramic views of the countryside. The building is structured around different sections that house the various domestic facilities.

The warm climate made thick stone walls a sensible choice for the elevations. This building system is inspired by traditional, popular architecture and gives the structure increased thermal inertia. The result is that in winter the heat given off by the heating system does not escape through the walls, nor does the cold enter through them. In summer the fiercest rays of the sun lose their strength as they pass through the thick stone.

The architecture of California is typically a blend, a mixture of trends ranging from the Mexican vernacular, incorporating the modern innovations of Richard Neutra and other architects of his period, and adopting the technological advances of the present day.

The entire building is governed by a minimalization of feature. This formal reduction can also be seen in the choice of materials, of which there are basically three: stone, wood, and glass. The interior design and furnishings are also plain but powerful: the simplification of form produces a direct and forceful effect.

A system of pillars on the exterior defines the outside leisure area. The swimming pool serves a number of functions: it is not only a place where you can enjoy a swim, but it also has a cooling effect and produces reflections of light and color that make it a genuine delight for the senses.

The detailed design of the swimming pool gives it a key role. The sheet of water merges with the landscape around and the reflections of light and color make this an ideal spot to enjoy magnificent sunsets.

Plain and simple elegance is the keynote of the spacious interiors. Their simplicity makes the few decorative objects present all the more striking in this minimal yet powerful setting.

House in Lambertville

Location: *Lambertville, New Jersey, United States*
Year of construction: *1988*
Architects: *John Keenen, Terence Riley*
Photography: *Eduard Hueber*

Situated in a summer resort, this design reflects the wishes of the clients, who wanted a holiday house some distance away from their permanent home. One of the requirements was an outside room, completely sheltered by glass, that would be an ideal place to eat out of doors in good weather or to spend time relaxing on warm summer nights. To meet the requirements of this specific program, the architects decided on a style of building largely forgotten during the 20th century: the casino-style social club.

This family dwelling is near the town of Lambertville, New Jersey, a small pre-revolutionary community on the banks of the Delaware river. The land falls away sharply and the house is built against the slope next to a stream that once fed an old mill. It is surrounded by dense vegetation consisting mainly of very tall trees. One of the advantages of the property is that it is only an hour's drive from New York.

The building has clean lines and is of limited dimensions, standing on a regular base formed by the main section, to which some small appendices have been added to form the whole.

The main room, the space between the low walls of an 18th-century mill, is a large, rectangular chamber inspired by the idea of the "casino" or social club.

To allow natural light to enter the areas inside, the architects have built a gallery that runs almost without interruption around the entire building.

Kirlin House

Location: *Napa Valley, California, United States*
Year of construction: *1987*
Architect: *Mark Mack*
Photography: *Reiner Blunck*

This building is constructed around two yards with different aspects: the south side is an outside area, sheltered in the winter, while on the north side the architect has designed a cool, shady area for the summer months.

A striking feature of the main elevation is the wall, divided into two sections, that encloses and protects the house. It stands like a medieval fortress, shielding every corner of the property. In the center of the wall is a timber-roofed, rectangular entrance that gives access to the yard. The ground here is covered by tiles in tones of ocher. There is also a blue structure leading directly to the wooden door of the main entrance.

The building is mainly rectangular in form, interrupted only by the patios and openings in the thick concrete walls that accentuate the enclosed nature of the structure. This is the access area and it was designed as a place to be

enjoyed in summer: water runs through stone channels into a small pool designed by Larry Shank.

Access to the property is on the north elevation through a wooden door in this wall. The interior is designed along the same principle of simplicity as the exterior. This gives unity and continuity to the structure as a whole. The most obvious example is the use of the same flooring material in both areas. This area is divided off by a concrete block that separates it from the other areas, but again spatial continuity is preserved, in this case by the timber roof that, from within, can be seen as a defined part of the whole.

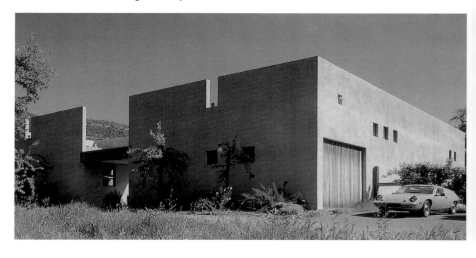

The south elevation from three different viewpoints, showing the vines and the angled roof that protects the interior of the house from the intense rays of the summer sun.

Right-hand page, bottom: View of the inner patio and the main door through the timber-roofed entrance area.

House in Sempach

Location: *Sempach, Lucerne, Switzerland*
Year of construction: *1988*
Architect: *Werner Hunziker*
Photography: *A. Zimmermann*

The rather surprising location of this modern design is the historic Swiss village of Sempach. Sempach has remained faithful to the traditional architectural style of the region and it took two years of intense debate with the local authorities – who believed that the structure and color of the building would ruin the countryside – before Werner Hunziker finally won approval from architectural circles. Yet even now the building still makes some of the area's inhabitants rather uncomfortable.

It is a private house, surrounded by dense vegetation in summer and by a carpet of snow in the winter. The site is basically flat though with certain irregularities. On one side the building extends towards the wood, concealing the lawn at the rear.

The original idea for the structure was based on that of a cube, but it was eventually built as three 26 ft x 26 ft (8 m x 8 m) squares that were divided and rejoined to produce an original geometric form. The ground plan is a rectangle subdivided into squares.

The house is constructed on two levels. The first floor contains a den at the entrance, in the salient corner of the house. The northerly aspect required special treatment for this elevation to protect it from the harsh climate of the area. The architect opted for highly toughened glass and designed the external staircase opposite to act as a shield. The library lies between the den and the living room and includes a small area designed for reading; unlike most rooms with large windows, this one gives on to the interior.

Detail of the glass and aluminum structure.

The chrome chimney rises through an opening in the aluminum roof.

House in Napa Valley

Location: *Napa Valley, California, United States*
Year of construction: *1990*
Architect: *David Connor*
Photography: *Richard Waite*

This house, designed by David Connor, stands on a 200 acre (800,000 m²) site on a hillside in the Napa Valley, California. The house bears no relation to neighboring properties: the owners, Swiss wine merchants Thomas and Anna Lundstrom, wanted a house with personality that would also be a home. From the outside the building is noble, powerful, and elegant – solid white concrete contrasting with a comparatively simple interior.

In architectural terms the residence is surprisingly innovative: none of its elements relates to its surroundings, to the architect that designed it, or to its owners. Yet the interpretation remains American, the product of a blend of cultures, typical of a land that has opened its doors to so many. The house recalls the bow of a ship and has a swimming pool that splits the guest tower from the main building.

The architect was forced to modify the original design of the house, which is built on a definite slope and surrounded by areas of lawn and other plantings in curving swathes. The change was the result of the owners' decision to set up in business as wine merchants and required the original plans to be altered to produce a modern interpretation of the Palladian style.

The lawns that surround the building play a very important role. They were designed as a rural art project with the help of Hargreaves Associates and their color changes seasonally.

The exterior is powerful and elegant, while the interior is extremely simple and functional: two longitudinal wings with two passages through which light enters. This, together with the pale colors used in this part of the house, creates rooms that are bathed in light.

View of the swimming pool with its solid, rectangular lines. The paved surround is of the same material as used in the porch and guest tower entrance.

View of the main entrance. The interior is extremely simple and functional, contrasting with the stately exterior.

Detail of the stairway leading to the upper floor. The treads of the stairs are wooden, as is the flooring on the upper level. The doors are painted white and blend with the walls.

La Casa Colorada

Location: *Mexico*
Year of construction: *1995*
Architects: *Legorreta Architects*
Photography: *Undine Pröhl*

This design by Ricardo Legorreta combines most of the characteristics of his particular architectural vision. There is a formalization governed by geometric parameters with right angles determining almost all the lines of the building. A series of principal spaces interconnect and abut, their intersections producing openings in various stretches of wall, new structural elements, porches, and even planters.

The mild climate allows the full use of outdoor areas. These are not left entirely exposed as protection from direct sunlight is needed. The building therefore has a number of porches, terraces, pergolas, and vertical screens that act as sun filters.

The influence of Luis Barragán, the architect's mentor, is apparent everywhere: the blend of traditional resources and contemporary architecture is obvious. One example is the exposed stone structure around the entrance.

A centuries-old building system is given a modern interpretation with a more detailed finish that smooths out imperfections and leaves edges clearly defined.

The colors used on the various surfaces give each environment its own quality, its own character, making it easily identifiable. This wide chromatic range also produces a great interplay of light through the reflection of the water features found in various parts of the property.

The furnishings also express this dichotomy between a vernacular tradition and the latest design ideas. The rich use of vegetation brings freshness to a very hot location.

Light floods in through the many openings. Window shades filter the sunlight, preventing the interior from becoming overheated.

House in Uruguay

Location: *Uruguay*
Year of construction: *1993*
Architect: *Antonio Horacio Ravazzani*
Photography: *Undine Pröhl*

South American architecture has always been known for its ability to adapt the characteristics of the modern movement to the architecture of the vernacular tradition. In practice this means that technological and formal advances are adapted to fit with traditional building methods.

This country house by Antonio Horacio Ravazzani is a good example of the trend. Constructed of stone with large surfaces of glass, it is in an elevated position and enjoys fine panoramic views of the surrounding countryside.

In formal terms the structure of the house recalls that of an industrial warehouse: a tall body incorporating mezzanines and subdivisions to house the domestic facilities. The roof is metal and is supported by a system of trusses resting on solid stone partitions and the metal structure that provides the framework for the glazed openings.

The ground plan is regular. At one end of the rectangle are the living room and dining room. A spiral staircase leads to the floor above: a mezzanine providing a further leisure area that, thanks to its height, enjoys fine views across the Uruguayan countryside.

The openings in the solid part of the elevation are purposely small to limit the amount of light entering and to make the domestic facilities and private rooms more intimate.

The mezzanine approached via the spiral staircase is built of the same material as the exterior of the house. A metal structure supports a timber framework that in turn supports the stone flooring.

The communal areas can
be easily identified as
they share a single space
with no vertical or
horizontal divisions to
obstruct the overall view.
Artificial light is limited
to lamps suspended from
the roof trusses.

Residence in "La Azohía"

Location: *Murcia, Spain*
Year of construction: *1998*
Architect: *José Tarragó*
Photography: *Eugeni Pons*

At first sight what appears unusual about this house is the monochrome character of all its environments, but in fact its most striking feature is the ambiguity of the arrangement of its spaces. Internally the rooms are totally permeable in a visual sense; interconnected and open to the outside, they do not allow introspection of any kind. Conversely, the outside patios are designed as if they were rooms in the interior and are surrounded by walls that separate them from the surrounding countryside.

Externally, the building makes use of vernacular know-how, incorporating the devices of traditional architecture to alleviate the effects of an extreme climate: thick walls give the building thermal inertia; the walls are whitewashed to reflect the sun's rays; the enclosed spaces are designed to enjoy maximum shade. On the other hand, the interior – including the patios – has a modern, almost futuristic feel.

The furnishings are in a combination of white and various shades of ocher and include exclusive designer pieces. The kitchen opens into the living room that is characterized by pureness of line, formal restraint, and the smooth, unsullied whiteness of the closets.

The external spaces are an
extension of the interior
living room. In summer the
patio doors slide back,
making the two areas one
continuous whole.

The wall openings, the skylights in the ceiling, and the tonality of the furnishings create an environment filled with light.

Finca in Mallorca

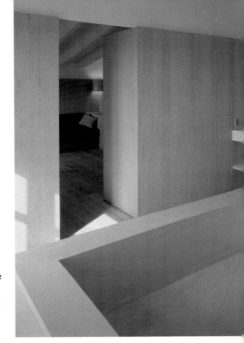

Location: *Mallorca, Spain*
Year of construction: *1998*
Architect: *Vincent van Duysen*
Photography: *Alberto Emanuele Piovano*

This house is a conversion of a traditional old Mallorcan house in the interior of the island. The facade and the two adjoining structures (the superintendent's residence and the owner's den) have been preserved intact. Inside the house, however, the aim has been to create an ascetic, very modern atmosphere.

An impressive timber partition separates the caretaker's house from the main house and creates a large but intimate patio area. The architect also designed the yard, creating a direct link with the house by utilizing the same flooring material for both: a combination of concrete and local stone. A large basin made from a single block of stone has been placed in an alcove and provides a strikingly dramatic touch.

The main house communicates the same atmosphere. The furnishings, designed specifically for each room, are smooth, bare forms, almost monastic in their simplicity. Materials such as wood, stone, ceramics, and marble have been delicately combined to create an elegant, relaxed atmosphere. The entrance is an empty room with wood-paneled walls that conceal the access to the guest bathroom. There is also access to the kitchen-dining room and the staircase which leads to the floor above, where the bedrooms are situated.

This house demonstrates the timelessness of the minimalist approach, which is not out of place in a traditional setting.

Boat Pavilion

Location: *Streatley-on-Thames, Great Britain*
Year of construction: *1999*
Architects: *Brookes, Stancey, Randall*
Photography: *Peter Durant, ARCBLUE*

The enveloping transparency of this building and its relationship with the water are reminiscent of a garden pavilion. The structure was in fact designed as a place to relax and adjoins the spacious garden of the property for which it was built. It offers a wonderful vantage point from which to watch the waters of the Thames flow quietly by.

The first two plans failed to get approval from the authorities as they did not fully comply with planning regulations. However, the client, a former shipowner, persisted and a third, exquisitely subtle design was finally constructed.

From the opposite bank, the structure appears minimal, being positioned perpendicularly to the river. The building projects some distance over the water to give the impression of floating. Two concrete pillars arise from a common foundation to connect with two girders projecting from the ground from which the structure extends almost without interruption out beyond the edges of the river bank. The metal structure and huge glass panels that form the parallelepipedal shell provide maximum transparency and delightful views.

A number of areas around the structure have also been carefully designed. These are principally the platform leading to the main entrance and the steps descending to the river and landing stage.

The powerful expression of the
bearing structure that carries
this impressive projection, and
the fine lines of the metal
framework of this parallepipedal
structure, are two of the key
elements of the design.

HOUSES IN THE MOUNTAINS

This chapter presents a selection of houses from all over the world, built in the mountains and of special architectural interest. All are modern interpretations of those early buildings that, for a number of very specific historical and economic reasons, were at one time located in this very special environment. The result is a transmutation of traditional building values and elements, into which renowned architects later incorporated new technological discoveries, producing structures capable of withstanding all kinds of adverse climatic and geographical conditions without foregoing any of the comfort and convenience that modern society demands. In order to understand the modern concept that defines these buildings, we therefore first need to analyze the distinguishing features of the houses of the past.

The principal characteristics of the few dwellings constructed in this inhospitable environment have, for many years, defined what is known as the traditional style. The first of these is, without doubt, the variety of form that resulted from the conflict between the creative imagination and the necessary functional aspects, the wide range of materials available, and the position the building was given. The traditional structures with their enormous, sloping roofs and solid masses of masonry were designed to inspire a sense of security.

These typical features have shown modern architects that in order to withstand the rigors of the climate and the topographical problems encountered in this environment, a building must be unpretentious. In fact many of the solutions devised in the past have withstood the test of time.

Today this type of building normally utilizes materials from the site itself or from the local area, depending on the degree of isolation. The timber frame construction, for example, commonly used in the 18th century, has been readopted by a group of modern architects, as it allows great variety in design and layout. In the interior, the widespread use of wood stems from the desire to give rooms warmth and character. The different layouts are chosen to give the building the feeling of a refuge: external traffic areas that would be at the mercy of the hostile environment are avoided. Great care is also taken in the choice of site and positioning of the house: poor placement in relation to the slope and the cardinal points could make a building uninhabitable.

Another element incorporated into many modern buildings is a stone plinth that not only isolates the building from the ground, but also provides a solid base for the chimney. Historically, people who moved to the mountains did so out of necessity because they needed to be near pasture and look after their animals. Today, however, the reasons are very different. People make a free choice to live in the mountains. They build houses either for occasional use – during holiday periods – or settle there permanently, making their mountain dwelling their main home.

The view also plays an important role – a house in the mountains must provide a panoramic view of the surrounding countryside. This predilection is the result of a more contemplative attitude to life and was not a requirement of the architecture of the past. In former times the view was not taken into account and openings were therefore of very limited size to afford better protection against the cold.

Today, however, houses in the mountains are designed with large windows that open defiantly, challengingly, onto the world outside.

The contribution made by modern architecture in this respect is precisely the infinite freedom with which the traditional responses to the problems encountered are given a fresh interpretation. All of that brings us to an analysis of how such buildings are adapted to fit the landscape. A building need not necessarily be adapted to blend into its immediate environment, as if it wished to conceal itself or felt subservient to its surroundings. Integration is not only a visual matter, but also a technical one.

Today, architects commissioned to build in the mountains regard tradition as a very useful source from which to develop their ideas. All the houses that appear here demonstrate that good architecture cannot be achieved with a servile attitude. On the contrary, the finest, most exquisite examples are those where the architect combines imagination with intelligence and adopts an approach that addresses the specific conditions imposed by the environment. The most appealing houses are those adapted to the landscape and lifestyle of the area where they are built.

Casa Negro

Location: *Contadero, Mexico*
Year of construction: *1995*
Architects: *Alberto Kallach, Daniel Álvarez,*
          Gustavo Lipkau, Rosa López
Photography: *Paul Czitrom, Luis Gordoa,*
          Marta Irene Alcántara

The nature of the site, on the south side of a valley, was a determining factor in the creative process. Architect Alberto Kallach had to construct a house on a steeply sloping site covered in oaks and buddleia. The strategy he adopted was to divide the project into four habitable units that would fit conveniently into the site.

To ensure minimum disturbance to the natural environment, the four structures are supported on platforms that follow the line of the natural pathways. Three are sited on paths that already existed, free of vegetation, where the incline was less pronounced.

Another important decision was to avoid building large retaining walls that would damage the roots of nearby trees. It was decided that the platforms would not penetrate the ground but float above it on reinforced concrete stands that would act as both supports and tanks, storing water collected from roofs and patios.

Concrete, steel, wood, and glass are the materials used to give form and finish to the four living units.

These units and the external levels and spaces are connected by a system of steps, ramps, and bridges that provide opportunities to enjoy this unusual location as you move between areas.

Casa Negro is a group of habitable units of varying dimensions and materials in dialogue with its surroundings: the mountainside, the sky, and the vegetation.

The entrance to the house is at the west end of the uppermost structure. A wooden pergola and the urbanized space below act as transitional elements between exterior and interior. The living room and dining room are located in this first unit and look out onto the rich vegetation. The utility areas are behind the passageway that backs on to them.

The units and the external levels and
spaces are connected by a linking
system of steps, ramps, and bridges
that provide opportunities to enjoy this
location as you move between areas.
The two lower buildings contain
additional elements with a den and
swimming pool on the lower part
of the site.

The second living unit
contains the bedrooms
and private areas. These
enjoy the same aspect as
the living room and
dining room, with access
via a passageway at the
rear, lit by a skylight. A
stairway links this floor
with the level above,
where the master
bedroom is located.

Casa Coll-Vallés

Location: *Barcelona, Spain*
Year of construction: *1997*
Architects: *Fidela Frutos, J.M. Sanmartín,*
     Jaume Valor
Associates: *Construcciones Técnicas Lliçà (builder),*
     Alex Soler (furnishings)
Photography: *Eugeni Pons*

From the outset this project was conditioned by the topography and the site: an extremely steep slope on the one hand and, on the other, an almost triangular plot. Regulations requiring a minimum 10 ft (3 m) distance between building and boundary placed severe restrictions on the positioning of the house. At the same time there was a desire to preserve the existing trees in the scheme and, at the clients' request, to include a swimming pool to be set against the backdrop of the landscape.

The house has a southerly aspect, dictated by the slope of the land, optimum views, and the maximum hours of sunshine. It comprises one floor partly below ground level and two double-height units superposed vertically. The lower section contains the living area and the upper part the bedrooms.

As regards the external appearance of the building, the architects admit that their intention was to treat the building as a single unit, that is to say, as one unified whole, without allowing the arrangement of the interior spaces or the functional aspects of the building to impinge on the exterior. One result of this is the avoidance of the (differently-sized) windows of the various rooms appearing in the elevations.

The north elevation (which is free of openings) has a frieze of metal sheeting that continues across the curved roof. This same material also conceals the windows but here the sheeting contains tiny perforations.

On the south elevation flat, continuous surfaces in a variety of materials have been used: window shades, glass, and polycarbonate. These surfaces create a number of horizontal bands at varying angles. The side elevations are uniform surfaces of whitewashed plaster with virtually no openings. Their appearance is not unlike a simplified section of the house.

View of the living room showing the double space connecting with the kitchen.

Detail of the master bedroom showing the stairs ascending to a small mezzanine fitted above the bathroom and below the curved ceiling.

Cheesecake Consortium

Location: *Mendocino County, California, United States*
Year of construction: *1994*
Architects: *Richard Fernau, Laura Hartman,*
David Kau
Associates: *Tim Gray, Kimberly Moses,*
Emily Stussi (design team), Dennis
McCroskey (structure),
Jim Boudoures (contractor)
Photography: *Richard Barnes*

This project was for the construction of a group of houses in a wood in Mendocino County, north of San Francisco, for a group of friends (4 couples and 3 singles), aged between 40 and 60, who had decided to spend their later years together for companionship and mutual support.

Most of Fernau and Hartman's projects show a tendency towards division into a number of different spaces or buildings so that, as a whole, the development blends more easily into the surrounding landscape. This strategy allows a heterogeneous approach that fosters dialogue between the different structures and contrast between their forms and finishes. The final result is not a single interpretation but an open system of relationships.

This development is based on three structures, each of which has a number of elements: a two-story building with communal areas on the lower floor and two apartments on the upper floor, a residential wing with five apartments and a laundry and library, and, lastly, a workshop area with facilities for car repairs, photo processing, marquetry work, and table tennis.

All the areas have been designed to allow alteration or extension at a later date, in accordance with the occupants' needs. Likewise, all the rooms have been made easily accessible for the elderly, with ramps and elevators able to accommodate wheelchairs.

"We asked the architects to make the communal areas large enough for our families so we could invite them for meals," said one of the members of the Cheesecake Consortium.

The four trees that had to be sacrificed during construction were used to make the balconies, the furniture, and the dining table – all designed by Davin Joy.

Casa Cabernet

Location: *Napa Valley, United States*
Year of construction: *1999*
Architects: *Legorreta Architects*
Photography: *Lourdes Legorreta*

The staggered positioning of the building is to adapt it to the gentle incline. The house is divided into four parts connected by intermediate spaces bounded by curving walls that merge with the topography to create a sculptural whole.

The Casa Cabernet provided Legorreta with a fresh opportunity to demonstrate that architectural intervention in a landscape of great natural beauty is not necessarily detrimental. The result is this splendid house standing on an attractive hilltop in Santa Helena, between woodland and vines. It is yet another example of the great wisdom this architect has acquired during his long career as a builder of dreams.

The integration of the project into the landscape is achieved by the division into a number of different structures and the careful siting within the existing topography. This approach also increases the opportunities to provide fine views, both of the house from the surrounding woods and of the countryside from within the property itself.

Walls play a key role in Legorreta's architecture and this is apparent in the Casa Cabernet. On the one hand, they act as an element connecting the outside and inside of the building. This is true, for example, of the curving wall already mentioned: after following its course on the exterior, it penetrates the building and, on the interior, defines the space occupied by the kitchen. On the other hand, walls can be used to allow light to pass into the interior and give it meaning, creating areas of great beauty and peace through natural illumination.

The outstanding quality of the spaces created stems from the quest for elements that would allow the owners to see their dream fulfilled: to enjoy and be happy in the house they had built.

The scheme of the house is simple: living rooms, a master bedroom, a terrace with swimming pool, and two guest bedrooms. The principal challenge was retaining a close relationship with the surrounding woodland without relinquishing the privacy of the house itself.

The elevations are designed chiefly from an interior perspective, acting as frames for the most attractive views. The color used almost throughout was chosen for its similarity to the red soil of the area and was called *Cabernet* as a tribute to the grape variety grown on the property.

There was the opportunity
of choosing the type of
furniture best suited to the
property and some items
were sent by boat directly
from Mexico. The
widespread use of wood in
both furniture and
carpentry work brings
warmth to a house clearly
designed on a human scale.

The interior spaces enjoy magnificent views framed by openings designed from an internal perspective rather than as compositional features of the elevations. The furniture was specially chosen or designed to blend with the other elements of the house.

Casa Nirvana

Location: *Valldoreix, Barcelona. Spain*
Year of construction: *1996*
Architect: *Jordi Casadevall*
Photography: *Jordi Miralles*

This property was located as a matter of strategy on the most elevated part of the plot, close to the northern boundary. This made it possible to preserve an existing group of Mediterranean pines that are useful against the heat and enhance the environmental quality of the site. These initial decisions on siting formed the foundation of an outstanding achievement, clear in its conception and functionally effective.

The first floor of the house is a 130 ft (40 m) – long, stone-faced parallelepiped. On this base are placed two cubic metal structures that contain the living areas used by the owners and their guests, and transform the flat roof into an external space with its own identity. The lack of alignment in relation to the base and the deliberately contrasting materials and color of the two elements accentuate their individual characters. The solidity and rigidity of the base stands out against the pavilions that bring lightness and movement to the whole.

Casa Nirvana is a clear example of a house in which the flow of the interior space is not at odds with the autonomy of its different parts. The two internal stairways are a good example of this: they offer almost direct access from the exterior and create an excellent link between the pavilions and the rest of the house and the garage, without sacrificing any of the intimacy.

The boundary between interior and exterior is permeable, creating fluid communication and a broad visual perception that includes the yard.

The lower floor is defined in stone. On this base are placed two metal cubes containing the bedrooms. Their lack of alignment accentuates the change of material and function.

On the north elevation some horizontal openings have been made to provide soft illumination to the longitudinal passageway, while isolating it visually from the road. By contrast, on the south elevation, the bedrooms and various living and eating areas spill onto the yard and swimming pool area – some through porches, others directly. In some cases the openings are so vast that it becomes difficult to distinguish interior from exterior.

Von Stein Residence

Location: *Sonoma County, California, United States*
Year of construction: *1994*
Constructor: *Fine Carpentry*
Architects: *Fernau and Hartman Architects*
Associates: *Timothy Gray, Beth Piatnitza, Anni Tilt*
(design team); Emily Stussi, Kimberly
Moses, Sarah De Vito
Photography: *David Heawitt/Anne Garrison*

Right-hand page:
View of the *Innenhof*, an outdoor
living and eating area. Each of the
exterior spaces has its own
identity, determined by
architectural detail, the degree of
protection against the sun, and
the type of vegetation.

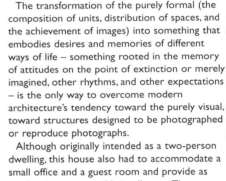

The transformation of the purely formal (the composition of units, distribution of spaces, and the achievement of images) into something that embodies desires and memories of different ways of life – something rooted in the memory of attitudes on the point of extinction or merely imagined, other rhythms, and other expectations – is the only way to overcome modern architecture's tendency toward the purely visual, toward structures designed to be photographed or reproduce photographs.

Although originally intended as a two-person dwelling, this house also had to accommodate a small office and a guest room and provide as much privacy as possible in all areas. The solution adopted is a loft apartment house with two separate buildings creating a series of shared exterior spaces.

The hillside in Sonoma County descends towards the southwest, with views of the vineyards in the Valley of the Moon, where the sun is fierce and sometimes unbearable.

The most striking feature of the scheme is the two towers. The taller one contains a door through which the main traffic routes pass. It looks out over the best views and has a den-bedroom and balcony where you can relax and enjoy the landscape. The smaller of the towers, standing among the trees, next to an enclosed, mystical yard, is at the highest corner of the property. Perfectly situated to enjoy the views and the cooling breeze, this spot is designed as the guest area.

The fierce Californian sun shines brightly on the yellow walls of the main building. The architects have designed different forms of protection from the sun: metal canopies, roll-up drapes, and wooden pergolas.

View of the tower where the master bedroom is located. The projecting area is a small viewpoint which forms part of the bedroom.

Different levels are a feature of the Von Stein Residence. Light streams in to the lower floor.

View of the kitchen. There are two types of flooring in the house: parquet and polished concrete. Contrary to expectation, the concrete is in the living room and the parquet flooring is in the kitchen.

Right-hand page:
View of the living room. The master bedroom is constructed like a balcony over the living room. Large, translucent, sliding panels make it possible to connect the two areas or separate the bedroom from the living room.

Type/Variant House

Location: *Wisconsin, United States*
Year of construction: *1996*
Architects: *Vincent James, Paul Yaggie*
Associates: *Nancy Blanfard, Nathan Knuston, Andrew Dull, Steve Lazen, Krista Scheib, Julie Snow, Taavo Somer, Kate Wyberg*
Photography: *Don F. Wong*

Bluish stone was chosen for the base of the house as the color is very similar to that of the bark on the lower trunks of the tall trees in the surrounding woodland.

This house is in fact a collection of spaces that correspond to the rhythms and patterns of domestic life. Using structures similar to wooden boxes, a series of different, linking architectural environments has been created. Each has its own specific proportions, aspect, and natural light. Despite being of strictly orthogonal composition, the articulation of the different units produces a continually changing succession of views of the surrounding area. Similarly, the turns and angles of the different rooms of the building create a number of semienclosed exterior spaces.

Geometrically, the composition is based on interlinking parallelepipeds at different heights and with different positions. The largest rooms, terraces, and balconies form the central area of each body, and it is in these spaces that family members come together; at the junctions and intersections between the units, the spaces tend to be more enclosed and smaller, making them more secluded and intimate.

Both the rooms and the courtyards are designed as uncomplicated, accessible spaces, simple in form, that take on life with daily use and the changing seasons. The system of construction, like the finishes chosen, takes its inspiration from the typical rural architecture of the northern United States.

The end result is both abstract and friendly, thus meeting the requirements of the owners, who wanted a warm and rustic home.

The materials on the exterior – mainly copper sheeting from the Douglas company and bluish stone – are arranged in different ways and bring a great variety of rhythm and texture to the elevations. The copper cladding has not been treated to withstand the elements, the intention being to allow it to age naturally.

View of the inner courtyard in the south wing and the walkway above on the second floor. This courtyard lies between the garage and the kitchen. The wall on the left has been adapted to act as a woodstore.

Natural light enters the
house through vertical
wooden window shades
that act as a filter against
the direct rays of the sun.
The positioning of the
openings in the elevations
creates a variety of effects
in the interior.

In the interiors, there is no attempt to conceal blemishes. Many of the wooden panels still show the marks left by the construction process.

Bernhard Burger House

Location: *Bregenz, Austria*
Year of construction: *1994*
Architects: *Karl Baumschlager & Dietmar Eberle*
Photography: *Eduard Hueber*

The Burger House stands on a site with a steep south-north slope which overlooks Lake Constance.

The building has a simple structure: the ground plan is an almost perfect 20 x 30 ft (6 x 9 m) rectangle, developed on four levels with the lower floor partly below ground level. Access is from the south via a gently sloping ramp to the middle floor where the entrance hall, visitors' washroom, master bedroom, and main bathroom are located.

The kitchen, dining, and living areas share an open space on the floor above. The kitchen work surface is situated in an extension that runs the entire length of the west wall. This area is lit by a large linear skylight, which also creates a distinction between the different environments of the upper floor.

The arrangement of the house is based on its section, the different functions being divided into relatively small stories. In the Burger House, however, the functional distribution is different from the usual typology: the utility space in the basement level has been converted into a type of loft or attic room, while the main reception area is located on the top floor, to take advantage of the views over the lake.

The master bedroom,
a simple space with
drapes for privacy.

The main door, skylight,
and elevation viewed from
the stairway landing.

Kitchen, dining-living
room, and second balcony.

Waldman House

Location: *Charlottesville, Virginia, United States*
Year of construction: *1996*
Builder: *G. Viquer & P. Radis*
Architect: *Peter Waldman*
Associates: *John Fitzerald*
Photography: *Peter Waldman*

Located in a wood near Charlottesville (Virginia), this house is the home of architect Peter Waldman, who also designed it and teaches at the nearby University. The lack of a client to consult gave him a different relationship with the project.

Not far from the site is a clear precedent for the Waldman House: Monticello, a project started by father of the American constitution, President, and architect Thomas Jefferson. Work on the house still continues after two hundred years.

In some ways, in a case such as this, the house becomes a full-scale working model, a prototype. As a result, some of the houses that architects have built for themselves (like Robert Stern's house for his mother, the Hedjuk House, and the Gehry House) have played a leading role in many of the esthetic revolutions of recent years.

This experimental vocation gives the project an experimental aspect. This may seem obvious, but in fact it is not, because insofar as it is considered to be a trial exercise, a working instrument or a form of study, the end result is subject to a different type of judgement.

In the Waldman House everything has a sense of the dramatic. But what changes your perception of the spaces is Peter Waldman's collection of unusual objects: unclassifiable machines that seem to originate in some protoindustrial era, eclectic furniture acquired from antique stores, puppets, and disturbing miniatures.

The large picture windows in the elevations face east and west, giving fine views of sunrise and sunset from the interior. The surrounding trees create an excellent natural sun filter.

One of the more unusual elements is the roof skylight, constructed from translucent fabric.

There are almost no openings
on the front elevation. It is
covered in copper sheeting
that blends perfectly with
the colors of the landscape.

The Waldman House is built
in sloping woodland near
Charlottesville, Virginia.

The conical skylight is 10 ft (3 m) high with a diameter at the base of 6½ ft (2 m).

The objects in the house have been specially chosen to create a dramatic, theatrical effect. The balustrades, radiators, pipes, and lamps appear to date from the early 20th century.

Bridge House

Location: *Olive Bridge, New York, United States*
Year of construction: *1996*
Architect: *Peter Gluck*
Photography: *Paul Warchol*

The house acts as a bridge, providing access between different areas of the wood.

Peter Gluck uses a wide variety of materials, colors, and finishes. He also works with clear geometric elements that interrelate in a complex manner.

This house in the woods of Olive Bridge near New York is a holiday retreat, a kind of private hotel to which the owners invite their family and friends. Peter Gluck had to adapt to a site that, though stimulating in many ways, also had a steep incline. Rather than trying to adapt the building to the topography, the house Gluck designed is placed on the site with almost no modification.

The building consists of three separate, well-defined units with different characters that blend together. This approach is typical of Gluck's recent work: from a functional or schematic division he constructs a complex group of different but interrelated buildings.

In this instance the structures consist of a two-story cube faced with artificial stone, a traditional ridge-roofed building, and a bridge or tunnel raised on piles and clad in corrugated metal sheeting.

The house acts as a bridge or link between two different areas.

House in Maine

Location: *Maine, United States*
Year of construction: *1989*
Architects: *Andrea P. Leers, Jane Weinzapfel*
Photography: *Michael Moran*

This house in West Bath (Maine) stands on the area's rugged coastline, at the highest point of a north-south peninsula on top of a rocky promontory 8 ft (2.5 m) from the water. This wonderful location offers stunning views of the ocean and nearby island. The brief Andrea P. Leers and Jane Weinzapfel received from the owners was to create a house that would be a year-round refuge, easy to maintain and with all modern domestic conveniences.

The house is constructed on a T-shape plan and comprises three distinct, compact structures arranged vertically within the buildable boundaries of the site. First there is the main section with the entrance, dining room, and living room on the lower floor, and two bedrooms on the second floor, one of which is a guest room.

The second section is a tower that has the kitchen on the lower floor, a Japanese-style bathroom on the second floor, and a den on the top floor. The third part is the porched area that runs the length of the main section and is the area most used in summer.

The design solution adopted by the architects takes its inspiration from a number of different sources: the basilica of former times, the modern industrial unit, the barn, and the lighthouse. The house and its site are closely interrelated. The main unit follows the north-south axis of the land and is closed on the north side and open on its south part to the sun and ocean views.

Sectional view of the house.

The floor on the first story is wood painted in shades of gray. The decorative carpets are bright and colorful.

The interior of the main unit has natural pine paneling; the areas of painted plaster within this timber shell – the walls of the stairs and the fireplace – subdivide the space.

The tower walls are of painted plaster to emphasize the division from the main unit. In this way the wood combines with the reddish and blue tones of the paint to create different environments that vary from warm to cold, to informal.

Garey House

Location: *Kent, Connecticut, United States*
Year of construction: *1991*
Architects: *Gwathmey Siegel & Associates Architects*
Photography: *Richard Bryant/Arcaid*

The Garey House stands in a wonderful mountain location in Kent (Connecticut), surrounded by steep, craggy hillsides with a fast-flowing river. From this varied topography the architects chose a site in a woodland clearing on a gentle slope close to a waterfall.

The structure, which has an L-shape plan, is divided into two distinct areas – the swimming pool area and the living space. These are defined by a steep slope contained by a stone wall. The American architects have placed a set of steps as an architectural feature at this dividing point. This serves a double function, acting as a spatial link and providing access between the outdoor leisure area and the house itself.

Externally, the building has the appearance of a number of superposed vertical and horizontal units. The glass elevation of the cylindrical body stands out, however, because of its height – it occupies almost the entire wall space – and because it contrasts with the straight lines that dominate the building as a whole. The semicircular facade stands like a vast picture window divided into large panels by reddish wooden bars that match the doors and windows of the rest of the building. The brightness of the color stands out against the cold gray tones that dominate the external walls.

This unusual volumetric composition is translated on the interior into a number of superposed levels performing a wide range of domestic requirements. The result is a building rich in spatial variety.

The structure consists of reinforced concrete walls painted white on the interior and rendered on the exterior. The pool terrace is paved with grayish slabs that highlight the chromatic uniformity of the elevations.

Right-hand page:
The house opens onto the exterior through large glass panes that fill the elevation, creating a light, transparent atmosphere in the interior.

In the kitchen all the walls are fitted with closets with dark wood doors alternating with the windows; these allow the maximum amount of sunlight to enter and create a warm and pleasant atmosphere.

893

Houses in Igls

Location: *Igls, Austria*
Year of construction: *1990*
Architect: *Peter Lorenz*
Photography: *Giancarlo Gardin*

The village of Igls in the Austrian Tyrol is a very popular tourist resort not far from the city of Innsbruck. Peter Lorenz designed these houses on the basis of a number of concepts fundamental to the architecture of the 1990s: a minimum built area, maximum quality in the plans and construction, and low cost.

The site where these buildings stand is long and narrow, and the presence of a large electricity pylon at the far end presented an added problem. Lorenz's design has a southwest aspect, while the north elevation, where the main entrance is located, is more secluded. By giving the houses this outlook the architect successfully manages to avoid the pylon interfering with the mountain views from the windows.

The development has two identical buildings, each of which consists of four floors and two one-family dwellings.

The architect has partially rotated the roofs of both buildings to take maximum advantage of the windows on the southwest elevation. This produces warm, bright interiors and an attractive interplay of light and shade. The doors and windows of each of the houses are strategically placed to make the most of the natural light. On the exterior, the rotation of the roof gives a dynamic feel to the whole structure.

The roofs are rhomboid in form, with metallic surfaces that reflect the color of the sky. Each building has the same basic structure, with slight variations to meet the individual character of each house.

Side view of one of the
unroofed balconies, showing
the extension of the support
structure.

The main differences
between the houses lie
in the finishing touches,
particularly in the design of
the balconies and verandas.
The metal and glass
structure of this balcony
gives it the appearance
of a greenhouse.

Right-hand page:
The doors and windows of
the houses have been
strategically placed to
enjoy maximum sunlight.

In the interior a number of
colorful art works decorate
the white walls.

House in Orta Lake

Location: *Orta Lake, Italy*
Year of construction: *1987*
Architect: *Alessandro Mendini*
Photography: *Occhiomagico*

Alessandro Mendini's design for what has come to be known as "The House of Happiness" was the result of his friendship with the owner, a well-known Italian industrial designer, and his understanding of the needs and personality of his friend.

Mendini has a keen interest in the psychological and anthropological aspects of architecture and this is what inspired the owner to entrust him with this delicate task. Moreover, as far as the owner was concerned, the fact that Mendini had never designed a house before made him the ideal candidate, as he would feel greater motivation when faced with a new challenge.

One of the main factors to be taken into account was that the house must be designed to suit the lifestyle of its occupants. The use of color, the form of the rooms, and the symmetry or lack of it are key elements that were decided by mutual agreement between the architect and the owner as they greatly impact upon the quality of life the house can offer. Hence the name "The House of Happiness": the pursuit of happiness being a key element of the design from the outset. The name later took on a second meaning: "happy" not only in the sense of a house designed for comfort and convenience, but also in the sense of authentic, well-conceived, and free.

The structure of the building had to be different and experimental, a house full of the unexpected, free of rigid plans. The aim was to give visitors a feeling of continuous surprise and the expectation of new discoveries in every room.

Right-hand page:
The wooden ceiling and
parquet floor bring
warmth to the gym.

Light, sinuous form and
contrasting materials give
this room its character.

The main living room is
dominated by the
fireplace designed by
Ettore Sottsas.

House in Porza

Location: *Porza, Switzerland*
Year of construction: *1987*
Architects: *Franco Moro, Paolo Moro*
Photography: *Filippo Simonetti*

This building, with its avant-garde features, is inspired by the desire to make the structure an integral part of the site without changing the nature of the land itself. The site, being at the very top of a hill, has a pronounced slope. Surrounded by trees and mountain vegetation, the house, with the strong zigzag features of its elevations and its horizontal ground-penetrating structure, stands out clearly and defiantly between the green of the wood and the blue of the sky.

As topographical integration was a determining factor, the building has been structured in three different parts, each corresponding to separate components of the site. At road level there is an underground garage. On the flat, the basement – partly below ground level – forms the foundation for a panoramic balcony that, from this elevated position, looks out over the countryside, the views uninterrupted by the underlying structures. The house itself, built into the slope, is arranged on two levels and opens out like a fan, taking in the whole of the view and collecting solar energy. This staggered deconstruction of the building maintains the organic relationship with the natural profile of the land.

The geometric arrangement is achieved by the vertical removal of the two halves of a cube, cut diagonally and inserted in a stepped manner along the inclined plane of the ground.

This one-family house reinterprets the Ticino style of architecture in a different and modern way, adapting it to its mountain environment.

Left-hand page:
The main entrance to the
building lies inside
exposed stone walls that
fan outward on both sides
to form a wall that
encloses and protects this
area of the house. After
crossing the space
between the walls, steps
lead up to a glass door.

The living area, dining
room, and kitchen are
located on the lower floor.
A staircase with wooden
flights and black metal
banisters leads to the
upper floor where the
bedrooms and their
corresponding bathrooms
are located.

House in Lake Ossiach

Location: *Carintia, Austria*
Year of construction: *1988*
Architect: *Manfred Kovatsch*
Photography: *Reiner Blunck*

This single-family house stands 1,150 ft (350 m) above Lake Ossiach, on a steeply sloping site that drops vertiginously down to the water's edge. This elevated position provides panoramic views of the stunning landscape that surrounds the building on all sides.

The plan of the building is clearly irregular, though tending towards the rectilinear. It comprises four distinct levels that appear to be inserted into a supporting timber frame, rather like the decks of a ship. Various flights of stairs that differ in length according to the angle of the building constitute the main supporting elements. The steps on the valley side go to all four levels while those on the gully side go to only two. Manfred Kovatsch has taken advantage of the sloping terrain on which the building stands: on top of the base structure – a framework of beams joined to the foundations above ground level – he has placed long, wide steps that mark the entrance. These serve a double purpose: in good weather they are an ideal spot to sit and enjoy the sun and their hollow structures also serve as storage areas.

One of the magical qualities of this building is that it lives and grows with the family and is continually developing.

One of the architect's aims – also shared by the owners – was to give the house a natural splendor. The most successful feature is the roof – steeply pitched to cope with the weather.

The choice of woods (larch and fir) was determined by the proximity of these types of trees. Larch provides protection against the weather, while the internal skeleton of the building, sheltering under the roof and its covering, is built of spruce.

Interior view of the upper level showing, in the background, the covered balcony with a spectacular view over the lake.

View of the kitchen on
the first floor.

View of the dining area.

Detail of the interior of
the rooms on the upper
level, showing the
unusual position of
the bathtub.

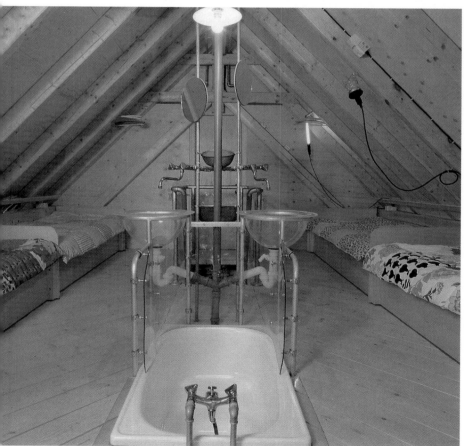

Cookston House

Location: *Rustic Canyon, California, United States*
Year of construction: *1987*
Architect: *Ray Kappe*
Photography: *Reiner Blunck*

The majority of houses architect Ray Kappe has built on hills are linked horizontally with the landscape. With Cookston House, however, the interpretation is vertical, and the construction is in concrete, with a castle-like structure surrounded and overhung by trees.

The house is particularly unusual for Rustic Canyon and takes advantage of an area of flat land extending from the long access road.

While the boundary of other houses here is defined by the road, Cookston House appears to have been dropped into acres of stunning countryside and is only connected to the roadway by a large doorway of concrete, glass, and steel that is secured symbolically to the structure of the building.

The owners wanted a house constructed of concrete with rounded forms, and Kappe seized this opportunity to create a piece of architecture very different from the earlier work that had earned him his reputation as an architect. The main criterion that inspired the building was energy efficiency.

The combination of curved roofs, projecting balconies, and a rounded bay in the rear wall space creates a contrast of composition when juxtaposed to the south elevation, which is constructed entirely of glass. The building is divided in a north-south direction by a central east-west axial wall and although the formal arrangement is dictated by considerations of energy efficiency, the structure as a whole is impressively situated and provides a sensitive response to the surrounding canyon views.

Kappe uses active and passive systems in his work, in line with Californian energy regulations. His aim was to create living environments that were energy efficient without highlighting the lifestyle and principles normally associated with the climate of southern California.

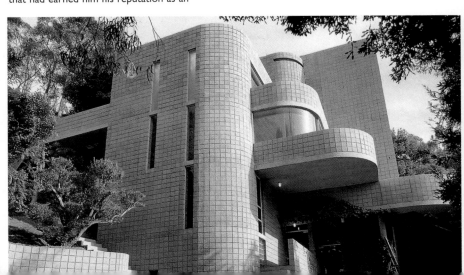

The staircase is metal with transparent steps. The entire area is brightly lit by the vast glass structure of the south elevation.

Right-hand page:
The bedroom is located inside a curved glass structure.

House in Inn Valley

Location: *Inn Valley, Bairbach, Austria*
Year of construction: *1990*
Architect: *Jörg Streli*
Photography: *Tim Hursley*

This single-family house has an irregular ground plan and is divided in three distinct levels that are staggered to adjust to the slope of the land. Despite its linear development, the various rooms are arranged around a small hallway that fills the entire height of the structure to form a public space shared by all the sections. The house has a basement, partly underground, that includes an area for leisure activities, a sauna, and the building's heating equipment. A staircase, forming a kind of bridge on the second floor, connects with the different levels from this central entrance hall and leads to the lower floor. The enormous living room is located on this floor and extends the entire length of the house, forming one continuous space with the small, friendly dining area; only the stove separates one area from the other while, paradoxically, also acting as a link between the two. These two public areas are designed as social spaces and look out onto the valley, enjoying beautiful views and plenty of natural light. Also on this floor is a garage with direct access from the road, a large balcony extending out from the living room, and a bathroom. The bedrooms are located at the rear and on the third floor to give the sleeping quarters greater privacy.

The architect's primary aim in constructing this house was to provide a panoramic outlook over the spectacular valley scenery while structuring the site to fit the sloping terrain.

The small windows on the upper floor give the bedroom greater privacy.

Axonometric projection.

The roofing consists of a layer of untreated larch covered by copper sheeting, bringing a sheen to the roof.

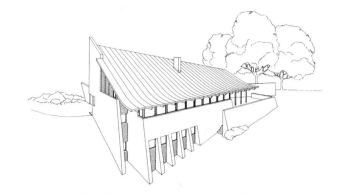

The door and window
frames are made of larch.
Below the tiled floor
with its protective cotton
rugs is an underfloor
heating system.

Right-hand page:
View of part of the living
room and dining room,
showing the cozy table
arrangement in the
background.

House in Lake Marion

Location: *Massachusetts, United States*
Year of construction: *1987*
Architect: *Peter Forbes*
Photography: *Tim Hursley*

The inspiration for this single-family property came from the owners' passion for boats and sailing. Taking this as his guiding principle, American architect Peter Forbes designed a building that would resemble an observation tower, facing out over a large, picturesque lake that disappears into the distance.

The house is splendidly located on top of a hill in an area of woodland with very tall pine trees that are hardy enough to withstand the harsh climate. It stands high above beautiful Lake Marion, in the state of Massachusetts.

The building is on four separate levels, and although the foundations stand on a rectangular base, the upper floors are slightly adapted to take an oval form that also incorporates a tower with a square ground plan – the vertebral element of the whole structure. The basement, partly concealed below ground level, is designed as a utility and workshop area and includes the garage. A porch opens on one side to create an outdoor space sheltered from the strong winds. A staircase right in the center of the building, inside the tower, leads to the second floor where the living areas are located: a large living room with fireplace, the dining room, and the kitchen. The spatial continuity of these areas is interrupted only by the flight of stairs.

921

The architecture of this building
grows out of the hillside,
extending upward to the tall
chimneys and staggered roofs via
the apse-shape porches at each
end of the building and
culminating in the central tower.

The central element of the building is the three-story tower that rises above the rest of the structure. Inside, the central staircase moves from one side to the other, crossing the tower and at the same time connecting the different spaces that form the final composition.

In the interior of the building, the flooring, the stair treads, and the banisters are all made of wood, while the walls and ceilings are of whitewashed plaster, white being the dominant color throughout the house.

Heschl House

Location: *Agarone, Switzerland*
Year of construction: *1987*
Architect: *Luigi Snozzi*
Photography: *Francesc Tur*

Heschl House is built on densely wooded hillside in the Magadino meadowland, which is gaining popularity as a site for second homes.

As a result of local regulations, the owners were obliged to build their property on an uneven area of ground. Heschl House is designed with a square ground plan and has a four-sided roof giving it a certain similarity with the architectural style of the other houses in the valley, all of which date from the 19th century. The arbor – a feature typical of Snozzi's work – affords excellent views over the entire wood and a panoramic view of Lake Lugano.

Although the building, designed as a house inside a house, adopts many of the features of the traditional farmhouses of the area, the square ground plan is irregular and reinterpreted in a modern style. The main entrance gives onto a hallway on the main floor, which is built out from the hillside.

The windows have black metal frames and connect the living room with the balustraded balcony. This is partly covered and serves as a lookout over the impressive vegetation of the surrounding area. The house has a four-sided, pyramidal roof covered in dark gray tiles supported on a flat structure.

The walls have relatively few windows and give a more solid appearance. A one-story covered porch area has been built onto one of these elevations. With its table and chairs it provides an ideal spot to relax on summer days.

Right-hand page:
The living room from
different angles. The
small square windows
bring natural light
into the room.

View of the rear of the
building showing the
pyramidal roof and
covered porch.

Country House in the "Cerros de la Santa"

Location: *Belvís de Monroy, Cáceres, Spain*
Year of construction: *1998*
Architects: *Estudio de Arquitectura*
Picado-De Blas-Delgado
Photography: *Eugeni Pons*

This country-style property is located on a plot in the outskirts of the town and was constructed on a minimum budget based on square footage. From the outset the aim was to make the most of the exceptional views over the Vera Valley and the main window is therefore west-facing, looking out toward the sun setting behind the medieval castle on a hilltop less than a mile away. Having studied the given parameters – climate, location, and client requirements – a two-part scheme was proposed. On the one hand there is a large communal area around which the whole design is structured and, on the other, the remaining rooms that serve and make sense of the first.

The main room is 13½ ft (4.2 m) high and includes the traffic areas, areas for communal use, the main load-bearing walls, and has, of course, magnificent views. The east-west axis, so apparent in the ground plan, dissolves on entering the living area as this extends into deeper, lower spaces. The relationship between interior and exterior spaces is made more fluid by this and is accentuated by the natural light entering via these outer areas. The external structure reflects a building system based on load-bearing concrete walls.

To achieve greater
integration with the
surroundings, the building
is painted in tones of
greenish brown, helping
it to blend unnoticed
into the landscape.

931

Casa Palmira

Location: *Cuernavaca, Mexico*
Year of construction: *1994*
Architect: *Alberto Kalach*
Photography: *Martairene Alcantara, Pep Avila*

Designed to be surrounded by gardens, this house stands alongside a gully in Palmira, Cuernavaca, Mexico. As it takes years for a garden to develop, the property effectively lies unfinished, like a forgotten seed.

The house is a pavilion surrounded by green spaces. For primarily functional reasons it was designed as a compact structure but it still fills the site.

Each part of the property has its own yard and the structure as a whole is contained within four long walls and two concrete towers. To reach the small hallway you cross a little sloping courtyard paved with local stone, entering via a covered passageway that will eventually be covered with bougainvillea. The living room is a deep terrace opening onto the yard on the northwest, surrounded by acacia and jasmine. The dining area is enclosed by long walls and adorned with abelias and heavenly bamboo in a courtyard filled with orange trees. The den shares a terrace with the swimming pool and the bedrooms are submerged in the rich vegetation of the yard.

In time plants will fill the spaces allocated to them in the design. The mud walls, the concrete, and the wood that acted as a framework will age and become part of the yard itself.

The concrete walls and
the wood used for the
framework will age
as the plants grow and
gradually take over
the surroundings.

Casa Palmira is designed
as a combination of
interior spaces, yards,
patios, and a pool.

937

Ekler House

Location: *Budakalász, Hungary*
Year of construction: *1994*
Architect: *Dezsö Ekler*
Photography: *Dezsö Ekler*

Right-hand page:
View of the house from the Danube
showing the structural composition
based on two large
pillars of exposed brick.

This secluded house in a wooded area of Budakalász, Hungary, stands on the shores of the Danube. It is built on an irregular-shape corner plot and has two floors, each 1,050 sq ft (98 m²). The symbolic references to the river and the mountain geography of the region are apparent in the structural forms. The house rises out of the ground in an oval form, like the silhouette of a boat, with load-bearing walls of rough exposed brick, culminating in a roof typical of mountain architecture. It also has a terrace looking out over the river and toward the woods.

Some windows are a mixture of curved and oblique lines, as part of a scheme that embraces the design of the whole elevation. Likewise, some of the internal partition walls end in angles rather than straight lines.

Wood is the dominant material in the interior. The walls are brick, finished in plaster and painted, and stone is used on some corners. The floors, ceilings, stairs, certain items of furniture – such as the oval table forming part of the partition dividing the kitchen and dining room, and the shelves – are all made of wood. An early 20th century cast-iron banister, reclaimed, like many of the materials used, creates a contrast with the continuity of the wood.

Rear elevation. The second floor projects out over the
curved walls of the lower floor. The change in treatment
of the external surfaces also marks the divide between
the two stories, with wood planking on the upper floor
and exposed brick on the lower.

Two pillars in traditional exposed brick support
the end of the balcony and the roof.

View of the Danube from the upper balcony.

Detail of the roof showing the timber structure.

Right-hand page:
Wood is the dominant material
in the interior and is used for
floors, ceilings, and stairs.
The walls are finished in plaster
and painted, with exposed stone
elements at the corners.

View of the early 20th-century cast-iron banister.

The internal staircase seen from the second floor.

Foot of the internal staircase leading to the floor above.

Left-hand page:
View of the rustic marble fireplace that dominates the living room. The entrance hall and stairs in the background form one continuous space.

Büchel House

Location: *Vaduz, Liechtenstein*
Year of construction: *1996*
Architects: *Baumschlager & Eberle*
Associates: *Elmar Hasler, Nic Wohlwend, D.I. Plankel*
Photography: *Eduard Hueber*

The house is located in a contrasting landscape, with a steep, rocky cliff on one side and on the other the valley filled with fruit trees lying below Vaduz castle.

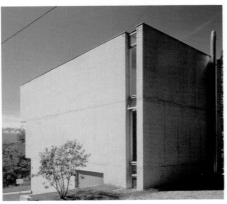

Büchel House stands alone and unconcerned in this outstanding countryside location. It rises proudly, changing the way the landscape is perceived. It was only after much debate between the architects and their clients that this unusual design was finally approved.

To make the most of the topography of the site and also to preserve the existing fruit trees, the designers opted for a compact, three-story structure rather than a horizontal development that would occupy a larger surface area and be detrimental to the existing vegetation.

The decision to use inverted staggering on the front elevation may appear to be the result of some trivial esthetic consideration, but in fact it is a masterly stroke, increasing the surface area of each floor but keeping the area of land actually built on to a minimum.

The design pays special attention to the functional requirements of the building and gives each part a specific type of elevation. Three of the elevations are constructed of exposed concrete but are given an extremely fine, almost delicate finish. The north side, subject to very cold temperatures and poor light, is completely enclosed. There are only two openings on this elevation: the garage door and a tall, narrow slit of a window that emphasizes the verticality of the structure. The west elevation is of freer design with openings that do not follow such a rigid arrangement.

The inward-looking nature of the first three elevations disappears completely on the south side that looks out over the valley. The house opens onto magnificent views framed by large, tall windows.

The house is conceived as an
entity designed for a specific
location: the impressive wall of
rock left by quarrying acts as a
backdrop to the house,
providing continuity of
texture with the exposed
concrete of the walls.

Each detail is the product of a careful, precise design process. One example is this wall of glass with its wooden, foldback, sliding screens.

Rosebery House

Location: *Brisbane, Australia*
Year of construction: *1997*
Architects: *Brit Andresen & Peter O'Gorman*
Associates: *John Batterham, Lon Murphy*
Photography: *John Linkins, Brit Andresen*

The Brisbane gorges are magical, mysterious places: deep, leafy remnants of the original landscape now reduced by mankind's efforts to adapt the land for building.

Wild and densely wooded, the plot where Rosebery House now stands presented the architects with a number of problems. The ravine is at its steepest on the north, the side favored in the southern hemisphere as it offers better light and warmer temperatures. Another obstacle was the amount of water on the site: overcoming it meant extra expense.

With a limited budget, architects Brit Andresen and Peter O'Gorman had to intervene in this landscape without destroying any of its inherent qualities. Their first priority was to survey and study the area exhaustively to ensure that their plans would not cause damage. To emphasize the long, narrow nature of the gorge and the connection it forms between hill and river, they designed a narrow building positioned along the north-south axis of the site. They located it at the east end of the plot, facing away from neighboring properties and taking advantage of the trees on the west side to give privacy and scale to the building.

One of the key aims of the project was to bring light from the north into the deepest, darkest recesses, beneath the canopies of the trees. This was achieved by creating three units linked by semicovered platforms that allow light to enter the rooms of the house. Extensive use of glass and wooden window shades gives the effect of light filtered through the trees.

The interior spaces can be seen to merge into the adjacent woodland. The boundaries between the building and the exterior spaces are blurred, giving magnificent views of the trees in the gorge.

Right-hand page:
The structure of the building is based on a system of load-bearing timber beams and pillars. The terraces and balconies are partly covered by strips of eucalyptus wood, providing protection against the rays of the sun that can be very strong in these latitudes. The platforms that connect the different pavilions play an important role as they also provide outdoor living areas.

Andresen & O'Gorman have managed to turn this unusual location to their advantage. Their design is based on respect for nature intervening in the landscape in a nondestructive manner.

The functional scheme is based on three pavilions connected by walkways or semicovered terraces. The lower level contains a small apartment for guests or, at a future date, for younger family members requiring greater independence. The semicovered terraces provide shelter from the heat of the sun. They are ambiguous areas where the boundaries between interior and exterior become blurred.

YG House

Location: *Katta-gun, Japan*
Year of construction: *1997*
Architect: *Atelier Hitoshi Abe*
Photography: *Syunichi Atsumi*

Hitoshi Abe, the visible head of Atelier Hitoshi Abe, belongs to a later generation of architects. Born in 1962, he is a contemporary of Shigeru Ban and Kazuyo Sejima. For four years he worked for the Coop Himmelblau before founding the Atelier Hitoshi Abe, together with Yosikatu Matuno and Hideyuki Mori.

In the early 1990s the Atelier undertook a number of large-scale projects such as the Miyagi Stadium and the Miyagi water tower. During the second half of the 90s, at the same time as the commission for the YG House, they took on projects on a more domestic scale such as the M-house, Gravel-2, and the "neige lune fleur" restaurant.

The YG House was designed in the form of a 295 ft (90 m) long strip, folding in on itself three times to create a large central space. Six units are placed along this perimeter band containing the necessary utilities to make it a living space: a fireplace-closet, a kitchen, a washroom-laundry, a bathroom, a shoe closet, and a store.

The double-height enclosed space, the indisputable nucleus of the house, is unusual within the building. The other spaces are enclosed – and only opened when there is a functional need – whereas the central space communicates with the exterior, through the views it affords and the light it allows to enter, establishing different relationships with its surroundings.

The house retains a very close relationship with the site where it is built. On the north side the entrance area runs parallel to the curve of the land and remains in contact with it. Entering the house obliquely, we find that the south end of the structure rises away from the ground and, following the centripetal movement of the interior, we skirt round the central space – now at its full height – by ascending the stairs, passing around the chimney stack and following the walkway, moving further and further away from ground level.

With the YG House the Atelier Hitoshi Abe has endeavored to transform an abstract mental concept into a physical entity within a determined context.

The YG House was designed to be used
by guests of the company that
commissioned it, mainly as weekend
accommodation. It stands on a huge
15,000 sq ft (1,392 m²) site and is
located at the top of a south-facing
slope. The house itself occupies 1,320
sq ft (123 m²) and is divided into two
floors and surrounded by trees.

A house occupied on a casual basis only
requires a limited amount of furniture.
The resulting austerity, however, is
counterbalanced by the warmth of the
wood used both in the structure and
finish of the interiors.

The ascending spiral staircase is highlighted by two design elements: the white walls of the staircase and fireplace contrast with the dark cedar of the floors and walls, marking out the route to follow; while on the exterior, the expressive angled roofs illustrate what happens inside.

Into House

Location: *Espoo, Finland*
Year of construction: *1998*
Architect: *Jyrki Tasa*
Photography: *Jussi Tianen & Jyrki Tasa*

This design by Jyrki Tasa combines a poetic exercise with a rational development. The most advanced precision techniques have been applied to transform the symbolic forms of this modern, sensual, and imaginative structure into reality.

Standing on a tall hill facing west toward the sea, Into House appears to perch on the rock, clinging to it, and sheltered by a curving white wall pointing in the direction of the evening sun.

The building is clearly organized into sectors. Although this system is methodical and practical, the use of steel – powerful and poetic – and of wood – beautiful and inviting – creates a warm and friendly environment and removes any sense of rigidity or lack of movement.

The road leads the visitor to the protective white wall at the rear of the property. From the winding approach road you can catch occasional glimpses of sections of the undulating eaves and the tall columns of the west elevation that hint at the dual nature of the building.

The main entrance is a narrow glass opening in the elevation reached by a metal bridge over the pool. This bridge marks the point at which you leave behind neighboring houses and other developments and prepare to enjoy nature, either in terms of the house itself or, in its untamed state, from the terraces and balconies.

The hallway acts as a visual and functional link with the other areas of the house, its great height and tall glass windows offering magnificent views of the sea. The entire house can be seen and read from this one space that connects the public living areas with the more private rooms.

Into House stands proudly
on top of a solid rocky
outcrop. The design is a
metaphor of the traditional
nomadic structures. The
metal roof rests on
cylindrical poles like a
protective canopy.

Right-hand page:
The structure unfolds
like a fan, enclosing
within it a warm and
welcoming house, its
back turned to the cold
north aspect.

The staircase is a piece of precision engineering. A sheet of pine pleating is supported on a light structure of steel tubes and metal cables.

The material that dominates the interior is wood. The floors are of cherry wood and the vertical partitions are pine. This finish creates environments that are practical and functional but also comfortable and esthetically expressive. The natural light that streams through the skylights and picture windows brings out the varied textures of the wood in all their splendor and changing character.

Ravenwood House

Location: *North Woods, Minnesota, United States*
Year of construction: *1998*
Architect: *David Salmela*
Associates: *Carrol & Franck,*
Hurst & Heinrichs, Coen & Stumpf
Photography: *Peter Kerze*

Jim Brandenburg discovered this secluded spot in 1979 on an assignment for *National Geographic* to photograph a waterfall close to where Ravenwood now stands. This site lies within the Superior National Forest and on the border of the *Boundary Waters Canoe Area*. It is also the setting for Jim's later best-selling portrait of wolves, *Brother Wolf*, published in 1993.

In 1981 Jim and his wife Judy, who were living in Minneapolis at the time, built a holiday home here in the middle of the woods. Constructed from the trunks of cedar trees, it comprised four small units – a log cabin, a guest house, a sauna, and a washroom – arranged in a staggered fashion down one side of the hill.

As time went by, the Brandenburgs decided to extend the cabin so that they could live in it for longer periods of time, and they contacted David Salmela. What Jim Brandenburg had in mind – probably a result of his Norwegian roots – was a typical Viking long house. Salmela adopted this concept but added a number of pitched roof buildings in a style that would blend in with the existing structures, and positioned these around an exterior courtyard.

The original cabin now has a kitchen on the lower floor and a double bedroom on the upper. The main 4,570 sq ft (425 m²) building constructed 45 degrees southwest of the first is linked to it by the lower-floor kitchen and gallery.

The building comprises three clearly differentiated areas: a double-height space with a store and bathroom; a second two-story space with a living room on the lower floor and a guest bedroom on the upper floor; and a third, three-story area containing, from the ground up, the main den, a work space with computers, and, suspended above, an attic area.

Salmela, who is a great admirer of the architects Aalto, Asplund, Eliel, and Eero Saarinen, shares Brandenburg's taste for Nordic tradition. In Ravenwood he uses two materials – turf roofing with a cedar-wood covering – that were used for centuries in Scandinavian buildings.

In 1997 Ravenwood was awarded a
national prize by the AIA (American
Institute of Architects) and a regional
prize by the Minnesota AIA. This
recognition was well deserved. David
Salmela's work develops out of a desire
to interpret the wishes and tastes of his
clients and when he achieves this, the
result is almost magical.

Furniture House

Location: *Yamanaka, Japan*
Year of construction: *1998*
Architect: *Shigeru Ban*
Photography: *Hiroyuki Hirai*

The minimalist approach of this project was a way of ensuring the minimum possible disturbance to the natural environment while establishing the most appropriate language for dialogue with the landscape. The 1,180 sq ft (110 m²) house stands in the Yamanaka mountains in Japan. An independent, autonomous structure, it contrasts with the rich vegetation of its surroundings. Japanese architect Shigeru Ban wanted the house to be an expression of extreme Oriental simplicity and developed the structure from the divisions and storage area of the project.

The construction system of Furniture House uses prefabricated units that are the height of the building and work both structurally and as elements that define space. Unlike the carpentry work that would have been available on site, these units are produced under conditions of total mechanization and control, producing better results in terms of quality. The units function as furniture and as structural elements, making it possible to reduce the materials and labor needed as well as onsite construction time. These advantages are reflected in considerable savings in project cost. The units used in Furniture House are 8 ft (2.4 m) high and 3 ft (90 cm) wide. The depth, which is determined by their use and location in the building, varies between 18 in. (45 cm) in the case of bookshelves and 28 in. (70 cm) for other storage and shelving requirements. Arranged in accordance with the structure and composition of the rooms, they produce vertical and horizontal tensions.

The construction system not only gives the required degree of refinement, but, in keeping with this concept, its effect on the natural environment is minimal – including the way in which the house is constructed.

The building recalls the 17th-century work of Kamo no
Chomei, whose buildings were created in sections and
could be completely dismantled. Through this
experimental approach, Ban is reinterpreting the classical
tradition of Japanese architecture in a modern way.

The elegance of the plan, which recalls the earliest houses
of Mies van der Rohe, stems from a highly intelligent
distribution of space that eschews any clear differentiation
of the functional elements of the house. The boundaries
between traffic and living areas and between interior
and exterior are virtually nonexistent or only indicated
in the most subtle manner.

The six structural panels used as dividing screens create different living areas within one continuous space. The architect simply places these elements so that the tensions produced direct the movement and the eye toward a large platform, while the wide sliding windows that move on concealed rails in the floor and ceiling help to link the space with the surrounding landscape.

Barry's Bay House

Location: *Ontario, Canada*
Year of construction: *1994*
Architects: *Hariri & Hariri*
Associates: *Paul Baird, Grandon Yearick, Brigid Hogan, Aaron McDonald*
Photography: *John M. Hall*

This weekend holiday home offers a wide formal repertoire using different applications of a single material: wood. This richness, reflected both externally and in the interior space, derives from a minute observation of the intrinsic nature of the landscape. The two New York-based architects from Iran who designed it adopted an approach committed to abstracting these features and applying them to the building as an entity as well as to the most subtle of details. The location is a rural plot in Ontario, Canada, sloping gently down to the peaceful waters of Lake Kamaniskeg. It is planted with evergreens and tall birches. The setting is tranquil, meditative, with the ever-present horizon defined by the shores of the lake contrasting with the trees along the shoreline.

The project began as a commission to enlarge an old, prefabricated A-frame cabin that had become too small for the six-person family that owned it. The old cabin was preserved at the client's request, for sentimental reasons, and is now used as accommodation for guests and younger family members. The original structure therefore became a starting point and an important element in the whole. The false shutters and pink paintwork on the walls were removed and the asphalt tiles were replaced by galvanized steel panels better suited to the language of the new structure. The interior, however, was altered hardly at all. The living room was changed around to create space for a new and larger kitchen and a dining area was created on the lower level.

The new cabin is a 98 ft (30 m) long timber structure extending along the western boundary of the property, only 6½ ft (2 m) away from the original cabin. It accommodates the master bedroom, a library, a reading room, a large living room, and a boat store.

The principal materials used in this property are red cedar for the interior and exterior, white maple for the floors, and galvanized metal panels for the roof.

Two-family duplex

Location: *Basilea, Switzerland*
Year of construction: *1996*
Architect: *Harry Gugger*
Associate: *Lukas Egli*
Photography: *Margherita Spiluttini*

This design for a pair of semidetached houses in the outskirts of Basilea creates a close dialogue with the surroundings through the power of its form, introduced subtly into the landscape. The particular nature of the site required an extensive study of the typology of multifamily dwellings. The principles of sequence and levels traditionally adopted, either for houses in rows or apartment blocks, did not provide an adequate solution in this case.

The plot extends longitudinally in a westerly direction until it meets the access road. It stands in a clearing, the other boundaries being marked by dense vegetation on the adjacent properties. The site is unusually dynamic and this is accentuated by the inherent proportions of the property itself and by a line of old fruit trees that serves as a reminder of the region's predominantly agricultural past. These temporal links give the place a powerful, almost mysterious hold over the imagination.

On the exterior, the two dwellings are characterized by the homogeneity of the whole. The structure is removed from the ground by a concrete base that offsets the incline of the slope. It appears to be a single-family unit with nothing of the crossover arrangement of the interiors betrayed in the outer shell. The complex internal arrangement of two superposed dwellings of equal size enables both sets of occupants to take advantage of the different aspects of the property and of the relationship between lower floor and exterior space.

The relationship with the surroundings reaches full expression in the interior. The windows act as a series of paintings, not only reflecting the natural world, but also transposing it into the interior itself. With the windows open, the rooms are transformed into loggias. The access points are designed to the same effect, leading onto timber planking that transforms the base of the building into a deck. A simple language and a limited number of elements are sufficient to create a close link between landscape and architecture.

Wilson Residence

Location: *Vermilion Lake, United States*
Year of construction: *1998*
Architect: *David Salmela*

The objective behind this project was to design a house suited not only to the location, the region, and the client's needs, but that would also have a contemporary look.

The Wilson Residence is located on a rocky point on the shores of Vermilion Lake and has stunning views of the lake and surrounding countryside. For the family who live here the geographical nature of the site and its situation evoke the landscape of Sweden. It was built as a country retreat by the present owner's grandfather, who emigrated from Sweden in the early 20th century. As a child, the present owner spent his summers at the old house, where he developed a passion for boat-building. After living on the eastern and western seaboards of the United States while pursuing their careers in engineering, he and his wife, also of Swedish descent, decided to take early retirement and fulfil their common dream: to construct a house and devote their time to boat-building.

A first line of parallel forms flanks the main living room, the most important area of the house, around which the remaining spaces are structured. The master bedroom looks west while the remaining rooms face east. The formality of the two units is suddenly broken by the rocky outcrop of the mountain and the systematic change in the window pattern. The main living room appears to stand in front of a Victorian-style window screen, like a covered terrace, and acts as a transitional space between the interior of the house and the natural space outside. In contrast, the courtyard is on a smaller scale, enclosing and concealing the view of the lake until you enter the house.

The success and power of this design lie in its ability to be both modern and traditional, to have a classical appearance organized with an apparently spontaneous lack of symmetry.

The house is constructed around lines of sight, the best sources of natural light, the desire to create a distinctive access, and architecturally expressive lines.

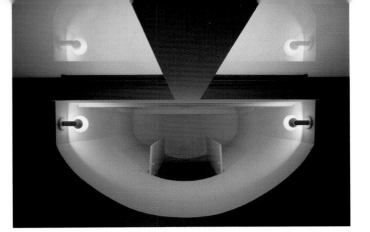

In the interior we find
restful spaces that are an
invitation to stay and
contemplate the landscape
framed in the large
windows. The white of the
walls and ceilings merges
with the pale wood detail
of the floor, the balustrades,
and the interior pergola
suspended over the living
room. Highlights of color
are introduced through
the use of furnishings and
rugs in tones of gray and
navy blue.

Loken Residence

Location: *Duluth, Minnesota, United States*
Year of construction: *1996*
Architect: *David Salmela*
Associates: *Rod & Sons Carpentry*
Photography: *Peter Kerze*

This project is the result of improvements and extensions to a house that already stood on this mountain site and was originally used as a small family summer home. The Loken Residence stands just a few yards from Big Sucker – a stony river with lots of waterfalls that flows through the site – and about a mile from Lake Superior in Minnesota. The topographical conditions of the site, some 330 ft (100 m) above the lake, give it a stunning panoramic view of the lake and surrounding area.

The original building, which dates from 1910, had undergone a number of poorly-planned changes, remodeling work, and extensions. Over the course of the years the damage these changes had inflicted on the structure and its foundations gradually became more apparent. When the current owner decided to undertake a building project to satisfy his needs and those of his family, he saw this as an opportunity to restore the old building to its original character. This became the springboard for the project.

A number of different factors played their part in the design process: the history of the place and its traditional vernacular cabin architecture, the changes to the original house, the family's Norwegian roots and their passion for Scandinavian design, and the need to provide their horses with shelter and to create a display area for their enormous collection of timepieces. However, the most powerful influence of all was simply the curiosity and tremendous interest the clients showed in the architectural process.

The dominant material in both interior and exterior is wood, the plastic capabilities of which have been used to their full advantage. The traditional typology of the mountain cabin, very common in the area, has been reinterpreted here to produce interior spaces that are clean and simple. On the exterior, however, a wide formal repertoire can be found that slots comfortably into space in the surrounding landscape.